This volume examines the complex and vitally important ethical questions connected with the deployment of nuclear weapons and their use as a deterrent. A number of the essays contained here have already established themselves as penetrating and significant contributions to the debate on nuclear ethics. They have been revised to bring out their unity and coherence, and are integrated with new essays. The book's exceptional rigor and clarity make it valuable whether the reader's concern with nuclear ethics is professional or personal.

Part I explores the morality of nuclear deterrence from each of the two dominant traditions in moral philosophy, deontology and consequentialism, and points out a number of interesting ethical dilemmas. Deontological objections to deterrence are examined with precision and ingenuity, and a new and plausible consequentialist principle of rational choice is proposed that justifies certain forms of nuclear deterrence. Part II criticizes a variety of alternatives to deterrence – unilateral nuclear disarmament, world government, strategic defense against ballistic missiles, and nuclear coercion – and argues for mutual nuclear disarmament as a realistic and desirable long-run alternative.

MORAL PARADOXES
OF NUCLEAR
DETERRENCE

Gregory S. Kavka
University of California, Irvine

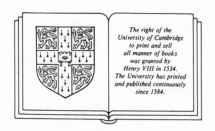

The right of the
University of Cambridge
to print and sell
all manner of books
was granted by
Henry VIII in 1534.
The University has printed
and published continuously
since 1584.

Cambridge University Press

CAMBRIDGE

NEW YORK   NEW ROCHELLE   MELBOURNE   SYDNEY

Published by the Press Syndicate of the University of Cambridge
The Pitt Building, Trumpington Street, Cambridge CB2 1RP
32 East 57th Street, New York, NY 10022, USA
10 Stamford Road, Oakleigh, Melbourne 3166, Australia

First published 1987

Printed in the United States of America

Library of Congress Cataloging-in-Publication Data

Kavka, Gregory S., 1947–

Moral paradoxes of nuclear deterrence.

Bibliography: p.

1. Deterrence (Strategy) – Moral and ethical aspects.
2. Nuclear warfare – Moral and ethical aspects.
I. Title.
U162.6.K38   1987   172′.42   87–13149

British Library Cataloguing in Publication Data

Kavka, Gregory S.

Moral paradoxes of nuclear deterrence.

1. Deterrence (Strategy) – Moral and
ethical aspects. 2. Nuclear warfare –
Moral and ethical aspects.
I. Title.
172′.42   U22

ISBN 0 521 33043 2 hard covers
ISBN 0 521 33896 4 paperback

For a "Pair o' Docs" – Georgine Kavka, M.D.,
and Jerome Kavka, M.D. – and one of their
offspring – Audrey Kavka Moretti, M.D.

Contents

Preface

On December 2, 1942, under the stands of Stagg Field at the University of Chicago, the first controlled nuclear chain reaction was achieved. A few years later and a few blocks away, I was born as a member of the first generation to live its entire life under the threat of atomic destruction. My subsequent interest, as a young adult, in the moral issues raised by the existence of nuclear weapons, and the policy of nuclear deterrence based on the threat to use these weapons, resulted from two factors: the immense importance of the subject and the intellectual difficulty and complexity of the basic questions.

When I began my work on these questions in the early seventies, they were largely being neglected by other scholars. During the early sixties, there had been a brief flurry of writings on the moral aspects of nuclear war and deterrence, mainly by theologians. Ten years later, there was mostly silence. By the early eighties, when most of the essays in this book first appeared in print, this situation had changed drastically – with several anthologies and a few monographs by philosophers on nuclear ethics becoming available. Apparently philosophers, like almost everyone else, were alarmed by the escalating superpower nuclear arms race and the hawkish rhetoric and military procurement policies of the new U.S. administration. This shows, I believe, their good sense.

Most of the chapters in this book were originally written for publication in professional journals and anthologies of writings by philosophers. Nevertheless, they should be intelligible to other academics and to general readers who are willing to take the time to read them carefully. Chapters 3, 8, and 10 make use of elementary game theory and decision theory. Chapter 4 might be the best place to start for readers without philosophical background who are trying to gain a quick sense of the style and message of the book. I have tried, without extensive rewriting, to make the language of the essays nonsexist. As a result, I frequently employ the rather clumsy device of using feminine and masculine pronouns in alternate passages. I hope that this will not prove distracting.

During the period when much of this book was written, I suffered both long-term and short-term radiation effects. Recovering from these, even to the limited (and perhaps temporary) extent I have, has been extremely difficult and required a great deal of assistance from my doctors, family, friends, colleagues, university, and society. In the event of even a small-scale nuclear war, the resources will not be available to provide such assistance to the many survivors suffering significant radiation effects and other medical problems. Appreciation of this fact, together with my own experience of radiation-caused illness, has reinforced my prior belief in the moral necessity of humankind's avoiding nuclear war and attaining nuclear disarmament.

This collection of essays is far from being a systematic and comprehensive treatise on nuclear ethics. I present it anyway because Cambridge University Press's gracious offer to publish the essays together constituted, in view of my own uncertain future, an irresistible "window of opportunity" to express my thoughts on this important subject. Some of the arguments offered here are inconclusive, and many significant questions are left unanswered. I have tried, nonetheless, to clarify some central issues in nuclear ethics and to bring us closer to an adequate understanding of them. Where I have succeeded, I hope others will learn from what I have written; where I have failed, I hope others will be encouraged to do better.

I thank the relevant editors and publishers for permission to reprint revised versions of previously published essays as chapters in this book.

The original sources are:

Chapter 1. "Some Paradoxes of Deterrence," *Journal of Philosophy* 75 (June 1978). Reprinted with permission.

Chapter 2. Contains a few paragraphs from "Deterrent Intentions and Retaliatory Actions," in Douglas MacLean (ed.), *The Security Gamble* (Totowa, N.J.: Rowman & Allanheld, 1984). Reprinted with permission.

Chapter 3. "Deterrence, Utility, and Rational Choice," *Theory and Decision* 12 (March 1980). Copyright © 1980 by D. Reidel Publishing Company. Reprinted with permission.

Chapter 4. "Nuclear Deterrence: Some Moral Perplexities," in Douglas MacLean (ed.), *The Security Gamble* (Totowa, N.J.: Rowman & Allanheld, 1984). Reprinted with permission.

Chapter 6. "Doubts About Unilateral Nuclear Disarmament," *Philosophy and Public Affairs* 12 (Summer 1983). Copyright © 1983 by Princeton University Press. Reprinted with permission.

Chapter 7. "Nuclear Weapons and World Government," *The Monist* 98 (in press). Reprinted with permission.

Chapter 8. "Space War Ethics," *Ethics* 95 (April 1985), © 1985 by The University of Chicago. All rights reserved. And "A Critique of Pure Defense," *Journal of Philosophy* 83 (November 1986). Reprinted with permission.

Chapter 9. "Morality and Nuclear Politics: Lessons of the Missile Crisis," in Avner Cohen and Steven Lee (eds.), *Nuclear Weapons and the Future of Humanity* (Totowa, N.J.: Rowman & Allanheld, 1985). Reprinted with permission.

I am also grateful for generous support for my work from the University of California's Institute on Global Conflict and Cooperation, the National Endowment for the Humanities, the University of California Regents, and the School of Humanities of the University of California, Irvine. In addition to those cited in the notes of the individual chapters, I have benefited from discussions with Virginia Warren, Carlos Colombetti, George Draper, Paul Graves, and other colleagues and students in the philosophy department and the Global Peace and Conflict Studies Program at the University of California, Irvine. John Bickle assisted mightily, under difficult conditions, in the preparation of the manuscript. Jonathan Sinclair-Wilson of Cambridge University Press encouraged the project in its late stages and helped see it through to completion. Daniel Ellsberg very kindly took the time to discuss with me several of the chapters and some of his own related work. And Jefferson McMahan provided extensive and very helpful comments on nearly every chapter, enabling me to make the book much better than it otherwise would have been.

My greatest debt is to the doctors at M.D. Anderson Hospital, Orange County Regional Head and Neck Institute, and the University of California, Irvine Medical Center, who have worked hard to preserve and prolong my life, and to family, friends, and colleagues who have helped me during my illness and medical treatments. (Daniel Rotman, Ralph Cygan, M.D., and – again – Virginia Warren deserve special mention in this regard.) Without their efforts, this book would never have been completed.

Introduction

The possession of large numbers of enormously destructive nuclear weapons by the superpowers and other nations raises a number of important and difficult moral questions. Under what circumstances and in what ways, if any, would it be morally permissible for a nation to use such weapons in warfare? Does morality allow, as a form of defense by deterrence, threatening to use such weapons? Which possible nuclear deterrence policies are morally superior to which other such policies, and for what reasons? The essays in this book focus on the latter sort of questions – those involving nuclear threats and deterrence – rather than questions concerning the actual use of nuclear weapons.

These and related moral issues have been much debated over the last forty years, but the debate has generally failed to constitute an informative and productive dialogue. In particular, the views of moralists (primarily philosophers and theologians) have not had much apparent influence on the views of strategists (international relations theorists, military planners, responsible government officials and their advisers) or ordinary citizens.[1] The commonsense view of the person in the street is that nuclear deterrence is obviously justified because it is a necessary means of national defense in a world in which other nations, including some hostile ones, possess such weapons. Strategists tend to share this view together with the belief that nuclear deterrence is, in any case, an established fact of international life and that therefore the only relevant question is which form of nuclear deterrence is best.[2] By contrast, most moralists who have written on the subject tend to regard nuclear deterrence as a highly questionable practice because it involves threats to kill large numbers of innocent people and runs risks of carrying out these threats. According to many of them,

nuclear deterrence is not morally justified and we in the West are
obligated to dismantle our nuclear arsenals, unilaterally if
necessary.

My own view, sketched in these essays, is a reasoned and limited
vindication of common sense. I share with the woman in the street,
and the strategists, the belief that some possible forms of nuclear
deterrence are morally permissible because they are necessary for
national defense. Nuclear deterrence is justified in the short run as a
lesser evil because, as Part II of this book argues, all of its major
alternatives are either more undesirable, infeasible, or feasible only
in the long run. At the same time, I follow my fellow moralists in
taking very seriously both the formidable moral objections to
nuclear deterrence and the moral arguments for unilateral nuclear
disarmament. My overall conclusion is that nuclear deterrence
would be morally justified if practiced under the proper restrictions
– most importantly, if its most destabilizing features were eliminated
and it was practiced as a stopgap measure while bilateral nuclear disarmament was being vigorously pursued. Even this qualified endorsement of deterrence is tentative, however. For moral conclusions about nuclear deterrence are not reached as easily as either side
in the nuclear debate tends to assume. Indeed, the main theme of
Part I of this book is that moral arguments for and against deterrence
tend to focus on only one side of significant moral dilemmas and
paradoxes, and that a deeper understanding of nuclear ethics
requires giving serious attention to both sides.

THE ARGUMENT OF THIS BOOK

This is a book in applied ethics. No attempt is made here to develop
or argue for any systematic moral theory. Instead, attention is paid
to both utilitarian considerations and relevant deontological principles in attempting to evaluate the moral status of nuclear deterrence.[3] It is the contention of Part I that in carrying out this
evaluation, serious conflicts and dilemmas arise both within and between utilitarian and deontological ethics.

The choice among possible nuclear defense policies of a superpower may affect the survival and happiness of billions of people.
With so much at stake, it is plausible to suppose that consideration of
the likely consequences of various policies should play a decisive
role in their moral evaluation. In Chapters 1 and 2, it is emphasized

that the utilitarian costs and benefits of making deterrent nuclear
threats may be very different from the costs and benefits of carrying
out those threats if deterrence fails. Given this divergence, and the
importance of what is at stake, we should not apply absolute deontological prohibitions in evaluating the moral status of nuclear
deterrence. More specifically, even if it is wrong under any circumstances to deliberately kill many innocent civilians, it is not
necessarily wrong to threaten (or intend or risk) such killings, provided such threats are necessary to deter great evils and a valid
utilitarian justification for making them exists. In Chapter 3 it is
pointed out that, because of great uncertainty about the outcomes of
the two policies, a utilitarian comparison between nuclear deterrence and unilateral nuclear disarmament is not an easy one to make.
Practicing deterrence risks a greater disaster, an all-out superpower
nuclear war. But disarming unilaterally would risk, with greater
probability, lesser disasters such as world domination by the rival
superpower, a nuclear strike by the rival superpower, or a smaller
nuclear war between the rival superpower and one or more of the
remaining nuclear powers. Since it is not irrational to prefer the less
probable risk under these circumstances, a utilitarian defense of
nuclear deterrence is possible.

Chapter 4 makes the point that there is a conflict, in evaluating
deterrence, between plausible deontological principles. An unlimited right of national defense clashes, in a nuclear world, with an
absolute prohibition on threatening the lives of innocent people. To
settle this conflict, we must either introduce utilitarian considerations, or – as I hope to do in future work – explore further the
foundations and limits of the right of national defense. While the
first four chapters stress the difficulty of morally evaluating the
practice of nuclear deterrence, the fifth chapter considers some
dilemmas that democratic citizens may face in acting in light of their
evaluations. It is pointed out that several moral problems may arise
for the citizen who believes that his government's nuclear weapons
policies do not satisfy the conditions neessary to render a deterrence
policy morally permissible.

Part II develops the argument that nuclear deterrence is justifiable
as a lesser evil by discussing the main kinds of alternatives to
deterrence. Chapter 6 argues that unilateral nuclear disarmament by
the United States is more undesirable than nuclear deterrence
because of the relatively high risk it would entail of world domina-

tion by the Soviets, a Soviet nuclear strike on the United States, or a nuclear war between the Soviets and other nuclear powers. World government is rejected as an alternative in Chapter 7 on the grounds that it is, for all practical purposes, impossible to bring about, even if desirable. In Chapter 8, it is observed that building strategic defenses would be dangerously destabilizing and that the apparent moral advantages of strategic defenses are largely illusory. Chapter 9 considers nuclear coercion, as practiced, for example, by each superpower in the Cuban Missile Crisis. It argues that nuclear coercion is immoral because it is highly dangerous, and seeks to understand why U.S. leaders practiced it, nonetheless, in the missile crisis. My favored alternative to continued nuclear deterrence – bilateral nuclear disarmament – is discussed in Chapter 10. Arguments that bilateral nuclear disarmament is impossible or undesirable are rebutted. This, together with the morally troublesome features of nuclear deterrence, justifies viewing nuclear deterrence as fully permissible only when conjoined with a sincere and sustained pursuit of bilateral disarmament.

SYMMETRY AND THE SOVIETS

Nearly all the chapters of this book were originally written as independent essays. Gathered together they form a book, but one with significant gaps – some important issues are left undiscussed, some significant assumptions are not fully articulated. In the remainder of this introduction, I shall try briefly to fill in some of these gaps. Where possible (e.g., in Chapters 1 through 4, 7, and 10), the two superpowers are treated in a roughly symmetrical manner. In these cases, the general conclusions reached are applicable to both superpowers, and are not dependent upon controversial ideological assumptions about who the bad guys and good guys in international politics are. But there are, of course, very important differences between the two superpowers that sometimes affect the scope and conclusions of my arguments. A utilitarian comparison between nuclear deterrence and unilateral disarmament, for example, ultimately rests on some assumptions about the likely behavior of one's potential foe under various possible circumstances. And the two superpowers have foes (namely each other) whose behavioral dispositions may not be the same. Also, in a concrete situation like the missile crisis, a great deal more information may be available about the actions and motives of one side because of differences in degrees of secrecy. Further, some moral issues may apply especially to one side of the East–West political divide because of internal political differences (e.g., Soviet citizens cannot safely protest government defense policies as Westerners can), or differences in strategic policies or capabilities (e.g., some U.S. leaders, but not the Soviets, appear to favor replacing the 1972 ABM treaty with strategic defenses). Where these relevant asymmetries affect the content or scope of my arguments (e.g., in Chapters 5, 6, 8, and 9), my general procedure is to adopt the Western perspective.

There are two general assumptions about international politics that underlie my approach here. One is the descriptive assumption that there would be a great danger (i.e., a fairly high probability) that if the United States disarmed unilaterally of nuclear weapons, the Soviets would try to use the enormous nuclear preponderance that resulted to blackmail and dominate the world or much of it. Some reasons for believing this assumption are offered in Chapter 6. The assumption is also based on my view of the current superpower conflict as partly ideological and partly a traditional conflict among great powers for influence, security, and dominance. In this conflict, the Soviets are especially dangerous because of their ideology of worldwide revolution and the lack of domestic political constraints on their foreign policy behavior. The United States is especially dangerous because its leaders and citizens got used to a predominant political-military position in the world after World War II and may be inclined to take not very sensible risks to maintain that position despite changed conditions.

An alternate way to express my basic descriptive assumption is in terms of two models of Soviet international behavior. The bank-robber model of Chapter 6 imagines the Soviets as potential robbers of Western treasures who have been deterred by tight Western security measures. The contrasting elephant-dance model derives from the old joke about the woman who sees her wildly costumed neighbor doing a strange and noisy dance on his lawn and asks him what he is doing. "Keeping away the elephants," he says, and she responds, "But there aren't any elephants around here." He replies, "See how well it works!" According to this model, extensive Western security measures (including our nuclear arsenal) are as unnecessary as this man's dances, since the Soviets would not be in our backyards if these measures were absent. My assumption is that it is quite likely that the bank-robber model is the superior model of Soviet behavior. I don't claim there is certainty about what the Soviets would do. I doubt that obtaining such certainty is possible short of doing the crucial (and dangerous) experiment of unilaterally disarming and seeing what actually happens. But I am encouraged about my assessment of what is likely by the fact that a number of knowledgeable people I have discussed it with (including socialists and leftist critics of U.S. foreign and defense policies) agree with this assessment.

A general assumption about values also underlies the argument of these essays. It is the rather modest assumption that domination of the world by the Soviets would very probably be a very bad thing for the people of the world. The more doubtful assumption that U.S. domination of the world, or the universal adoption of Western values, would be a good thing is not required for my arguments. And, indeed, though I myself strongly prefer Western to Soviet values, I would be disinclined to accept the latter assumption. A world with a plurality of political systems, or one dominated by a third system that embodies the strengths of both liberalism and socialism (if this is possible), would probably be a better world than one dominated by either of the current superpowers. In any case, it is fortunate that my arguments for the permissibility of nuclear deterrence require only the modest value assumption. For as a political philosopher, I am aware of both the difficulty of establishing controversial claims about values and the foolishness of engaging in ideological debate in an introduction.

STRATEGIC ISSUES

These essays focus on the fundamental question as to whether any policy of nuclear deterrence involving the threat (and risk) of killing many innocent civilians can be morally permissible. Little attention is paid to more specific questions about nuclear weapons procurement, targeting, strategy, and use. There are three reasons for this. First, as the discussion in the essays shows, it is hard enough to answer the fundamental question in a satisfactory way. Second, as a philosopher, I am not an expert on the factual matters relevant to answering the more specific questions (though I have devoted considerable time over a period of years to learn what I could). Third, on many of the relevant strategic issues, there is something like a consensus among most philosophers who have written about them. Usually, where there is a consensus, I am in agreement with it, and have little distinctive or novel to add to what others have said. Nonetheless, to avoid misunderstandings, I shall briefly state my views on some of the more important general strategic issues. Readers should especially note that on each of thse issues, there is a substantial divergence between current U.S. policy and the positions I – as one representative of the philosophical consensus – regard as justified.

One such issue concerns what concept should guide nuclear arms procurement, and the obviously correct answer here, in my view is *adequacy* or *sufficiency*. Forces adequate for deterrence (and perhaps providing sufficient incentive for the other side to engage in mutual nuclear disarmament) are what a superpower should seek. Sufficiency for war fighting or war winning are not appropriate goals, and are likely, if adopted, to lead to an accelerating nuclear arms race. Superiority is an unreasonable goal for similar reasons – its pursuit is highly likely to result in a continuing quantitative and qualitative nuclear arms race between the superpowers. Equality is a less objectionable goal than superiority, but because of definitional difficulties and perceptual biases (see Chapter 10), its pursuit may impede arms control and lead to continued weapons competition. The dangers of a nuclear arms race leading to war should be obvious. Qualitative weapons improvements can raise the relative advantage of striking first in a nuclear exchange, thus increasing the chances of war during a crisis. An ongoing nuclear arms race also poisons the political atmosphere between the competitors, making dangerous crises more likely. It also tends to raise the size of nuclear stockpiles and hence the potential destructiveness of all-out war. And its presentation of "windows of opportunity" combined with future possible "windows of vulnerability" may encourage one side to take dangerous military or political actions while the balance of strategic forces seems (temporarily) favorable. Given these dangers, sufficiency for deterrence is the preferred guiding concept for weapons procurement, as it is least likely to stimulate a nuclear arms race.[4]

A second strategic issue concerns the justifiable scope of nuclear deterrence. Strategic theorists distinguish between *minimum* deterrence, which threatens nuclear retaliation against nuclear (or other) attacks on the homeland, and *extended* deterrence, which threatens nuclear retaliation to protect allies, armed forces deployed overseas, or other "vital national interests" abroad. The utilitarian arguments for practicing minimum rather than extended deterrence are strong. A relatively small invulnerable force of weapons would be adequate for the purposes of minimum deterrence – hence the dangers of the nuclear arms race could be lessened or avoided if one or both superpowers adopted a minimum deterrence posture. Crisis stability would be great under a minimum deterrence system, since neither side would have much incentive to strike first. (The enemy's weapons are largely invulnerable and a strike on the enemy homeland is nearly certain to be answered.) Also, there are potentially feasible nonnuclear measures, at least for the United States, that would achieve the same purposes as extended deterrence (e.g., beefing up NATO conventional forces and perhaps narrowing the U.S. conception of vital national intersts that must and can be guarded by military means). Minimum deterrence remains necessary (in the absence of bilateral nuclear disarmament) because there is a plausible reason for one superpower to attack the other that does not apply to other targets: removing one's main rival from a position of power. In the case of other potential targets, the likely aim of aggression would be to gain territory or resources. This aim would be largely frustrated by using nuclear weapons in the attack. Large-scale conventional attacks, on the other hand, should be reliably deterrable by adequate conventional forces together with the residual risk that nuclear weapons deployed for minimum deterrence might nevertheless end up being used in a large, initially conventional, war.

This is not to say that a change to a minimum deterrence policy would be without risks or costs. The United States and its European allies might have to lower their high average standards of living a small amount to build up NATO conventional forces. The whole process would have to be carried out gradually to minimize the likelihood of dangerous responses by the Soviets or the Western Europeans – for example, crash nuclear armament policies by Western European nations followed by Soviet threats (or actions) directed against these policies. Such a shift would be decidedly safer if carried out as part of the bilateral nuclear disarmament process advocated in Chapter 10. But it would carry risks in any case. It is justified only because the greatest current dangers of nuclear war arise from extended deterrence policies – with the arms race being fueled by the strong credibility requirements of extended deterrent threats, and the most plausible routes to large-scale nuclear war involving use of tactical nuclear weapons on foreign battlefields.[5]

Two main objections can be offered to the preference for minimum over extended deterrence. One is that drawing the line of nuclear defense at U.S. borders is arbitrary, both logically and morally. Why shouldn't European as well as American freedoms be defended by the U.S. nuclear umbrella? Freedom-loving Europeans (and other allies) are no less deserving of nuclear defense than Americans. If it makes sense to threaten and risk nuclear war to defend Alaska, Hawaii, and California, why doesn't it make equal sense to do the same to defend England, West Germany, South Korea, and Japan?

The answer to this objection is that the degree of risk involved in the two cases is very different. Nuclear threats to defend the homeland are inherently more credible: they do not invite challenges and they do not require destabilizing procurement and deployment practices (such as forward basing of tactical nuclear weapons and the attainment of a plausible first-strike capacity) to enhance their credibility. To see the force in this reply, notice that freedom-loving Poles, Ukrainians, and Estonians are as deserving of having their freedoms secured by U.S. nuclear threats as are Western Europeans. But very few would favor attempting to liberate Eastern Europe and the non-Russian Soviet republics by U.S. nuclear threats! The reason is that these threats would be inherently incredible and extremely dangerous. This shows that the key determinant of whose freedoms it makes moral sense to secure by nuclear threats has little to do with who is deserving and has everything to do with the degrees of risk involved. In the case of the United States defending itself by minimum deterrence, the risks are quite small; while in the case of the United States attempting to liberate Eastern Europe by nuclear threats, the risks are prohibitively large. The risks of defending U.S. allies by extended deterrence fall in between and are not worth running if there are alternative means of defense available.

A second objection to minimum deterrence is based on the moral right of national defense discussed in Chapter 4. If allied nations can pool these rights and transfer them to their U.S. ally, then the United States would have the moral right to threaten potential enemies with nuclear attack to defend these allies as well as itself. This objection cannot be adequately treated without further investigations of the foundations and limits of the right of national defense. However, two apparent limitations of this objection are worth noting here. First, national defense by nuclear threats may be permissible only when there is no feasible alternative and, in the case of many U.S. allies, there may be feasible alternatives, such as effective conventional defenses. Second, a nation's right of national defense probably derives from the individual rights of self-defense of its citizens and does not apply to defense of the government or political system except insofar as these are freely chosen by the citizens. If this is true, the present line of argument could *at most* sanction nuclear defense of democratic allies (e.g., Western European nations) and not U.S. nuclear defense of undemocratic proxy governments in third world countries. So while no final answer can be given here, and the possibility is left open that extended deterrence to protect some (e.g., Western European) allies is permissible, when nuclear deterrence is defended in these essays, it is – unless otherwise specified – primarily minimum deterrence that I have in mind.

A third strategic issue concerns the targeting of nuclear weapons. The main debate here is between two targeting doctrines: aiming at military targets, or counterforce, versus aiming at enemy cities, or countervalue. The moral defect of countervalue targeting is that it involves threatening, intending (conditionally), and risking the killing of many millions of enemy civilians. The moral defect of counterforce targeting is that it is destabilizing, both in crises and over the long term. Counterforce targeting gives each side strong incentives to strike first in an intense crisis, for the side shooting first can hope to limit the damage it suffers with its counterforce weapons. And counterforce targeting fuels an ongoing arms race in which each side seeks to preserve its continuing second-strike capacity in the face of more and better weapons on the other side, and strives for a credible first-strike capacity of its own for purposes of damage limitation or extended deterrence.

Indeed, counterforce targeting is usually associated with extended deterrence, on the assumption that the credibility of extended deterrent threats requires a nuclear war-fighting capability that can limit retaliatory damage to the homeland. And countervalue targeting is usually associated with minimum deterrence, on the assumption that a second strike with a relatively small number of weapons must be aimed at cities if the prospect of it is to deter successfully. But there is a third targeting option, namely *flexibility*. This involves having strategic nuclear weapons that can be fired either at military targets away from cities or at cities (and military targets within or near them), depending upon the orders given at the time of attack. This, if technically feasible, is probably the superior targeting strategy, because it combines some of the main advantages of each of the other approaches. It allows for maximally deterrent countercity threats to be made, without facing an attacked party with the unpalatable choice of doing nothing or making devastating counterstrikes on enemy cities. (If making the countercity threats sufficiently credible requires actually intending to carry them out, this strategy raises some moral paradoxes that are discussed in Chapters 1 and 2.)

If strategic weapons are effectively invulnerable, this flexible targeting strategy is readily combinable with a minimum deterrence posture. Stable mutual deterrence by the threat of destroying cities would be possible if each side had a relatively small number of nuclear warheads on submarines and single-warhead mobile missiles. Under these conditions there would be little incentive to preempt, since the other side could devastate many of one's cities in response. But if there were an actual attack, the side attacked would still have the morally preferable option of firing its nuclear weapons only at military targets some distance from cities.[6]

The actual combat use of nuclear weapons remains to be considered here. On the morality of nuclear use, I am largely in agreement with the views of the U.S. Catholic bishops' Pastoral Letter of 1983.[7] Actual first use of nuclear weapons would be morally wrong. Strategic first use would be wrong because of the incredible amount of damage that would be done to humanity and civilization by a strategic nuclear exchange.[8] First use of tactical nuclear weapons would be wrong because of the considerable likelihood it would lead through escalation to large-scale nuclear war, and because even if escalation was somehow avoided, it would set a precedent for future nuclear use that would eventually produce escalation. Retaliatory use of nuclear weapons against cities would be wrong because of the deliberate large-scale killing of innocent civilians it would involve, without sufficient certainty of attaining potentially overriding ends (e.g., the saving of much greater numbers of civilians). Retaliatory use of nuclear weapons against military targets isolated from cities (what I call in Chapter 2 Scrupulous Retaliation) might be justified, but only if there were good reasons to think it more likely to result in damage limitation or intrawar deterrence than in further counterstrikes and escalation. Note, however, that an official nuclear policy of retaliating only in a morally proper way might not be an effective deterrent (or, in any case, as effective a deterrent as policies threatening more severe and more certain retaliation). This means that a sufficiently reliable policy of nuclear deterrence might require making threats to retaliate immorally. Indeed, if our threats of nuclear retaliation are unconvincing unless we mean to carry them out (or set up a strategic military system that will carry them out semi-automatically), we may actually have to intend immoral retaliation in order to deter reliably. This leads us to Chapter 1, in which some moral paradoxes that arise out of this observation about intentions are discussed.

PART I

Moral paradoxes of nuclear deterrence

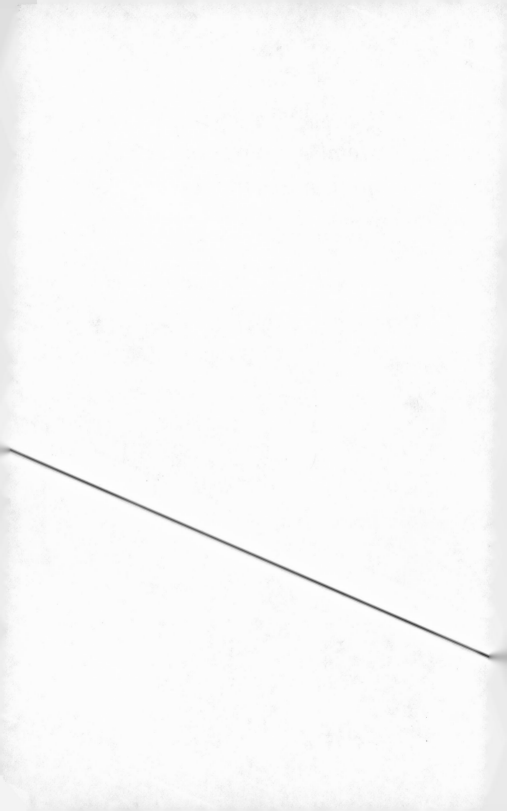

1. Some paradoxes of deterrence

Deterrence is a parent of paradox. Conflict theorists, notably Thomas Schelling, have pointed out several paradoxes of deterrence: that it may be to the advantage of someone who is trying to deter another to be irrational, to have fewer available options, or to lack relevant information.[1] I shall describe certain new paradoxes that emerge when one attempts to analyze deterrence from a moral rather than a strategic perspective. These paradoxes are presented in the form of statements that appear absurd or incredible on first inspection, but can be supported by quite convincing arguments.

Consider a typical situation involving deterrence. A potential wrongdoer is about to commit an offense that would unjustly harm someone. A defender intends, and threatens, to retaliate should the wrongdoer commit the offense. Carrying out retaliation, if the offense is committed, could well be morally wrong. (The wrongdoer could be insane, or the retaliation could be out of proportion with the offense, or could seriously harm others besides the wrongdoer.) The moral paradoxes of deterrence arise out of the attempt to determine the moral status of the defender's *intention* to retaliate in such cases. If the defender knows retaliation to be wrong, it would appear that this intention is evil. Yet such "evil" intentions may pave the road to heaven, by preventing serious offenses and by doing so without actually harming anyone.

Scrutiny of such morally ambiguous retaliatory intentions

An earlier version of this chapter was presented at Stanford University. I am grateful to several persons, especially Robert Merrihew Adams, Tyler Burge, Daniel Farrell, Robert Ladenson, Warren Quinn, and Virginia Warren, for helpful comments on previous drafts. My work was supported, in part, by a Regents' Faculty Research Fellowship from the University of California.

reveals paradoxes that call into question certain significant and widely accepted moral doctrines. These doctrines are what I call *bridge principles*. They attempt to link together the moral evaluation of actions and the moral evaluation of agents (and their states) in certain simple and apparently natural ways. The general acceptance and intuitive appeal of such principles lends credibility to the project of contructing a consistent moral system that accurately reflects our firmest moral beliefs about both agents and actions. By raising doubts about the validity of certain popular bridge principles, the paradoxes presented here pose new difficulties for this important project.

I. SPECIAL DETERRENT SITUATIONS

In this section, a certain class of situations involving deterrence is characterized, and a plausible normative assumption is presented. In the following three sections, we will see how application of this assumption to these situations yields paradoxical conclusions that conflict with widely accepted bridge principles.

The class of paradox-producing situations is best introduced by means of an example. Consider the balance of nuclear terror as viewed from the perspective of one of its superpower participants, nation N. N sees the threat of nuclear retaliation as its only reliable means of preventing nuclear attack (or nuclear blackmail leading to world domination) by its superpower rival. N is confident such a threat will succeed in deterring its adversary, provided it really intends to carry out that threat.[2] (N fears that, if it bluffs, its adversary is likely to learn this through leaks or espionage.) Finally, N recognizes it would have conclusive moral reasons *not* to carry out the threatened retaliation, if its opponent were to obliterate N with a surprise attack. For although retaliation would punish the leaders who committed this unprecedented crime and would prevent them from dominating the postwar world, N knows it would also destroy many millions of innocent civilians in the attacking nation (and in other nations), would set back postwar economic recovery for the world immeasurably, and might add enough fallout (and sun-blocking ashes and dust) to the atmosphere to destroy the human race.

Let us call situations of the sort that nation N perceives itself as being in, *Special Deterrent Situations (SDSs)*. More precisely, an agent is in an SDS when he reasonably and correctly believes that the following conditions hold. First, it is likely he must intend (conditionally) to apply a harmful sanction to innocent people, if an extremely harmful and unjust offense is to be prevented. Second, such an intention would very likely deter the offense. Third, the amounts of harm involved in the offense and the threatened sanctions are very large, and the relevant probabilities and amounts of harm are such that a rational utilitarian evaluation would substantially favor having the intention.[3] Finally, he would have conclusive moral reasons not to apply the sanction if the offense were to occur.

The first condition in this definition requires some comment. Deterrence depends only on the potential wrongdoer's *beliefs* about the prospects of the sanction being applied. Hence, the first condition will be satisfied only if attempts by the defender to bluff would likely be perceived as such by the wrongdoer. This may be the case if the defender is an unconvincing liar, or is a group with a collective decision procedure, or if the wrongdoer is shrewd and knows the defender quite well. Generally, however, bluffing will be a promising course of action. Hence, although it is surely logically and physically possible for an SDS to occur, there will be few actual SDSs. It may be noted, though, that writers on strategic policy frequently assert that nuclear deterrence will be effective only if the defending nation really intends to retaliate.[4] If this is so, the balance of terror may fit the definition of an SDS, and the paradoxes developed here could have significant practical implications.[5] Further, were there no actual SDSs, these paradoxes would still be of considerable theoretical interest. For they indicate that the validity of some widely accepted moral doctrines rests on the presupposition that certain situations that could arise (i.e., SDSs) will not.

Turning to our normative assumption, we begin by noting that any reasonable system of ethics must have substantial utilitarian elements. The assumption that produces the paradoxes of deterrence concerns the role of utilitarian considerations in determining one's moral duty in a narrowly limited class of situations. Let us say that *a great deal of utility is at stake* in a given situation if either (1) reliable expected utilities are calculable and the difference in expected utility between the best act and its alternatives is extremely large, or (2) reliable expected utilities are not calculable and there are extremely large differences in utility between some possible outcomes of different available acts. Our assumption says that the act favored by utilitarian considerations should be performed whenever a great deal of utility is at stake. This means that, if the difference in expected, or possible, utilities of the available acts is extremely large (e.g., equivalent to the difference between life and death for a very large number of people), other moral considerations are overridden by utilitarian considerations.

This assumption may be substantially weakened by restricting in various ways its range of application. I restrict the assumption to apply only when (i) a great deal of *negative* utility is at stake, and (ii) people will likely suffer serious injustices if the agent fails to perform the most useful act. This makes the assumption more plausible, since the propriety of doing one person a serious injustice, in order to produce positive benefits for others, is highly questionable. The justifiability of doing the same injustice to prevent a utilitarian disaster that itself involves grave injustices, seems more in accordance with our moral intuitions.

The above restrictions appear to bring our assumption into line with the views of philosophers such as Robert Nozick, Thomas Nagel, Richard Brandt, and Michael Walzer, who portray moral rules as "absolutely" forbidding certain kinds of acts, but acknowledge that exceptions might have to be allowed in cases in which such acts are necessary to prevent catastrophe.[6] Even with these restrictions, however, the proposed assumption would be rejected by supporters of genuine moral absolutism, the doctrine that there are certain acts (such as vicarious punishment and deliberate killing of the innocent) that are always wrong, whatever the consequences of not performing them. (Call such acts *inherently evil*.) We can, though, accommodate some absolutists. To do so, let us further qualify our assumption by limiting its application to cases in which (iii) performing the most useful act involves, at most, a small risk of performing an inherently evil act. With this restriction, the assumption still leads to paradoxes, yet is consistent with absolutism (unless that doctrine is interpreted to include absolute prohibitions on something other than doing acts of the sort usually regarded as inherently evil[7]). The triply qualified assumption is quite plausible; so the fact that it produces paradoxes is both interesting and disturbing.

II. PARADOXICAL INTENTIONS

The first moral paradox of deterrence is:

(P1) There are cases in which, although it would be wrong for an agent to perform a certain act in a certain situation, it would nonetheless be right for that agent, knowing this, to form the intention to perform that act in that situation.

At first, this strikes one as absurd. If it is wrong and the agent is aware that it is wrong, how could it be right for her to form the intention to do it? (P1) is the direct denial of a simple moral thesis, the Wrongful Intentions Principle (WIP): *To form the intention to do what one knows to be wrong is itself wrong.*[8] WIP seems so obvious that, although philosophers never call it into question, they rarely bother to assert it or argue for it. Nevertheless, it appears that Abelard, Aquinas, Butler, Bentham, Kant, and Sidgwick, as well as recent writers such as Anthony Kenny and Jan Narveson, have accepted the principle, at least implicitly.[9]

Why does WIP seem so obviously true? First, we regard the person who fully intends to perform a wrongful act and is prevented from doing so solely by external circumstances (e.g., a person whose murder plan is interrupted by the victim's fatal heart attack) as being just as bad as the person who performs a like wrongful act. Second, we view the person who intends to do what is wrong, and then has a change of mind, as having corrected a moral failing or error. Third, it is convenient, for many purposes, to treat a prior intention to perform an act as the beginning of the act itself. Hence, we are inclined to view intentions as parts of actions and to ascribe to each intention the moral status ascribed to the act "containing" it.

It is essential to note that WIP appears to apply to conditional intentions in the same manner as it applies to nonconditional ones. Suppose I form the intention to kill my neighbor if he insults me again, and fail to kill him only because, fortuitously, he refrains from doing so. I am as bad, or nearly as bad, as if he had insulted me and I had killed him. My failure to perform the act no more erases the wrongness of my intention, than my neighbor's dropping dead as

I load my gun would negate the wrongness of the simple intention to kill him. Thus the same considerations adduced above in support of WIP seem to support the formulation: If it would be wrong to perform an act in certain circumstances, then it is wrong to form the intention to perform that act on the condition that those circumstances arise.

Having noted the source of the strong feeling that (P1) should be rejected, we must consider an instantiation of (P1):

(P1′) In an SDS, it would be wrong for the defender to apply the sanction if the wrongdoer were to commit the offense, but it is right for the defender to form the (conditional) intention to apply the sanction if the wrongdoer commits the offense.

The first half of (P1′), the wrongness of applying the sanction, follows directly from the last part of the definition of an SDS, which says that the defender would have conclusive moral reasons not to apply the sanction. The latter half of (P1′), which asserts the rightness of forming the intention to apply the sanction, follows from the definition of an SDS and our normative assumption. According to the definition, the defender's forming this intention is likely necessary, and very likely sufficient, to prevent a seriously harmful and unjust offense. It follows that doing so involves only a small risk of performing an inherently evil act.[10] Further, in an SDS, a great deal of utility is at stake, and utilitarian considerations substantially favor forming the intention to apply the sanction. Applying our normative assumption yields the conclusion that it is right for the defender to form the intention in question.

This argument, if sound, would establish the truth of (P1′), and hence (P1), in contradiction with WIP. It suggests that WIP should not be applied to *deterrent intentions,* that is, those conditional intentions whose existence is based on the agent's desire to thereby deter others from actualizing the antecedent condition of the intention. Such intentions are rather strange. They are, by nature, self-stultifying: if a deterrent intention fulfills the agent's purpose, it ensures that the intended (and possibly evil) act is not performed, by preventing the circumstances of performance from arising. The unique nature of such intentions can be further explicated by noting the distinction between intending to do something and desiring (or intending) to intend to do it. Normally, an agent will form the intention to do something because she either desires doing that thing as an end in itself, or as a means to other ends. In such cases, little importance attaches to the distinction between intending and desiring to intend. But, in the case of deterrent intentions, the ground of the desire to form the intention is entirely distinct from any desire to carry it out. Thus, what may be inferred about the agent who seeks to form such an intention is this. She desires *having the intention* as a means of deterrence. Also, she is willing, in order to prevent the offense, to accept a certain risk that, in the end, she will apply the sanction. But this is entirely consistent with her having a strong desire not to apply the sanction, and no desire at all to apply it. Thus, while the object of her deterrent intention might be an evil act, it does not follow that, in desiring to adopt that intention, she desires to do evil, either as an end or as a means.

WIP ties the morality of an intention exclusively to the moral qualities of its object (i.e., the intended act). This is not unreasonable since, typically, the only significant effects of intentions are the acts of the agent (and the consequences of these acts) that flow from these intentions. However, in certain cases, intentions may have autonomous effects that are independent of the intended act's actually being performed. In particular, intentions to act may influence the conduct of other agents. When an intention has important autonomous effects, these effects must be incorporated into any adequate moral analysis of it. The first paradox arises because the autonomous effects of the relevant deterrent intention are dominant in the moral analysis of an SDS, but the extremely plausible WIP ignores such effects.[11]

III. THE PRISON OF VIRTUE

(P1') implies that a rational moral agent in an SDS should want to form the conditional intention to apply the sanction if the offense is committed, in order to deter the offense. But will he be able to do so? Paradoxically, he will not be. He is a captive in the prison of his own virtue, able to form the requisite intention only by bending the bars of his cell out of shape. Consider the preliminary formulation of this new paradox:

(P2') In an SDS, a rational and morally good agent cannot (as a matter of logic) have (or form) the intention to apply the sanction if the offense is committed.[12]

The argument for (P2') is as follows. An agent in an SDS

recognizes that there would be conclusive moral reasons not to apply
the sanction if the offense were committed. If he does not regard
these admittedly conclusive moral reasons as conclusive reasons for
him not to apply the sanction, then he is not moral. Suppose, on the
other hand, that he does regard himself as having conclusive reasons
not to apply the sanction if the offense is committed. If, nonetheless,
he is disposed to apply it, because the reasons for applying it
motivate him more strongly than do the conclusive reasons not to
apply it, then he is irrational.

But couldn't our rational moral agent recognize, in accordance
with (P1'), that he ought to form the intention to apply the sanction?
And couldn't he then simply grit his teeth and pledge to himself that
he will apply the sanction if the offense is committed? No doubt he
could, and this would amount to trying to form the intention to
apply the sanction. But the question remains whether he can succeed
in forming that intention, by this or any other process, while
remaining rational and moral. And it appears he cannot. There are,
first of all, psychological difficulties. Being rational, how can he dispose himself to do something that he knows he would have conclusive reasons not to do, when and if the time comes to do it?
Perhaps, though, some exceptional people can produce in themselves dispositions to act merely by pledging to act. But even if one
could, in an SDS, produce a disposition to apply the sanction in this
manner, such a disposition would not count as a *rational intention* to
apply the sanction. This is because, as recent writers on intentions
have suggested, it is part of the concept of rationally intending to do
something, that the disposition to do the intended act be caused (or
justified) in an appropriate way by the agent's view of reasons for
doing the act.[13] And the disposition in question does not stand in
such a relation to the agent's reasons for action.

It might be objected to this that people sometimes intend to do
things (and do them) for no reason at all, without being irrational.
This is true, and indicates that the connections between the concepts
of intending and reasons for action are not so simple as the above
formula implies. But it is also true that intending to do something
for no reason at all, in the face of recognized significant reasons not
to do it, would be irrational. Similarly, a disposition to act in the face
of the acknowledged preponderance of reasons, whether called an
"intention" or not, could not qualify as rational. It may be claimed

that such a disposition, in an SDS, is rational in the sense that the agent knows it would further his aims to form (and have) it. This is not to deny the second paradox, but simply to express one of its paradoxical features. For the point of (P2′) is that the very disposition that *is* rational in the sense just mentioned, is at the same time irrational in an equally important sense. It is a disposition to act in conflict with the agent's own view of the balance of reasons for action.

We can achieve some insight into this by noting that an intention that is deliberately formed, resides at the intersection of two distinguishable actions. It is the beginning of the act that is its object and it is the end of the act that is its formation. As such, it may be assessed as rational (or moral) or not, according to whether either of two different acts promotes the agent's (or morality's) ends. Generally, the assessments will agree. But, as Schelling and others have noted, it may sometimes promote one's aims *not* to be disposed to act to promote one's aims should certain contingencies arise. For example, a small country may deter invasion by a larger country if it is disposed to resist any invasion, even when resistance would be suicidal. In such situations, the assessment of the rationality (or morality) of the agent's intentions will depend upon whether these intentions are treated as components of their object-acts or their formation-acts. If treated as both, conflicts can occur. It is usual and proper to assess the practical rationality of an agent, at a given time, according to the degree of correspondence between his intentions and the reasons he has for performing the acts that are the objects of those intentions. As a result, puzzles such as (P2′) emerge when, for purposes of moral analysis, an agent's intentions are viewed partly as components of their formation-acts.

Let us return to the main path of our discussion by briefly summarizing the argument for (P2′). A morally good agent regards conclusive moral reasons for action as conclusive reasons for action *simpliciter*. But the intentions of a rational agent are not out of line with her assessment of the reasons for and against acting. Consequently, a rational moral agent cannot intend to do something that she recognizes there are conclusive moral reasons not to do. Nor can she intend conditionally to do what she recognizes she would have conclusive reasons not to do were that condition to be fulfilled. Therefore, in an SDS, where one has conclusive moral reasons not to apply the sanction, an originally rational and moral agent cannot have the intention to apply it without ceasing to be fully rational or moral; nor can she form the intention (as this entails having it). We have observed that forming an intention is a process that may generally be regarded as an action. Thus, the second paradox can be reformulated as:

(P2) There are situations (namely SDSs) in which it would be right for agents, if they could, to perform certain actions (namely forming the intention to apply the sanction), and in which it is possible for some agents to perform such actions, but impossible for rational and morally good agents to perform them.

(P2), with the exception of the middle clause, is derived from the conjunction of (P1′) and (P2′) by existential generalization. The truth of the middle clause follows from the consideration of the vengeful agent, who desires to punish those who commit serious harmful and unjust offenses, no matter what the cost to others.

(P2) is paradoxical because it says that there are situations in which rationality and virtue preclude the possibility of right action. And this contravenes our usual assumption about the close logical ties between the concepts of right action and agent goodness. Consider the following claim. *Doing something is right if and only if a morally good person would do the same thing in the given situation.* Call this the Right-Good Principle. One suspects that, aside from qualifications concerning the good person's possible imperfections or factual ignorance, most people regard this principle, which directly contradicts (P2), as being virtually analytic. Yet the plight of the good person described in the second paradox does not arise out of an insufficiency of either knowledge or goodness. (P2) says there are conceivable situations in which virtue and knowledge combine with rationality to preclude right action, in which virtue is an obstacle to doing the right thing. If (P2) is true, our views about the close logical connection between right action and agent goodness, as embodied in the Right-Good Principle, require modifications of a sort not previously envisioned.

IV. DELIBERATE SELF-CORRUPTION

A rational moral agent in an SDS faces a cruel dilemma. His reasons for intending to apply the sanction if the offense is committed are, according to (P1'), conclusive. But they outrun his reasons for doing it. Wishing to do what is right, he wants to form the intention. However, unless he can substantially alter the basic facts of the situation or his beliefs about those facts, he can do so only by making himself less morally good; that is, by becoming a person who attaches grossly mistaken weights to certain reasons for and against action (e.g., one who prefers retribution to the protection of the vital interests of innocent people).[14] We have arrived at a third paradox:

(P3)   In certain situations, it would be morally right for a rational and morally good agent to deliberately (attempt to) corrupt himself.[15]

(P3) may be viewed in light of a point about the credibility of threats that has been made by conflict theorists. Suppose a defender is worried about the credibility of her deterrent threat, because she thinks the wrongdoer (rightly) regards her as unwilling to apply the threatened sanction. She may make the threat more credible by passing control of the sanction to some *retaliation agent*. Conflict theorists consider two sorts of retaliation agents: people known to be highly motivated to punish the offense in question, and machines programmed to retaliate automatically if the offense occurs. What I wish to note is that future selves of the defender herself are a third class of retaliation agents. If the other kinds are unavailable, a defender may have to create an agent of this third sort (i.e., an altered self willing to apply the sanction), in order to deter the offense. In cases in which applying the sanction would be wrong, this could require self-corruption.

How would a rational and moral agent in an SDS, who seeks to have the intention to apply the sanction, go about corrupting himself so that he may have it? He cannot form the intention simply by pledging to apply the sanction; for, according to the second paradox, his rationality and morality preclude this. Instead, he must seek to initiate a causal process (e.g., a reeducation program) that he hopes will result in his beliefs, attitudes, and values changing in such a way that he can and will have the intention to apply the sanction should the offense be committed. Initiating such a process involves taking a rather odd, though not uncommon attitude toward oneself: viewing oneself as an object to be molded in certain respects by outside influences rather than by inner choices. This is, for example, the attitude of the lazy but ambitious student who enrolls in a fine college, hoping that some of the habits and values of his highly motivated fellow students will rub off on him.

We can now better understand the notion of "risking performing an inherently evil act" introduced in Section I. For convenience, let "an inherently evil act" be "killing." Deliberately risking killing is different from risking deliberately killing. One does the former when one rushes an ill person to the hospital in one's car at unsafe speed, having noted the danger of causing a fatal accident. One has deliberately accepted the risk of killing by accident. One (knowingly) risks deliberately killing, on the other hand, when one undertakes a course of action that one knows may, by various causal processes, lead to one's later performing a deliberate killing. The mild-mannered youth who joins a violent street gang is an example. Similarly, the agent in an SDS, who undertakes a plan of self-corruption in order to develop the requisite deterrent intention, knowingly risks deliberately performing the wrongful act of applying the sanction.

The above description of what is required of the rational moral agent in an SDS, leads to a natural objection to the argument that supports (P3). According to this objection, an attempt at self-corruption by a rational moral agent is very likely to fail. Hence, bluffing would surely be a more promising strategy for deterrence than trying to form retaliatory intentions by self-corruption. Three replies may be given to this objection. First, it is certainly conceivable that, in a particular SDS, undertaking a process of self-corruption would be more likely to result in effective deterrence than would bluffing. Second, and more important, bluffing and attempting to form retaliatory intentions by self-corruption will generally not be mutually exclusive alternatives. An agent in an SDS may attempt to form the retaliatory intention while bluffing, and plan to continue bluffing as a "fallback" strategy, should self-corruption fail. If the offense to be prevented is disastrous enough, the additional expected utility generated by following such a combined strategy (as opposed to simply bluffing) will be very large, even if the agent's attempts to form the intention are unlikely to succeed. Hence, (P3) would still follow from our normative assumption. Finally, consider the rational and *partly corrupt* agent in an SDS who already has the intention to retaliate. (The nations participating in the balance of terror may be examples.) The relevant question about such an agent is whether she ought to act to become less corrupt, with the result that she would lose the intention to retaliate. The present objection does not apply in this case, since the agent already has the requisite corrupt features. Yet, essentially the same argument that produces (P3) leads, when this case is considered, to a slightly different, but equally puzzling, version of our third paradox:

(P3′) In certain situations, it would be morally wrong for a rational and partly corrupt agent to (attempt to) reform herself and eliminate her corruption.

A rather different objection to (P3) is the claim that its central notion is incoherent. This claim is made, apparently, by Thomas Nagel, who writes:

> The notion that one might sacrifice one's moral integrity justifiably, in the service of a sufficiently worthy end, is an incoherent notion. For if one were justified in making such a sacrifice (or even morally required to make it), then one would not be sacrificing one's moral integrity by adopting that course: one would be preserving it.[16]

Now the notion of a justified sacrifice of moral virtue (integrity) would be incoherent, as Nagel suggests, if one could sacrifice one's virtue only by doing something wrong. For the same act cannot be both morally justified and morally wrong. But one may also be said to sacrifice one's virtue when one deliberately initiates a causal process that one expects to result, and does result, in one's later becoming a less virtuous person. And, as the analysis of SDSs embodied in (P1′) and (P2′) implies, one may, in certain cases, be justified in initiating such a process (or even be obligated to initiate it). Hence, it would be a mistake to deny (P3) on the grounds advanced in Nagel's argument.

There is, though, a good reason for wanting to reject (P3). It conflicts with some of our firmest beliefs about virtue and duty. We regard the promotion and preservation of one's own virtue as a vital responsibility of each moral agent, and self-corruption as among the vilest enterprises. Further, we do not view the duty to promote one's virtue as simply one duty among others, to be weighed and balanced against the rest, but rather as a special duty that encompasses the other moral duties. Thus, we assent to the Virtue Preservation Principle: *It is wrong to deliberately lose (or reduce the degree of) one's moral virtue*. To many, this principle seems fundamental to our very conception of morality.[17] Hence the suggestion that duty could require the abandonment of virtue seems quite unacceptable. The fact that this suggestion can be supported by strong arguments produces a paradox.

This paradox is reflected in the ambivalent attitudes that emerge when we attempt to evaluate three hypothetical agents who respond to the demands of SDSs in various ways. The first agent refuses to try to corrupt himself and allows the disastrous offense to occur. We respect the love of virtue he displays, but are inclined to suspect him of too great a devotion to his own purity relative to his concern for the well-being of others. The second agent does corrupt herself to prevent disaster in an SDS. Though we do not approve of her new corrupt aspects, we admire the person that she was for her willingness to sacrifice what she loved – part of her own virtue – in the service of others. At the same time, the fact that she succeeded in corrupting herself may make us wonder whether she was entirely virtuous in the first place. Corruption, we feel, does not come easily to a good person. The third agent reluctantly but sincerely tries his best to corrupt himself to prevent disaster, but fails. He may be admired both for his willingness to make such a sacrifice and for having virtue so deeply engrained in his character that his attempts at self-corruption do not succeed. It is perhaps characteristic of the paradoxical nature of the envisioned situation, that we are inclined to admire most the only one of these three agents who fails in the course of action he undertakes.

V. ACTS AND AGENTS

It is natural to think of the evaluation of agents, and of actions, as being two sides of the same moral coin. The moral paradoxes of deterrence suggest they are more like two separate coins that can be fused together only by significantly deforming one or the other. In this concluding section, I shall briefly explain this.

Our shared assortment of moral beliefs may be viewed as consisting of three relatively distinct groups: beliefs about the evaluation of actions, beliefs about the evaluation of agents and their states (e.g., motives, intentions, and character traits), and beliefs about the relationship between the two. An important part of this last group of beliefs is represented by the three bridge principles introduced above: the Wrongful Intentions, Right-Good, and Virtue Preservation principles. Given an agreed-upon set of bridge principles, one could go about constructing a moral system meant to express coherently our moral beliefs in either of two ways: by developing principles that express our beliefs about act evaluation and then using the bridge principles to derive principles of agent evaluation – or vice versa. If our bridge principles are sound and our beliefs about agent and act evaluation are mutually consistent, the resulting systems would, in theory, be the same. If, however, there are underlying incompatibilities between the principles we use to evaluate acts and agents, there may be significant differences between moral systems that are *act-oriented* and those which are *agent-oriented*. And these differences may manifest themselves as paradoxes which exert pressure upon the bridge principles that attempt to link the divergent systems, and the divergent aspects of each system, together.

It seems natural to us to evaluate acts at least partly in terms of their consequences. Hence, act-oriented moral systems tend to involve significant utilitarian elements. The principle of act evaluation usually employed in utilitarian systems is: in a given situation, one ought to perform the most useful act, that which will (or is expected to) produce the most utility. What will maximize utility depends upon the facts of the particular situation. Hence, as various philosophers have pointed out, the above principle could conceivably recommend one's (i) acting from nonutilitarian motives, (ii) advocating some nonutilitarian moral theory, or even (iii) becoming a genuine adherent of some nonutilitarian theory.[18] Related quandaries arise when one considers, from an act-utilitarian viewpoint, the deterrent intention of a defender of an SDS. Here is an intention whose object-act is anti-utilitarian and whose formation-act is a utilitarian duty that cannot be performed by a rational utilitarian.

A utilitarian might seek relief from these quandaries in either of two ways. First, she could defend some form of rule-utilitarianism. But then she would face a problem. Shall she include, among the rules of her system, our normative assumption that requires the performance of the most useful act, whenever an enormous amount of utility is at stake (and certain other conditions are satisfied)? If she does, the moral paradoxes of deterrence will appear within her system. If she does not, it would seem that her system fails to attach the importance to the consequences of particular momentous acts that any reasonable moral, much less utilitarian, system should. An alternative reaction would be to stick by the utilitarian principle of act evaluation, and simply accept (P1)–(P3), and related oddities, as true. Taking this line would require the abandonment of the plausible and familiar bridge principles that contradict (P1)–(P3). But this need not bother the act-utilitarian, who perceives her task as the modification, as well as the codification, of our moral beliefs.

Agent-oriented (as opposed to act-oriented) moral systems rest on the premise that what primarily matters for morality are the internal states of a person – character traits, intentions, and the condition of the will – and these should not be evaluated solely in terms of their consequences. The doctrines about intentions and virtue expressed in our three bridge principles are generally incorporated into such systems. The paradoxes of deterrence may pose serious problems for some agent-oriented systems. It may be, for example, that an adequate analysis of the moral virtues of justice, selflessness, and benevolence, would imply that the truly virtuous person would feel obligated to do whatever is necessary to prevent a catastrophe, even if this required a sacrifice of personal virtue. If so, the moral paradoxes of deterrence would arise within agent-oriented systems committed to these virtues.

There are, however, agent-oriented systems that would not be affected by our paradoxes. One such system could be called extreme Kantianism. According to this view, the only things having moral significance are such features of a person as character and state of will. The extreme Kantian accepts Kant's dictum that morality requires treating oneself and others as ends rather than means. This is interpreted to imply strict duties to preserve one's virtue and not to deliberately impose serious harms or risks on innocent people. Thus the extreme Kantian would simply reject (P1)–(P3) without qualm.

Although act-utilitarians and extreme Kantians can view the paradoxes of deterrence without concern, one doubts that the rest of us can. The adherents of these extreme conceptions of morality are untroubled by the paradoxes because their viewpoints are too one-sided to represent our moral beliefs accurately. Each of them is closely attentive to certain standard principles of agent *or* act evaluation, but seems too little concerned with traditional principles of the other sort. For a system of morality to reflect our firmest and deepest convictions adequately, it must represent a middle ground between these extremes by seeking to accommodate the valid insights of both act-oriented and agent-oriented perspectives. The normative assumption set out in section I was chosen as a representative principle that might be incorporated into such a system. It treated utilitarian considerations as relevant and potentially decisive, while allowing for the importance of other factors. Though consistent with the absolute prohibition of certain sorts of acts, it treats the distinction between harms and risks as significant and rules out absolute prohibitions on the latter as unreasonable. It is an extremely plausible middle-ground principle; but, disturbingly, it leads to paradoxes.

That these paradoxes reflect conflicts between commonly accepted principles of agent and act evaluation, is further indicated by the following observation. Consider what initially appears a natural way of viewing the evaluation of acts and agents as coordinated parts of a single moral system. According to this view, reasons for action determine the moral status of acts, agents, and intentions. A right act is an act that accords with the preponderance of moral reasons for action. To have the right intention is to be disposed to perform the act supported by the preponderance of such reasons, because of those reasons. The virtuous agent is the rational agent who has the proper substantive values, that is, the person whose intentions and actions accord with the preponderance of moral reasons for action. Given these considerations, it appears that it should always be possible for an agent to go along intending, and acting, in accordance with the preponderance of moral reasons; thus ensuring both her own virtue and the rightness of her intentions and actions. Unfortunately, this conception of harmonious coordination between virtue, right intention, and right action, is shown to be untenable by the paradoxes of deterrence. For they demonstrate that, in any system that takes consequences plausibly into account, situations can arise in which the rational use of moral principles leads to certain paradoxical recommendations: that the principles used, and part of the agent's virtue, be abandoned, and that wrongful intentions be formed.

One could seek to avoid these paradoxes by moving in the direction of extreme Kantianism and rejecting our normative assumption. But to do so would be to overlook the plausible core of act-utilitarianism. This is the claim that, in the moral evaluation of acts, how those acts affect human happiness often is important – the more so as more happiness is at stake – and sometimes is decisive. Conversesely, one could move toward accommodation with act-utilitarianism. This would involve qualifying, so that they do not apply in SDSs, the traditional moral doctrines that contradict (P1)–(P3). And, in fact, viewed in isolation, the considerations adduced in section II indicate that the Wrongful Intentions Principle ought to be so qualified. However, the claims of (P2) and (P3), that virtue may preclude right action and that morality may require self-corruption, are not so easily accepted. These notions remain unpalatable even when one considers the arguments that support them.

Thus, tinkering with our normative assumption or with traditional moral doctrines would indeed enable us to avoid the paradoxes, at least in their present form. But this would require rejecting certain significant and deeply entrenched beliefs concerning the evaluation either of agents or of actions. Hence, such tinkering would not go far toward solving the fundamental problem of which the paradoxes are symptoms: the apparent incompatibility of the moral principles we use to evaluate acts and agents. Perhaps this problem can be solved. Perhaps the coins of agent and act evaluation can be successfully fused. But it is not apparent how this is to be done. And I, for one, do not at present see an entirely satisfactory way out of the perplexities that the paradoxes engender.

2. A paradox of deterrence revisited

Since Chapter 1 was originally published in 1978, there have been a number of discussions, by philosophers and others, of the issues treated there. These discussions have focused on the first moral paradox of deterrence, concerning whether it can be permissible to conditionally intend impermissible retaliation, and – in particular – on the application of this paradox to the case of nuclear deterrence. In this chapter, I consider some of the points raised in these discussions and explain my current views concerning this paradox.

The paradox arises from our apparently having good reasons to endorse – as regards Special Deterrent Situations (SDSs) – each of the members of this inconsistent triad of propositions:

(1) It would be wrong to retaliate if the offense were committed.

(2) It is permissible to form the intention to retaliate should the offense be committed, since this is the only reliable way to prevent the offense.

(3) If it would be wrong to do something under certain conditions, then it is wrong to form the intention to do that thing should those conditions arise. (The Wrongful Intentions Principle [WIP])

Unfortunately, the best known and most influential discussion of these issues – that of the U.S. Catholic bishops[1] – appears to endorse all of these propositions (in the case of nuclear deterrence) without acknowledging their mutual inconsistency.[2] That is, the bishops seem to condemn nuclear use and approve nuclear deterrence

I am grateful to Daniel Farrell and David Lewis for helpful comments on an earlier draft of this chapter.

(under specified constraints), while holding fast to WIP. This is quite understandable considering that the bishops' Pastoral Letter is a collectively produced political document operating under the constraints of the popes' limited endorsement of nuclear deterrence, the Catholic tradition's emphasis on the moral importance of intentions, and the need to achieve consensus among diverse opinions within the Church. Nonetheless, the bishops' failure to address the inconsistency of the various principles of nuclear morality that they apparently endorse inhibits our ability to learn clear moral lessons from an otherwise sensible and informative document.

If the bishops failed to notice, or at least acknowledge, the first paradox of deterrence, other writers – operating under fewer constraints – have not. Some, call them Traditionalists, have held fast to propositions (1) and (3), and have concluded that forming retaliatory intentions in SDSs is, after all, morally impermissible. Others, whom we may call Retaliators, have embraced propositions (2) and (3), and have concluded that retaliation would be permissible if deterrence failed in an SDS. Yet others have denied that the paradox applies to nuclear deterrence. In the next three sections of this chapter, I discuss these positions in turn, firmly rejecting the first two and explaining why I do not fully agree with the last.

Before proceeding with these discussions, however, something must be said about the nature of the first paradox of deterrence. As suggested at the beginning of Chapter 1, the first moral paradox of deterrence is analogous to a paradox about rationality noted by strategic theorists: it may be rational (for purposes of deterrence) to form the intention to carry out an irrational act of retaliation. But the analogy is not perfect in all respects. In particular, the moral paradox may apply in situations in which the rational paradox does not. Suppose A must sincerely threaten deadly retaliation against a group containing potential offender B, in order to deter B from committing a horribly destructive offense. If the likelihood of deterrent success is high enough, and the offense is bad enough (relative to the harm contained in the retaliation), the moral paradox arises. For retaliating would wrongly impose deadly harm on the other members of B's group, while intending to retaliate is necessary, and very likely sufficient, to prevent the offense. But suppose A is utterly indifferent to the fate of the members of B's group, but does desire to see serious offenders suffer. Then, given the usual instrumental conception of rationality as choosing effective means to one's ends, it would be rational for A to retaliate against B's group (to secure revenge on B) if B committed the offense. Since here both forming the intention to retaliate and actually retaliating are deemed rational, there is no paradox of rationality. We have moral but not rational paradox, because morality rules out seriously harming innocent people in the pursuit of vengeance, while rationality, in itself, may not.[3]

Nor is this difference an unimportant one. For some nuclear deterrence situations may fit this pattern and involve us in moral, but not rational, paradox. Consider the example used in Chapter 1 to illustrate the moral paradox: a nation deciding whether to retaliate to a surprise nuclear attack that has left it with virtually nothing to defend. While we argued that such retaliation would be immoral, it would not be irrational if the potential retaliators are totally indifferent to the fate of those outside their nation. That the rational paradox may not arise here – though the moral one clearly does – is revealed by the form in which the rational paradox is often discussed by deterrence theorists. They consider the case of a limited first strike on a nation (or a strike against its allies) that renders retaliation irrational *because it would invite counterretaliation*. They do not seem to feel there is a similar problem about rational retaliation to an all-out first strike on the nation itself.[4] The implicit assumption operating here is that causing the destruction of one's own nation is irrational, while causing the destruction of other nations is not. A parallel claim about the morality of destroying one's own and other nations would not appeal to anyone but the most hardened nationalists. Hence the moral and rational versions of our first paradox apply to different nuclear scenarios.

Still, for purely theoretical purposes, the two paradoxes can be brought back together. We simply stipulate that the potential retaliator is not interested in revenge on the offender for its own sake, and that she knows that the reasons against retaliation will outweigh those for retaliation once the offense is committed. Then we have a paradox concerning the rationality of forming an intention to irrationally retaliate that is precisely analogous to our moral paradox. These two paradoxes should stand or fall together, and should have parallel solutions.

It has been necessary to clarify the relationship between the moral and rational versions of our first paradox because champions of different solutions have tended to focus on different versions. Opponents of forming retaliatory intentions in SDSs have stressed the immorality of forming such intentions, while the main defender of retaliation in SDSs argues the rationality of such retaliation. I will answer each in kind, arguing that the former are wrong about morality and the latter is wrong about rationality.

I. WRONGFUL INTENTIONS

Traditionalists reject proposition (2), the view that, in an SDS, it is permissible to form an intention to perform an immoral act of retaliation.[5] The argument for (2), presented in Chapter 1, depends upon this intention – which I call an *SDS deterrent intention* – having (at least) the following five features:

(A)   It is conditional – that is, of the form "If offense O occurs, I will do W."
(B)   It is a deterrent intention – that is, one formed to prevent the occurrence of its antecedent condition (O).
(C)   The offense O which the intending agent seeks to deter is an unjust and seriously harmful act.
(D)   The deterrent intention would very likely prevent O.
(E)   Given the magnitudes of O and W, and what is known about the likelihood of the deterrent intention (and alternative courses of action) preventing O, a rational utilitarian balancing of costs and benefits favors forming the intention.[6]

Unfortunately, in their discussions of the first paradox of deterrence, even some of the most sophisticated Traditionalists – such philosophers as Douglas Lackey, James Sterba, and Anthony Kenny – fail to take account of all these features of an SDS deterrent intention. Hence, their criticisms of proposition (2), insofar as they go beyond a mere reiteration of support for WIP, are largely off-target.

Consider first Lackey. He views the defender of deterrence as committed to the following principle: "It is always morally permissible to form an intention to do W if O provided that one has good reason to believe that O will not occur even if W is a wicked action which would be morally wrong to perform if O occurred."[7] And he proposes testing this principle by imagining whether someone who knows that he is unlikely ever to meet a member of a certain minority group may permissibly form the conditional intention to spit in the face of any member of this group that he does meet. But Lackey's principle, and example, take account only of feature A (conditionality) and part of feature D – its implication that the conditions for carrying out the intention are unlikely to arise. Lackey completely ignores the other crucial features of SDS deterrent intentions. Forming the intention to spit that Lackey describes is, as he suggests, clearly unjustified. But this is partly because that intention does not serve the purpose of deterring a seriously harmful and unjust offense that cannot otherwise be prevented. (Indeed, in Lackey's description, the intention serves no discernible purpose at all but that of expressing the agent's anti-minority feelings.)

To genuinely test proposition (2) by Lackey's case, we must alter that case so that the relevant intention possesses these additional features. This requires imagining fanciful circumstances, but is nevertheless instructive. Suppose you lived in, and could not escape, a community that hated a certain minority group. Members of this minority group are known to sometimes approach members of your influential family, unless these members make clear that such approaches would be firmly rebuffed. (The conventional method of firm rebuff is spitting in the face.) But you are closely watched by members of your family who caution you against having anything to do with minority-group members and credibly warn that they will massacre many members of this group if any of them ever approaches you. At the same time, you have good reason to believe that the minority group has some spies in your community who might well infer your true intentions about how to respond if approached. Further, you know that minority-group members are much less well deterred from making approaches by fear of violence than by fear of rebuff. So you cannot reliably expect to prevent approaches by publicizing your family's warnings, but you can prevent approaches by having – and making known – the intention to firmly rebuff them. In these circumstances, it seems to me that it would be permissible for you (if you could) to form the intention to spit in the face of any minority-group member who approached you – provided that this was done to prevent the killing of innocents that would likely follow such an approach. In any case, one has reason to reject proposition (2) and affirm Traditionalism only if one rejects the permissibility of forming the (conditional) intention to act immorally *in this sort of case.* Lackey's original version of the spitting case has no bearing on the truth or falsity of this proposition.

Sterba also uses an example to support Traditionalism and undermine proposition (2). The intention to do wrong that he focuses on is that of a gunman who sincerely threatens to shoot you if you do not hand over your money.[8] The gunman is only trying to prevent the occurrence of the circumstances in which he intends to carry out the threat (namely, your not handing over the money), and his threat is likely to succeed and not have to be carried out. Still, his forming the intention to shoot you if you do not surrender your money is wrong. This case, unlike Lackey's, captures the idea that proposition (2) ascribes permissibility to forming *deterrent* intentions that are likely to be successful; that is, it takes account of features A, B, and D.[9] But it ignores features C and E of an SDS deterrent intention – its prevention of an unjust, seriously harmful offense and its utilitarian justification. And, as in Lackey's case, if we add the ignored features, forming the SDS deterrent intention may plausibly be viewed as morally justified. Suppose that you wrongfully stole the money you possess from the gunman, and that taking it back at gunpoint is his only means of securing an emergency operation needed to save his child's life. Given these suppositions, what the gunman seeks to prevent by his intention – your keeping his money – is both unjust and has such serious bad consequences that a utilitarian justification of his forming the threatening intention is possible. But under these circumstances, it is no longer clear that his forming the intention is impermissible. Thus Sterba's example, like Lackey's, fails to come to grips with the case for proposition (2), because it ignores crucial features of an SDS deterrent intention.

Kenny describes a somewhat different argument as being "decisive against those who maintain that it is morally acceptable to have a conditional intention to do something which they agree to be morally unacceptable."[10] The argument seems to be this. If the agent were certain the condition would never arise, then he could not properly be said to have the intention to act (even conditionally). But if the agent lacks such certainty, as generally is the case, forming the intention is wrong (presumably because it can lead to the performance of the wrongful action, e.g., if the condition were to come about).

Depending upon one's interpretation of the slippery notion of intention, the first claim in this argument may or may not be true.

That is, it might be the case that inclinations or dispositions or reasons to act in certain ways in circumstances that one is certain will not arise are too "idle" ever to count as intentions (as opposed to wishes or fantasies). But this is beside the point in evaluating the morality of forming SDS deterrent intentions. For justification here depends only upon a *sufficient likelihood* of success in preventing the circumstances of fulfillment of the threat from coming about, as indicated in features D and E.

The second claim in Kenny's argument denies this; it asserts that anything less than certainty of successful deterrence would render forming the intention evil. But no support is ever offered for this claim, other than Kenny's reiterated endorsement of WIP.[11] Perhaps he is assuming that a morally good person would not – or could not – dispose himself to do wrong, even in circumstances he does not expect to arise. This may be so, as we saw in our discussion of the second moral paradox of deterrence in Chapter 1. But, as emerged in our second and third paradoxes, it does not follow that it is always wrong to form such dispositions. Indeed, one may be obligated to try to do so even at the cost of one's own virtue. This is a genuine (though paradoxical) possibility that Kenny fails to consider, much less argue against.

Lackey defends a weakened version of Kenny's second claim. He says that the acceptable level of risk of deterrence failure depends on the moral gravity of the retaliatory act, and that in the case of nuclear deterrence this implies we must be "nearly certain" of success if forming deterrent intentions is to be justified.[12] I would add that the acceptable risk level depends also on the moral gravity of the offense deterred, in which case something less than near certainty may suffice to justify nuclear deterrence. Lackey goes on to assert that the moral status of forming a deterrent intention to do W if O is the same as that of setting up an automatic retaliator which will do W if O occurs. This may be so, but what does it imply? The retaliator itself – poor machine that it is – has no intentions at all, conditional or otherwise, evil or otherwise. The intention of the agent who sets up the automatic retaliator is to prevent O by so doing. He does not himself intend to do W; at most he intends to risk being the initiator of a physical process that may end in W. *This* intention is wrongful only if that risk is not justified – which would seem to be primarily a matter of weighing costs, benefits, and probabilities. In other words, Lackey's arguments bring us back to a risk

– benefit calculation in determining the moral status of a deterrent intention. But, by feature E (or the definition of an SDS), the results of such a calculation support forming an SDS deterrent intention. There is no reason here to abandon proposition (2) and take the Traditionalist way out of the first paradox of deterrence.

Or perhaps there is. Gerald Dworkin, one Traditionalist who seems to have a very clear grasp of the logic of an SDS, contends that the characteristics of an automatic retaliation device reveal what is wrong with conditional intentions to retaliate immorally.[13] He considers the autoretaliator of our Chapter 4, a hypothetical device that can deflect half of incoming missiles to predetermined targets, with enemy cities chosen as deflection targets for purposes of deterrence. Deploying this device, Dworkin allows, is morally like practicing a policy of deterrence based on the conditional intention to retaliate. But both are to be contrasted with deploying a *bounce-back* device that is capable of deflecting half of incoming missiles to their point of origin, but nowhere else. For Dworkin, bounce-back is morally permissible while neither autoretaliation nor the conditional intention to retaliate is. This is because the bounce-back system, unlike autoretaliation, does not involve the immoral intention to kill civilians, though its existence might predictably lead to the deaths of as many civilians if there were an attack (since the potential attacker's missiles might be based near his cities). That is, bounce-backers do not impose a risk of death on civilians *as a means* of preventing attack, as autoretaliators (and conditional intenders) do.

We can best understand Dworkin's point, I think, by developing his suggestion that the difference between the intentions of the autoretaliator and the bounce-backer are cashable in terms of dispositions to act in certain counterfactual circumstances.[14] What distinguishes the autoretaliator is his willingness to impose risks on civilians for his deterrent ends. This is revealed by his not targeting his deflections (as he could) on oceans or deserts. The bounce-backer, as Dworkin conceives him, is different. His only available means of defense and deterrence – the bounce-back system – does impose risks on civilians.[15] But this risk is not chosen as a means, as is revealed by the fact that the bounce-backer would forgo (or accept less) deterrence rather than reinstate this risk if, for example, the enemy were to move all his missile bases far from cities (while the bounce-backer acquired a retargeting capacity so he could deflect missiles onto cities if he chose to do so). This is the real difference between the autoretaliator and the bounce-backer as portrayed by Dworkin: in certain nonactual circumstances, the former would place enemy civilians at risk to preserve deterrence, while the latter would not.[16]

Now this difference in action dispositions between bounce-backers and autoretaliators, as characterized by Dworkin, reflects a difference in values between the two and therefore may influence how we evaluate them as moral agents. But it does not follow from this that, in an SDS, only the bounce-backer acts permissibly. Perhaps they both do. For while the autoretaliator is willing to impose a risk on the innocent in an SDS, by definition of this sort of situation, this risk is highly unlikely to eventuate in actual harm and its imposition is favored by utilitarian considerations. It may be that agents willing to suffer harm themselves rather than impose such risks are morally superior, for they sacrifice their interests rather than jeopardize those of others. But those who redistribute risks onto others when an overall utilitarian balancing favors redistribution, and actual harm is highly unlikely, are generally not acting impermissibly. If, for example, one can escape likely serious injury from some dynamite that is about to explode only by tossing it out the window where it could injure passersby, it is permissible to do so. So acting does not reveal a willingness to use others as means in any objectionable sense, though one would be more virtuous if one heroically faced the explosion rather than expose others to risk. But even this conclusion about comparative virtue would be open to question if one's family was also in the room and was endangered by the dynamite. This implies that the case for the permissibility of risk imposition in an SDS is even stronger for collective agents than for individuals. For most members of collectives that practice deterrence favor doing so largely to protect each other, rather than simply to protect themselves.

The upshot of all this is that the differences Dworkin notes between the bounce-back system, on the one hand, and autoretaliation or deterrent intentions, on the other, are not good reasons for thinking that the latter policies would be immoral in an SDS. However, Dworkin does not rest his case entirely on these differences. He offers two other arguments for the Traditionalist position that we must briefly consider. One is that the retaliation threatener must be able to justify her policy to those she places at risk, by showing that this policy benefits them on the whole.[17] But clearly, this is too strict a requirement for permissible redistribution of risks: it would, for example, seem to imply that it is wrong to inflict substantial punishments on serious law violators. For many of them would be better off not suffering such punishments, even if this entailed an increased risk of being victims of the undeterred (or less deterred) crimes of others. Perhaps Dworkin means to apply this requirement only to risks or harms imposed on the innocent, but even here the requirement seems too strict. To justify quarantines must we be able to show that the contagious victims benefit on the whole from being confined? To justify private ownership and use of automobiles must we show that nondrivers benefit on the whole from such a practice? It is more plausible to suppose that benefits to some groups of a practice justify that practice if they sufficiently outweigh losses to other groups.[18] In at least some SDSs – those in which the utilitarian benefits sufficiently outweigh the costs – this condition will be satisfied.

Dworkin's final Traditionalist argument is that practices (such as deterrent threats) that impose risks of intentional harm are worse than practices that impose risks of accidental harm. He writes, "I do not believe that we would accept an institution which imposed the same risk of injury and death that [automobile] accidents cause, but risks brought about by actions aimed at injury or death."[19] But we do accept at least one such institution: private child rearing and the nuclear family. Every year, private families inflict significant and deliberate violence on thousands of children, and produce thousands of misguided offspring who eventually deliberately injure or kill others. Yet I think we would regard the nuclear family as justified – because of the benefits it provides to most and the central role it plays in their lives – even if we were convinced that some alternative mode of child rearing (e.g., in state institutions) would substantially reduce the rate of violent crime against children and adults. Similarly, if the overall benefits of a practice of deterrence in an SDS are substantial, we may regard that practice as justified even though it risks eventuating in harms done intentionally.

In summary, the Traditionalist arguments we have considered fail to establish that it is always immoral to form a conditional intention to do what is immoral. Many of them fail because they do not address the difficult cases for their position – deterrent intentions in SDSs. By focusing on disanalogous cases and red-herring principles, these arguments avoid rather than respond to the serious challenge to WIP raised in Chapter 1. Other Traditionalist arguments take account of that challenge, but do not answer it in a persuasive manner.

II. RATIONAL RETALIATION

In Chapter 1, strong arguments were presented for proposition (2), which asserts the permissibility of forming deterrent intentions in SDSs. In the last section it was contended that Traditionalists have not given any good reasons for rejecting these arguments and proposition (2). But this does not yet establish that we must reject WIP or embrace paradox. There is the Retaliator's alternative of rejecting proposition (1), which asserts the wrongness of retaliation if the deterrent threat fails.

The main expositor of this alternative position is David Gauthier.[20] He discussed the rational analogue of our first moral paradox, which may be formulated, for SDSs, in the following propositions:

(1′) It would be irrational to retaliate if the offense were committed, because this would cause harms without producing sufficiently compensating benefits.

(2′) It is rational to form the intention to retaliate should the offense be committed, since this is the only reliable way to prevent the offense.

(3′) If it would be irrational to do something under certain conditions, then it is irrational to form the intention to do that thing should those conditions arise.

Gauthier agrees that (2′) holds true in some SDSs, essentially for the reasons I have given in Chapter 1. He accepts (3′) because, like the traditionalists, he believes that actions, and the intentions from which they flow, must be evaluated together: either both are rational (moral) or neither are. He infers that (1′) is false. He does not deny that once deterrence fails, more bad than good (in the potential retaliator's scheme of values) would be produced by retaliating. Indeed, he stipulates this as a feature of the situations he is most interested in discussing. Rather, he says retaliation must be rational, or else, in view of the truth of (3′), rational agents would not be able to have the deterrent intentions they need to deter offenses in SDSs.

Before turning to consideration of Gauthier's arguments for the rationality of retaliation in SDSs, it will be useful to clear aside a confusion that lends his conclusion more initial plausibility than it deserves. We are used to thinking of deterrence operating in repeatable contexts – like that of criminal punishment – where one's future credibility and ability to deter depends heavily upon one's willingness to carry out one's retaliatory threats once deterrence has failed in the case at hand. Habituated to thinking this way, we may find it easy to suppose retaliatory actions following failed deterrence rational, as Gauthier suggests, in SDSs as well. But the difference between the two cases is crucial. The long-range deterrent effects that may render retaliation rational in a repeatable context are, by definition, either absent or outweighed in an SDS. Hence, in evaluating retaliation in SDSs, we should resist being swayed by intuitions appropriate only for repeatable contexts.

Gauthier, however, does not rely on such misguided intuitions. He offers, as far as I can discern, four arguments for the rationality of retaliation in SDSs – that is, against (1'). Let us consider and respond to these arguments in turn.

Gauthier argues that if (1') were true, it would be impossible for rational agents to form the rational deterrent intentions that they should have, according to (2'). This is true in one sense and false in another. Rational agents cannot form the intention to retaliate harmfully and pointlessly if they remain rational in all respects.[21] But they can seek to form that intention by exposing themselves to external influences that will render them irrational in the necessary respects. (Indeed, if Gauthier's account of rational retaliation is wrong but often persuasive, a rational agent in an SDS might seek to render himself appropriately irrational by reading Gauthier!) Thus, there are rational paradoxes analogous to the second and third moral paradoxes discussed in Chapter 1, namely:

(R2) There are situations (namely SDSs) in which it would be rational for agents to perform certain actions if they could (namely forming the intention to retaliate), and in which it is possible for some agents to perform such actions, but impossible for fully rational agents to perform them.

(R3) In certain situations (namely certain SDSs), it would be rational for a rational agent to deliberately (attempt to) make himself less rational.

The arguments for these propositions are precisely parallel to the arguments offered in Chapter 1 for their moral analogues. (R2) is true because a fully rational agent cannot intend to act against the balance of reasons, and hence cannot intend to retaliate in an SDS. (R3) is true because the agent's need for deterrence in an SDS may be so great that his ends are best fulfilled overall by making himself partly irrational and thus able to deter. So the answer to Gauthier's first argument is that a rational agent can, in principle, form the necessary intention to retaliate – though only by rendering himself less than fully rational.

This reply leads to Gauthier's second argument against (1'): this proposition precludes the unified assessment of the agent who forms and carries out a deterrent intention in an SDS. We must count him both rational and irrational. This is so, but there is nothing incoherent about it; the agent is simply rational and irrational at different times. In appreciating the case for having the deterrent intention and in setting out to form it, he is rational and acts rationally. Since, however, the intention is an intention to act irrationally (should deterrence fail), he can form this intention only by making himself irrational in certain respects. If he succeeds in doing so he becomes (partly) irrational. And if deterrence fails and he retaliates, he now acts irrationally. We are familiar with the same agents being rational and irrational, and acting rationally and irrationally, at different times. The only oddity about the present situation is that the agent rationally chooses at one time to try to make himself less rational at a later time. This is an oddity called for by the unusual structure of an SDS. It makes assessment of the agent's rationality over time more complex but not, as Gauthier suggests, impossible or incoherent.

Gauthier also claims that the rational agent is one who submits larger, rather than smaller, segments of her activity to rational scrutiny. This agent will assess actions in terms of the rational plans and intentions they flow from rather than from the effects they are likely to bring about. Now there may be something to this "wider segments" view. The general advantages of agents acting according to rules, plans, or policies rather than calculating on a case-by-case basis – for example, lower decision costs, more efficient coordination and cooperation – are well-known. But our normal view of rationality also implies being prepared to change previously formulated plans or intentions when there are significant stakes involved and relevant new information about outcomes is available. This is precisely the situation that arises when deterrence fails in an SDS. There is much harm to be done by retaliation, and the benefit that motivated formation of the intention to retaliate – prevention of the offense – is now unobtainable. Hence, nonretaliation is now the rational action and is the one our failed deterrer would perform if she somehow regained full rationality after the commission of the offense.

Gauthier's fourth and final argument is that rational agents would be better off – that is, better able to achieve their ends – if it were rational to retaliate. For this would make them more effective deterrers in SDSs and similar situations than they could be if (1′) were true. Let us grant that, given appropriate assumptions about the improbability of deterrence failing and the improbability of rational agents transforming themselves into irrational retaliators, agents would do better on average if they were retaliators than if they were not. This would show retaliation to be rational, as Gauthier claims, only if we assume that rational acts are those flowing from the most beneficial traits. But this assumption is not valid. To see this, let X stand for any trait that we can all agree is irrational (and leads to irrational actions), but not normally so damaging as to make its possessors' lives miserable. If an eccentric billionaire were to heap fortunes upon all and only those having X, this would benefit those possessing the trait, and could make it rational for others to try to acquire the trait, but would hardly make the trait itself (or its possessors or the acts flowing from it) rational. If the environment is structured to reward irrationality, success is no proof of rationality. In an environment studded with enough SDSs (or single-play prisoner's dilemmas[22]), the most rational actors would be unlikely to fare the best. We may regret this, but we cannot really improve things by attempting to redefine "rationality" so as to make it impossible by definition.

In the end, then, none of Gauthier's arguments against (1′) is persuasive. There is, however, an argument against *his* position that is, in my opinion, conclusive. Deterrent intentions in SDSs are a subclass of what I call *problematic intentions*. Problematic intentions are those whose direct effects (i.e., effects of carrying out the intention) are bad, but whose overall expected effects are good because of their good and important *autonomous* effects (i.e., effects of the agent having the intention that are independent of the intention being carried out). A deterrent intention in an SDS is problematic because the bad effects of carrying out retaliation are outweighed (when probabilities are taken into account) by the good autonomous effect – deterrence of the offense. Gauthier's view about rationality would imply a similar conclusion about problematic intentions in general as about deterrent intentions in SDSs: if it is rational to form and have them, it is rational to carry them out. But this cannot be right, as is shown by the following hypothetical example involving a problematic intention that is not conditional and has a desired autonomous effect other than deterrence.[23]

You are offered a million dollars to be paid tomorrow morning, if at midnight tonight you intend to drink a vial of toxin tomorrow afternoon that will make you very sick for a day. If you believe the offer and believe that the offerers can really tell whether, at midnight, you have the requisite intention, you would clearly have a good reason (in fact, a million good reasons) to form that intention. Suppose that you do so and bank the money the next morning – cashing in the desired autonomous effect of your intention. Would it then be rational for you to carry out your intention and drink the toxin? Surely not. If not, we have a divergence between the rationality of forming a problematic intention and the rationality of carrying it out – (3′) is shattered. Seeing no valid reason to suppose that this principle holds in the special case of problematic deterrent intentions in SDSs, I reject Gauthier's solution to the first paradox of deterrence.

III. NUCLEAR DETERRENCE AND RETALIATORY INTENTIONS

Our first paradox of deterrence has survived the attacks of the Traditionalists and the Retaliators. But does it apply to nuclear deterrence and tell us something about the moral status of that practice? Chapter 1 leaves this question open. It uses one conception of the nuclear balance of terror to illustrate the notion of an SDS (in which the paradox arises), and notes that the balance of terror may actually satisfy the definition of an SDS *if retaliatory intentions are necessary for successful nuclear deterrence*. The caution thus exhibited was appropriate. Nuclear deterrence occurs in an SDS, and thus exemplifies the first paradox, only if (i) its benefits outweigh its costs, (ii) it is actually necessary for defense, and (iii) its success requires possession of an actual intention to retaliate immorally should deterrence fail. In Chapters 3 and 6, it is argued that conditions (i) and (ii), respectively, may well be satisfied. In this section I will discuss whether intentions to retaliate immorally are necessary for successful nuclear deterrence.

Deterrence works, if it does, by persuading a potential aggressor that the risks of retaliation attached to the contemplated act of aggression outweigh its benefits. If the costs of suffering retaliation are immense, as they clearly are in the case of nuclear retaliation, the probability of that retaliation need not be very high to render aggression for any plausible political gain clearly a bad bargain. So even minimally rational governments will be deterred from engaging in aggressive acts that they believe might lead to their nation suffering nuclear retaliation. This analysis, plus experience with how high government officials actually regard nuclear weapons, has led to the idea that the existence of a nuclear retaliatory capability suffices for deterrence, regardless of a nation's will, intentions, or pronouncements about nuclear weapons use. This basic idea, called "existential deterrence,"[24] has led to various proposals for effective nuclear deterrence without immoral retaliatory intentions – bluffing, deterrence without threatening retaliation, and so on.[25] Here I limit my attention to two of the more interesting proposals, which I call, respectively, *No Intention* and *Scrupulous Retaliation*.

A *No Intention* nuclear retaliation policy is one practiced by a nation having the capability to retaliate if attacked (i.e., survivable nuclear weapons and plans for their possible use), but having no definite intention about whether or not to use this capability. It is not that the nation's leaders intend not to retaliate, they simply put off making up their minds about retaliation unless and until their nation is actually attacked.[26] By contrast, a *Scrupulous Retaliation* policy is one in which a nation intends to retaliate if subjected to nuclear attack, but only in a clearly moral fashion by limited strikes against military and economic assets located far from population centers.[27] Apparently, neither policy involves the conditional intention to retaliate immorally if attacked; hence neither can be shown to be wrong by direct application of WIP. If nuclear deterrence in either form were effective, it seems that we could practice nuclear deterrence (in that form) without being subject to the first moral paradox of deterrence.

There are two key questions to address here. Would these alternative forms of nuclear deterrence be as reliable as deterrence based on a conditional intention to immorally retaliate? Would there really be significant moral advantages to be gained by practicing one of these policies rather than a policy of deterrence by intention to immorally retaliate (*DITIR*, for short)? Let us consider these questions in turn.

No one really knows whether forms of nuclear deterrence that promise less retaliation (e.g., Scrupulous Retaliation) or retaliation with less certainty (e.g., No Intention) are less effective deterrents than policies threatening more retaliation with greater certainty. If our adversaries were always naive calculators who were prepared to attack us at any time their calculations showed the slightest gain in expected value for them in doing so, it would follow that a threat of greater retaliation with greater certainty would be a more reliable deterrent. If, to take the opposite extreme, our adversaries would always be deterred by the mere possibility of suffering significant nuclear retaliation, a threat of less (but still significant) retaliation with less certainty would be an equally effective deterrent. Doubtless, supporters of existential deterrence are correct that present nuclear adversaries under present circumstances are much closer to the latter extreme than the former – they are strongly disposed to err on the side of caution in deciding whether to use nuclear attack to achieve political-military gains or avoid political-military losses. But, as there is little prospect of achieving nuclear disarmament except over a relatively long period of time, we want our nuclear deterrence policies to be extremely *robust* – that is, effective under the greatest possible variety of circumstances. In particular, we want them to work even against non-risk-averse leaders who may come to power in nuclear-armed countries in the future, and in circumstances in which all the alternatives to using nuclear weapons may seem bleak and undesirable to our adversaries. We also want nuclear deterrence to work without a single instance of failure, including in changed political circumstances that might result from future environmental, population, or resource problems.[28] Now in theory, we might adapt our retaliatory policy to the dangers of the moment and maintain a policy of Scrupulous Retaliation unless and until non-risk-averse nuclear adversaries actually appeared.[29] But in the real political world there would very likely be a substantial time lag before such an adversary's true nature was perceived and appropriate changes in retaliatory policy were put into effect, just as it took a long time for the Western democracies to perceive, appreciate, and respond to the grave threat posed by Hitler. In a nuclear world, the consequences for humanity of a similar lag in appropriately responding to a non-risk-averse leader (or leaders) of a major power could be catastrophic.

Given the reasonable desire for robustness, the importance of avoiding a single failure, and this time-lag problem, it does not seem irrational to opt for the greater potential credibility provided by a nuclear policy of DITIR. We cannot know that circumstances will ever arise in which having such a policy will be necessary for successful deterrence, nor can we know that they will not arise. But given the momentousness of what is at stake – the avoidance of nuclear war – we should not risk practicing a less effective deterrent policy unless there clearly are overriding moral advantages to be gained by doing so.

Are there such advantages in the case of Scrupulous Retaliation? At first, it seems so, for such a policy appears to spare enemy civilians from the danger of our retaliation. But if Scrupulous Retaliation is a less robust and reliable deterrent this need not be so. In the event of nuclear war, our retaliation practices might (deliberately or accidentally) be much less scrupulous than our pre-war intentions. And the environmental effects of nuclear war (e.g., radioactive fallout or nuclear winter) might lead to the death of many of these civilians without our intending it. Thus, if Scrupulous Retaliation raises the probability of nuclear war enough, it may (compared to DITIR) actually *increase* the risks of nuclear destruction for enemy civilians. At the same time, if it is a less effective deterrent, it raises the risks to ourselves and our allies. Thus, if Scrupulous Retaliation does sacrifice robustness, as has been suggested, it possesses no clear moral advantages that would compensate for this sacrifice.

In addition, Scrupulous Retaliation poses the following moral-strategic dilemma. If sincerely proclaimed as official policy and reflected in force design and deployment changes, Scrupulous Retaliation is subject to being made even less effective by counter-moves. Adversaries may, for example, try to base their most valuable military and economic assets in or near cities so as to deprive us of meaningful retaliatory targets. Suppose, on the other hand, Scrupulous Retaliation were adopted in secret by high officials. This would leave lower-level officials, missile crews, and ordinary citizens (who would believe that the policy is still one of unrestricted retaliation) in the same state of "nuclear sin" they began in – only the leaders will have improved their moral state.

Before leaving the subject of Scrupulous Retaliation, I should emphasize that I have been discussing it – and questioning its supposed advantages – as a form of deterrent policy. As noted in the Introduction, once a nuclear war started, the morally proper policy to follow then would probably be to carry out only scrupulous retaliatory attacks, if any. To point out this divergence between permissible deterrent intentions and permissible retaliatory actions is, in essence, to restate the first moral paradox of deterrence.

What of the No Intention policy? Does this policy have any decisive moral advantages that might compensate for its potential lack of robustness? To answer this last question, we must consider why the intention to retaliate immorally with nuclear weapons is considered bad. Then we may determine whether, and to what extent, the No Intention policy is itself free from these bad-making characteristics.

One obvious reason for thinking DITIR bad is that it creates an actual risk of death (and other serious harms) for the many innocent people who would suffer attack if the intention were carried out. But would a No Intention policy create a lesser risk for these people? This depends upon a number of indeterminable empirical factors. How likely is it that the top leadership would decide not to retaliate (or to retaliate scrupulously) if their nation suffered a nuclear attack? If they decided not to retaliate, or to retaliate in a scrupulous or otherwise limited way, how likely is it that their decisions would actually be adhered to in the midst of a nuclear war? Does the relative lack of robustness of a No Intention policy increase the risk of nuclear war, and if so, by how much? Depending upon the answers to these questions, the No Intention policy may (or may not) actually *increase* the risks of nuclear destruction undergone by enemy civilians (and the risks of our being complicit in immoral nuclear retaliation).

As we saw in our discussion of the Traditionalists, however, there is a different possible explanation of the badness or evilness of intentions to retaliate immorally. Such intentions entail a willingness (under certain circumstances) to perform a wrong action, and hence reflect a flaw in the agent's values. In this view, the relevant question to ask about the No Intention policy is whether those who pursued it would possess better values than pursuers of DITIR.

Consider first the top leadership who, under the No Intention policy, have not made up their minds whether they would retaliate. Whether their values are better would seem to depend upon what they would decide if attacked. If they would in fact retaliate, it is hard to see that this reflects better on their values than if they had decided to do so ahead of time (perhaps influenced by considerations of deterrence[30]). We, and perhaps they themselves, do not know what they would decide in the event. Hence, while it is possible that a No Intention policy reflects superior values by top leadership in a given case, it need not, and we would not know whether in a particular case it did (at least until nuclear war had broken out).

What of lower-level officials, soldiers, and ordinary citizens? Does their going along with a No Intention policy reflect superior values to going along with threats of all-out retaliation? Again, it may or may not. If they support or acquiesce in a No Intention policy that could for all they know amount to the same wrongful acts in the event of war as a policy of all-out retaliation, it is hard to see in what way their values are superior. Perhaps if their support is based on the perceived likelihood that there would be no retaliation against civilians, and would be withdrawn if that perception changed, we could infer that the individuals in question had superior values. But if based on other grounds, it would seem that support for a No Intention policy, like support for DITIR, indicates a willingness to risk complicity in mass killing of the innocent. Thus, while a No Intention policy might reflect superior values on the part of some individuals, it need not. Indeed, depending upon the underlying reasoning, support for DITIR might reflect better values – for example, if the individual regards the two policies as equivalent in their effects, and views the No Intention policy as hypocritical and dishonest since "we'd surely retaliate anyway."

We have until this point considered the intentions of individuals. But what of the intentions of collectives such as nations? If WIP applies to them, it is relevant to inquire whether the No Intention policy avoids the *collective* intention to retaliate immorally if attacked. This is not easily determined, however, given that there is no generally accepted theory of what intentions are, even in the individual case. Chapter 1 assumed that rational intentions, at least, are dispositions to act derived from the agent's appreciation of the reasons for and against so acting. But it is not clear whether this account is correct, or even what exactly it means, when applied to the collective case.

Our difficulties in this matter are compounded by the fact that there is no simple formula for inferring group intentions from the intentions of individuals making up that group. Even all group members sharing the intention to do their part in a joint undertaking is not always sufficient to constitute a group intention. For even if the physical means of carrying out the intention are available, and each fully intends to do his best, it may be apparent that things are not sufficiently organized to get the job done. Thus, for example, there may be enough shelters to protect all, and each may be committed to doing her part to get herself and others into shelters in the event of attack. But if it is obvious that there are not sufficient workable organizational and operational plans to get people into shelters, so that chaos would be the likely actual result of attack, the nation could hardly be said to genuinely intend to protect itself and its citizens by means of shelters, if attacked. So even unanimous individual intentions plus physical capability need not add up to a group intention.

On the other hand, there may conceivably be a group intention to do X even if no individual member of the group intends to do (her part of) X. Suppose each member of a society secretly opposes the official policy of nuclear retaliation, but wrongly believes that all others favor that policy. Each intends not to do her part in retaliating, should the occasion arise. But it is predictable that enough would do their parts, if the occasion arose, because of the pressure of the perceived expectations of their comrades, and the (perhaps true!) belief that if one did not act (e.g., did not press the button firing the missile), someone else surely would.[31] In this case, it would seem appropriate to ascribe the intention to retaliate to the nation, though none of its members at present share that intention.

In light of all this, I am inclined to propose the following as jointly sufficient conditions for a group G *collectively intending* to do X if C occurs:

(a)   G has the physical capability to do X if C occurs.
(b)   G has plans to use this capability to do X if C should occur.
(c)   It is in fact likely that were C to occur, G would put these plans into effect and do X.

Note the rough analogy between the above account of rational intentions and this partial analysis of collective intentions. Conditions (a) and (c) correspond to having a disposition to act, while the notion of a plan in condition (b) roughly corresponds to the idea of being disposed to act in virtue of reasons for action.

The importance of this analysis, for our present concerns, is this. Suppose that the top leadership has not decided whether to carry out plans to immorally use their nuclear retaliation capacity if their nation suffers a nuclear attack – that is, the nation's policy is one of No Intention. But suppose that the leaders' values are such, or the nature of the command and control system is such, that it is likely that immoral retaliation would in fact take place if there were an attack. In this case, all the conditions in the above analysis are satisfied and the nation possesses a collective intention to retaliate immorally if attacked. In other words, a No Intention policy may, at the collective level, involve the intention to retaliate immorally. This means that if WIP applies to collective intentions, No Intention could have a moral advantage over DITIR only if command and control is highly reliable and top leadership possesses the right moral values (and could be expected to retain and act on those values during a nuclear war). Given the doubts of some experts about the ability of existing command and control systems to maintain nuclear restraint during alerts,[32] much less under nuclear attack, one may rightly wonder whether No Intention is a morally superior policy.

The task of this section was to evaluate the claim that the first moral paradox does not really apply to nuclear deterrence because – in virtue of existential deterrence – reliable nuclear deterrence without immoral retaliatory intentions is possible. Consideration of two representative alternative policies, Scrupulous Retaliation and No Intention, has suggested that only a more ambiguous conclusion than that embodied in the above claim is justified. Because of complex factual and conceptual uncertainties, we simply do not know whether the first paradox applies to nuclear deterrence or not. In the case of Scrupulous Retaliation, we do not know whether the potential loss in robustness it would entail is enough to eliminate it as a viable alternative policy, thus leaving intact the original argument for the permissibility of having immoral retaliatory intentions in the nuclear case. As regards the No Intention policy, there are several key uncertainties. Is it robust enough? Does it, at the individual level, involve the same moral paradox as DITIR, because many of the individuals involved in implementing the policy would likely have the same values that render the latter policy questionable?

Does the No Intention policy escape the first paradox of deterrence at the level of collective intentions? Without definite answers of the right sort to these questions, it is hasty – and quite possibly wrong – to conclude that our first paradox does not apply to nuclear deterrence.

IV. CONCLUSION

Traditionalists have given us no persuasive reasons for abandoning proposition (2). Retaliators have given us no persuasive reasons for abandoning proposition (1') – or, by analogy, proposition (1). Given the strong arguments for (1) and (2) offered in Chapter 1,[33] we are faced with the choice of embracing paradox or rejecting the Wrongful Intentions Principle. The latter is obviously the better choice. Strong intuitions support WIP, but these intuitions are doubtless based on the ubiquity of normal cases in which the intentions in question are nonconditional, nondeterrent, or non-SDS-deterrent. It is highly unlikely that originators of WIP considered the strange case of deterrent intentions in SDSs. The abnormality of this case is highlighted by the fact that some modern philosophical defenders of the WIP have failed to take account of many of its relevant features even when these have been clearly laid out in the literature. In any case, what seems to be the best way out of the first paradox of deterrence is to qualify WIP so that it does not apply to SDS deterrent intentions, or in general to problematic intentions. If this modification of WIP is justified, our paradox has served a constructive purpose by leading us to properly limit the scope of this important moral principle.

It is worth noting in addition that a proper understanding of the argument of Chapter 1 allows us to hold fast to some of the main Traditionalist intuitions underlying WIP, even while rejecting or modifying the principle itself. As the second and third paradoxes of Chapter 1 showed, there is some moral (or rational) defect in the agent who has succeeded in forming the relevant deterrent intention in an SDS. Thus, we may concede to the Traditionalists that there is something morally wrong with the intention itself (namely, it is an intention to act wrongly under certain circumstances) and with the character of the agent who has it (namely, possessing either the wrong values or the willingness to act wrongly under certain circumstances). But, as the arguments of Chapter 1 indicate, it does not follow from this that it is wrong for the agent to form this SDS deterrent intention. Hence, the unmodified version of WIP may be rejected while the main underlying intuitions are retained.[34]

Appropriately modifying WIP provides a theoretical solution to the first paradox of deterrence. But what does all this imply about the morality of nuclear deterrence? The arguments of the last section indicate that we do not know whether the paradox really applies to the case of nuclear deterrence. But if the proper solution to that paradox involves modifying WIP so it does not apply to SDS deterrent intentions, this does not really matter. If robust and reliable deterrence without immoral retaliatory intentions were possible, we could deter without running afoul of WIP. If not, and nuclear retaliatory intentions occur within an SDS, they fall outside the proper scope of the (modified) WIP. In neither case are they shown to be wrong in virtue of proper employment of the WIP.

This, of course, is not enough to determine that nuclear deterrence in some form is morally permissible. It remains to be shown that such deterrence can reasonably be viewed as having utilitarian benefits that exceed its costs. (Otherwise the nuclear deterrent situation is not a genuine SDS.) And there may be other deontological moral objections to nuclear deterrence that should be answered, besides the charge that it embodies wrongful intentions. Finally, deontological arguments *for* nuclear deterrence must be considered. In examining these matters further, in later chapters, we shall see that the first moral paradox of deterrence is not the only moral puzzle surrounding nuclear deterrence.

3. Deterrence, utility, and rational choice

The fundamental question of this book is whether practicing nuclear deterrence, in any form, is morally permissible. The present chapter is an attempt to deal with this question from the point of view of utilitarian moral theory.[1] For reasons given in the Introduction, I believe that the sort of minimum deterrence policy sketched there is, from the utilitarian perspective, far superior to the present deterrence policies of the superpowers.[2] With policies of the current type eliminated from contention as the choice recommended by utilitarian considerations, this chapter seeks to discover the best utilitarian policy by comparing minimum deterrence with the alternative of not practicing nuclear deterrence at all, that is, unilateral nuclear disarmament. It poses the issue as a problem of rational choice under conditions of uncertainty, reveals difficulties with the expected utility and maximum approaches toward solving it, and proposes an alternative principle of choice that may plausibly be applied to achieve a solution.

I begin with some simplifying assumptions. (Whether these assumptions distort or bias the analysis will be discussed in section V of this chapter.) Only the bilateral superpower balance of terror will be considered; complications due to the existence of other nuclear powers are ignored. As noted above, attention will be limited to a superpower's choice – hereafter called the *deter-or-disarm* choice – between the basic alternatives of (i) unilateral nuclear disarmament,

A remote ancestor of this chapter was presented to the Jacob Marschak Interdisciplinary Colloquium on Mathematics in the Behavioral Sciences, at UCLA, in the spring of 1976. I am grateful to the members of that group, and to Robert M. Adams, for their helpful comments. My work was partly supported by a Regents' Faculty Research Fellowship from the University of California.

and (ii) practicing some form of minimum deterrence (of the kind described in the Introduction) that involves the possession of nuclear weapons and the threat of their use against one's rival's homeland. Finally, it is assumed that a nation is choosing a policy for the foreseeable future, which is to be thought of as a significant but limited period, say thirty years.[3]

Our question is what now ought to be done by each participant in the balance of terror, given that participant's perceptions of the present political-military situation. The crucial elements of each superpower's perceptions are, presumably, these. First, it believes that its ideological-economic system promotes the well-being of those living under it to a much greater extent than does its opponent's system. Second, it believes its rival would probably impose its system on other nations if it could. Third, it regards complete bilateral nuclear disarmament as unattainable in the near future, largely because of its rival's unwillingness to disarm on reasonable terms. Our question is which of two nuclear policies – minimum deterrence or unilateral disarmament – would a utilitarian sharing a superpower's perceptions of the balance of terror wish that superpower to follow. Alternatively, we could ask whether a superpower would practice minimum nuclear deterrence (rather than unilaterally disarming itself of nuclear weapons) *if it were to decide the matter purely on utilitarian moral grounds.*

The dilemma a superpower would face if it looked at the balance of terror in this way is clear. It would recognize that it could greatly reduce (and perhaps eliminate) the danger of large-scale nuclear war by disarming unilaterally. But it would fear that if it did so, nothing would stand in the way of its rival dominating the world by the use of, or threat to use, nuclear weapons. Such a result would, given its view of its opponent's system, constitute an immense utilitarian disaster. On the other hand, it would realize that its continued participation in the balance of terror runs the risk of resulting in a different utilitarian disaster – large-scale nuclear war. How can this utilitarian moral dilemma be resolved?[4]

I. UNCERTAINTY

The fundamental principle of utilitarianism is that agents should act to produce as much long-run net utility for people as possible, where utility is conceived of as some objective quality such as pleasure or desire satisfaction.[5] This principle is generally interpreted to imply that, when the consequences of one's acts are not known with certainty, one should perform the act having the greatest expected utility. We cannot, however, determine the utilitarian status of nuclear deterrence by simply comparing the expected utilities of deterrence and unilateral nuclear disarmament. For application of the Expected Utility Principle (EUP) to this case would require us to have something we lack: reliable quantitative utility and probability estimates.[6]

Consider probabilities first. A distinction is often made between choices under risk, when the probabilities of the various outcomes following from the acts in question are known, and choices under uncertainty, when they are not known. The deter-or-disarm choice must be made essentially under conditions of uncertainty. This choice presents itself in a complex and unique historical situation. Assigning numerical probabilities to the possible outcomes of the available choices would require selecting an appropriate reference class of past situations to provide data on the relative frequencies of various outcomes. But the results will depend entirely upon the reference class selected. The probability of deterrence leading to war, for example, will turn out rather high if we choose past arms races among major powers as our reference class, but will seem very low if we choose earlier segments of the present balance of terror as our reference class. Lacking a natural reference class, such as we have when estimating the probability of rolling a six on a throw of a symmetrical die, and lacking a scientific theory of international relations that would allow us to deduce numerical probabilities of outcomes in some indirect manner, we cannot expect reasonable people to agree on the probability that minimum deterrence would lead to war, or that unilateral disarmament would lead to domination.

Serious problems also arise if we attempt to compare quantitatively the utilities of such outcomes as "large-scale nuclear war" and "rival's world domination."[7] In general, we face two problems in making quantitative estimates of utility: determining how utility is to be defined and measured, and actually carrying out the measurement process. Problems of the first sort aside, the practical difficulties of measurement in all but the simplest cases are so great that utility estimates must be based on crude simplifying assumptions (e.g., that negative utility is proportional to the number of casualties). In the present case, added to these standard difficulties is the fact that the nature of the specified outcomes is unknown, so that their effects on people (and hence their utility) cannot be accurately estimated. Lacking empirical data on the effects of large-scale nuclear war and world domination by the opposing superpower, we are in a poor position to estimate quantitatively the utilities of these outcomes. Indeed, as hinted at above, the term "world domination" is really shorthand for a wide variety of outcomes, such as tighter or lesser control of other nations by one's rival brought about by nuclear blackmail (implicit or explicit), nuclear attack, or victorious nuclear war against lesser nuclear powers. Obviously, the amounts of negative utility produced by these different outcomes, like the amounts of negative utility produced by different forms of large-scale nuclear war, will vary a great deal. In the sequel, therefore, we should remember that the terms "large-scale nuclear war" and "rival's world domination" cover a range of more specific outcomes, and should think of the utilities of these general outcomes as rough averages of the utilities of those more specific outcomes.

Without reliable quantitative utilities and probabilities to work from, we either cannot apply EUP, or must do so using unreliable estimates (i.e., guesses) that we have little confidence in.[8] The numbers emerging from such expected utility calculations can hardly form a sound basis of moral decision. Recognizing the problem of applying the traditional EUP under conditions of uncertainty, decision theorists have attempted to extend the scope of application of that principle by reinterpreting probabilities and utilities as entirely subjective.[9] They show that if an agent supplies sufficient data about his preferences between lotteries having specified probabilities of various outcomes, and these preferences satisfy certain plausible axioms, then quantitative subjective utility and probability measures for the agent can be constructd such that (i) the agent's expressed preferences maximize expected utility, (according to the constructed measures), and (ii) maximizing expected utility in accordance with the constructed measures in other decisions involving the given outcomes is the only way that the agent can make these decisions consistent with his expressed preferences and the axioms.

While this result is a substantial contribution to rational decision theory, it cannot be used to solve the deter-or-disarm problem from the point of view of utilitarian moral theory. This is partly because, when making choices of such vast utilitarian importance as the choice between deterring and disarming, consistency with other actual or possible decisions pales in significance in comparison with the problem of arriving at the proper decision in the case at hand. More important, applying subjective utility analysis to our problem presupposes the agent's ability to express meaningful preferences between lotteries involving such outcomes as large-scale nuclear war and world domination by the opposing superpower. Does she prefer a 10 percent chance of war to a 70 percent chance of domination? A utilitarian agent confronting these questions can only guess, and will have little, if any, confidence in these guesses. But the subjectivist analysis depends heavily on such guesses, though the agent herself is entirely unconvinced of their value as a basis for choice.

In essence, the subjective utility theorist and the utilitarian moralist differ in their conceptions of the problem that the latter faces.[10] The subjective utility theorist sees the utilitarian's problem in choosing between deterrence and disarmament as simply one of clarifying and making consistent the utilitarian's own subjective preferences. But the utilitarian, who wants to produce as much well-being and prevent as much suffering as possible, regards himself as attempting to deal with objective moral values in the face of extreme factual ignorance. If he knew the amounts of well-being and suffering that would be produced by war and by domination and the probabilities of these outcomes, or if he had what he regarded as reliable and objective scientific estimates of these quantities, he would probably be willing to use the traditional EUP in making his choice. Unlike the subjective utility theorist, he regards such knowledge and such estimates as possible in principle. But he does not in fact have them. Nevertheless, given the importance of the problem, he feels called upon to make a reasonable judgment based upon what he does know.

What then does he know that he could base a choice on? Aware of the enormous power of nuclear weapons, he presumably knows that a large-scale nuclear war would almost certainly be a worse utilitarian disaster than domination of the world by the opposing superpower (even if that domination were brought about by means of a small nuclear war). He does not know enough to determine or estimate accurately how much worse large-scale nuclear war would be, but he may rightly have confidence in the ordinal judgment that it would be worse to some unknown extent. A similar ordinal judgment may be made about the relevant (conditional) probabilities. While unable to determine how much more likely, he may be able to assume with confidence that it is more likely that unilateral disarmament would lead to domination than that practicing a policy of minimum deterrence for the relevant time period would lead to large-scale nuclear war. How can it be possible to arrive at such a judgment when we lack reliable quantitative estimates of the probabilities in question? The answer is that different methods of analyzing the same situation may yield differing numerical estimates, but nevertheless agree unanimously (or nearly so) in their ordering judgments. Thus, while different theories of international relations, or different experts making thoughtful overall judgments, or the choice of different plausible reference classes, may yield widely ranging numerical estimates of the (conditional) probability of war or domination by the other superpower, these methods may, on the whole, agree that one (in this case domination) is more probable than the other. This appears to be the way things stand with respect to expert opinion, as seen from the point of view of the United States.[11]

Let us call a choice between alternatives, any of which may result in disaster, a choice between *potential disasters*. Further, let us say a choice is made under *two-dimensional uncertainty* if the chooser has no reliable quantitative estimates of the relevant utilities and probabilities, but has confidence in his judgment of their ordinal rankings. What I am suggesting is that we view the deter-or-disarm choice as a choice between potential disasters under two-dimensional uncertainty. A choice of this sort is easily made if there is one alternative that minimizes both the probability of disaster occurrence and the degree of disaster, should one occur. However, in the deter-or-disarm situation, neither alternative possesses both features. Here one must choose, under two-dimensional uncertainty, between a smaller risk of a graver disaster and a greater risk of a smaller disaster. We have seen reasons for doubting that EUP can solve this choice problem for the utilitarian. In the next section, the desirability of applying another popular principle of rational choice is explored.

II. MAXIMIN

Among the most favored principles of rational choice under uncertainty is the Maximin Principle (MMP). It prescribes selecting the available alternative with the best worst outcome, that is, the one yielding the maximum minimum payoff. MMP is, in one respect, well suited for application to the deter-or-disarm problem: its use requires only ordinal rankings of the utilities of the various possible outcomes. On the other hand, as will be noted in Chapter 7, MMP, strictly interpreted, does not allow us to choose between minimum deterrence and unilateral disarmament. For it is *possible*, though highly unlikely, that unilateral disarmament could produce the worst outcome of all, namely human extinction. (This could happen, for example, by the rival power having a nuclear war with other powers that caused an extreme and long-lasting nuclear winter.) Thus, comparing deterrence and disarmament by their worst possible outcomes does not distinguish between them.

We could, however, modify MMP, so that it considers only outcomes that have a *significant probability* of following from the acts or policies in question. It is not implausible to assume that minimum deterrence has a significant probability of resulting in extinction (through large-scale nuclear war and it environmental effects) while unilateral disarmament does not. Given this assumption, a utilitarian following the modified MMP would favor unilateral disarmament over minimum deterrence, since the worst significantly probable outcome of the former (say, rival world domination secured by limited nuclear attack) is not as bad as the worst significantly probable outcome of the latter (say, large-scale nuclear war leading to extinction). To see if modified MMP can plausibly be applied in this way to solve our problem, it will be useful to look first at Rawls's use of MMP in his theory of justice.[12]

Rawls seeks to discover and justify principles of social justice by asking what principles governing major social institutions would be selected, in an original position of choice, by rational self-interested parties expecting to live under those institutions. Each party in the original position is assumed to know that the society in question will be subject to "moderate scarcity" of resources, but is assumed to lack knowledge of her own individual traits (e.g., abilities and goals) that could enable her to bias the principles in her own favor. Rawls contends that such parties so situated would follow MMP and attempt to assure for themselves the highest possible security level, by opting for social arrangements ensuring the best worst outcome. The resulting conception of justice is embodied in Rawls's *difference principle,* which says that inequalities in the distribution of primary goods (i.e., those goods such as income and liberty that it is rational for a person to want no matter what particular things she may want) are allowable only if they work to the greatest benefit of the least advantaged members of society. Rawls cites three main reasons for thinking the parties would follow a maximin strategy.[13] First, since there is no positive evidentiary basis for a party assigning a numerical probability to her ending up in a particular social class or position, EUP cannot reasonably be applied. Second, each party would know that she would receive an acceptable supply of primary goods under the difference principle, but she might not receive an acceptable supply if principles aimed at maximizing expected utility were chosen. Third, the parties do not substantially prefer the larger amounts of primary goods that they might obtain under other principles to the acceptable supply they would be assured of under the difference principle.

However, even if we accept this reasoning as sound, it would not follow that modified MMP yields the correct solution to the deter-or-disarm choice problem. For there are crucial differences between the deter-or-disarm choice situation and the situation faced by the parties in Rawls's original position, so that none of the three reasons Rawls offers for following a maximin strategy in the latter situation applies in the former situation. First, the deter-or-disarm situation is not one of complete uncertainty. There is a least one piece of probability data that is known: the ordinal ranking of the two relevant conditional probabilities. Second, while Rawls assumes moderate scarcity of resources so that one can be assured of receiving a supply of primary goods sufficient to sustain a minimally decent life if MMP is followed, there is no choice available in the deter-or-disarm situation that ensures an acceptable outcome. Third, in the deter-or-disarm situation, utilitarian choosers greatly prefer the favorable outcome they might achieve by following the nonmaximin policy (i.e., preservation of the status quo) to the security level outcome that could be assured by their playing a maximum strategy (i.e., world domination by the rival). To see how these differences affect the plausibility of applying MMP, let us alter Rawls's choice situation so that it comes to resemble the deter-or-disarm choice situation in these respects.

Let us suppose that there is some minimum amount X of basic primary goods (e.g., food and time free from labor), such that life for almost anyone receiving less than this amount would contain miseries outweighing its joys and would not be worth living.[14] *Extreme scarcity* may be said to exist in a society if there is no way of organizing production and distribution so as to yield a supply of basic goods equal to or larger than X to the members of the worst-off class. Imagine that the parties in the original position know that their society will be operating under conditions of extreme scarcity. If primary goods are distributed according to the difference principle, a substantial minority will receive an allotment of basic primary goods that is somewhat less than X. A more unequal distribution would minimize the number of persons receiving an allotment of less than X, but would ensure that the least advantaged would have less than under the difference principle, and would lead more miserable lives. Assume that enough of this information is known to the parties to allow them to infer that each is more likely to receive an allotment of X or greater if the more unequal distribution is chosen instead of the Rawlsian one, but the information is not complete enough to allow them to infer how much more likely. Here, following a maximin strategy would not appear to be rational. It seems to be worth risking receiving a very low level of basic primary goods, in order to obtain a better chance of receiving an allotment that would enable one to live a life that is minimally decent and worth living. To follow MMP, under these circumstances, would be to maximize one's chances of obtaining a disastrous and unacceptable outcome, and this does not seem reasonable. Hence, the propriety of applying MMP in the Rawlsian choice situation is decidedly less plausible when that situation is revised to resemble the deter-or-disarm choice situation in relevant respects. This suggests we should look beyond (modified) MMP in seeking a solution to our problem.

III. DISASTER AVOIDANCE

No generally satisfactory principle of rational choice under uncertainty has yet been found.[15] Fortunately, for our purposes, we only need a principle that is plausibly applicable to a very limited class of cases, those having the same relevant structural features as the deter-or-disarm choice. To aid discovery of such a principle, let us consider an example involving rational prudence.

A forty-year-old man is diagnosed as having a rare disease and consults the world's leading expert on the disease. He is informed that the disease is almost certainly not fatal but often causes serious paralysis that leaves its victims bedridden for life. (In the other cases, it has no lasting effects.) The disease is so rare that the expert can offer only a vague estimate of the probability of paralysis: 20 to 60 percent. There is an experimental drug that, if administered now, would almost certainly cure the disease. However, it kills a significant but not accurately known percentage of those who take it. The expert guesses that the probability of the drug being fatal is less than 20 percent, and the patient thus assumes that he is definitely less likely to die if he takes the drug than he is to be paralyzed if he lets the disease run its course. The patient would regard bedridden life as preferable to death, but he considers both outcomes as totally disastrous compared to continuing his life in good health. Should he take the drug?

The choice facing this patient has the same basic structure as the deter-or-disarm choice and is essentially like the choice facing the parties in the revised Rawlsian situation described above. If he ignores the very tiny chances of nontreatment resulting in death and treatment being followed by paralysis,[16] he must choose, under two-dimensional uncertainty, between a smaller probability of a larger disaster (the chance of death after taking the drug, which would correspond to large-scale nuclear war after deterrence) and a larger probability of a smaller disaster (the chance of paralysis after nontreatment, which would correspond to Soviet world domination after U.S. nuclear disarmament). Let us imagine the advice he would receive from three different friends (who also ignore the aforementioned "tiny chances"): an expected utility maximizer, a maximiner, and a disaster avoider.

The expected utility maximizer's advice: To choose rationally is to maximize expected utility. In this case, carefully consider the outcomes – death, bedridden life, and normal life – and estimate their relative values to you. Then estimate as best you can the probabilities that you will die if you take the drug and be paralyzed if you do not. Using these estimates, calculate the expected utility of each course of action and choose the one with the higher expected utility. Admittedly, it would be better if more information on the disease and the drug were available, but nonetheless, following EUP is the best you can do.

The maximiner's advice: Since you must choose essentially under conditions of uncertainty, you should act to make sure the worst does not happen. It would be silly to risk death for an indefinite improvement in your chances of continuing a normal life. At least if you refuse the drug, you know that the worst that might happen to you is paralysis.

The disaster avoider's advice: Since you regard paralysis as an extreme personal disaster, it would be wrong to sacrifice the extra chance of continuing a normal life, even to avoid the risk of death. Admittedly, if this were one of a series of like choices, the matter might be different. For you would quite likely perish if you were to take (different) potentially fatal drugs in each of a series of like cases. Since, however, this is a once-in-a-lifetime choice, and there is a very good chance of success, you ought to give yourself the best chance of obtaining an acceptable result and take the drug.

The first two friends advise, respectively, that the patient follow EUP and MMP. The third friend's advice conforms to the following Disaster Avoidance Principle (DAP): *when choosing between potential disasters under two-dimensional uncertainty, it is rational to select the alternative that minimizes the probability of disaster occurrence.* The reasoning of the third friend seems at least as cogent, and his advice seems at least as attractive, as the reasoning and advice of the expected utility maximizer and the maximiner. This suggests that DAP ought to be taken seriously, as an alternative to EUP and MMP, as a principle governing choices between potential disasters under two-dimensional uncertainty.[17] Further, it appears that DAP will have greatest credibility (compared to EUP and MMP) when all of nine special conditions are satisfied.[18] Each of these conditions is listed below (in italics), followed by a brief explanation of why it lends relative plausibility to the application of DAP.[19] (To preclude any possible misunderstanding, it should be emphasized that the following statements are not axioms from which DAP may be derived, but rather are statements of the limiting conditions for highly plausible applications of DAP.)

(1) *The chooser lacks reliable quantitative probability and utility estimates.* Under this condition, principles of choice such as EUP that rely on such estimates are relatively less attractive.

(2) *The chooser has confidence in his ordering of the (conditional) probabilities of the various outcomes.* This suggests that any principle such as MMP that ignores ordinal probability data is relatively less attractive.

(3) *All disastrous outcomes are regarded as extremely unacceptable, that is,*

as involving very large amounts of net negative utility. The truly disastrous nature of the lesser disaster makes it sensible to risk the worse disaster in hope of avoiding all disasters. The wisdom of following MMP is quite doubtful under these conditions, as this would maximize the probability of there being an extremely unacceptable outcome.

(4) *The disastrous outcomes are judged to be of roughly the same order of magnitude, that is the worse disaster may be many times worse than the lesser disaster, but it is not hundreds of times worse (or more).* If the larger disaster were a hundred or a thousand times as bad as the lesser one, principles such as MMP that emphasize disaster minimization rather than disaster avoidance would seem more attractive.

(5) *The chooser regards the utility disparity between the nondisastrous outcomes (e.g., between the status quo and mutual disarmament) as being small compared to the utility difference between the disastrous and nondisastrous outcomes.* If this were not so, a principle such as DAP that ignores the relative desirability of the different nondisastrous outcomes would be less attractive.

(6) *The choice is unique, that is, is not one in a series of like choices.* For a series of like choice, averaging principles like EUP are relatively more attractive

(7) *The probabilities of the disasters are not thought to be insignificant.* If the risks of disaster were thought to be negligibly small, principles such as EUP that take into account the relative merits of the nondisastrous outcomes would be relatively more attractive.

(8) *The probability of the greater disaster is not thought to be very large.* When this probability seems quite high, disaster avoidance is a rather forlorn hope and its importance pales in comparison with the goal of disaster minimization.

(9) *The probabilities of the disasters are not thought to be very close or equal.* If they were thought to be very close, following a strategy of disaster avoidance rather than disaster minimization would seem less plausible.

Are these nine conditions satisfied (or very nearly satisfied) by the deter-or-disarm choice situation? I believe it is not unreasonable to suppose that they are, though obviously the applicability of many of them could be debated at length. Rather than enter into such a debate, I shall simply state what each of the conditions would amount to when applied to the deter-or-disarm choice, as viewed from the perspective of the United States, and make a few brief observations about some of the more controversial conditions. The reader may then judge for herself the plausibility of regarding the deter-or-disarm choice as satisfying these conditions.

First, we do not have reliable estimates of the utilities of large-scale nuclear war and Soviet world domination, or of the probabilities that these outcomes would result from U.S. minimum deterrence (for thirty years) or U.S. nuclear disarmament. Second, we can be confident that the likelihood of Soviet domination if the United States disarms is greater than the likelihood of war if the United States practices minimum deterrence. Third, both war and Soviet domination would produce extremely large amounts of negative utility. Fourth, Soviet domination would produce negative utility of roughly the same order of magnitude (i.e., not hundreds of times less) as would war. Fifth, the amount of positive utility produced by U.S. nuclear disarmament, if it did not lead to Soviet domination, would be small compared to the amount of negative utility produced by either Soviet domination or war. Sixth, since (i) either disarmament or deterrence could lead to a disaster that would eliminate the opportunity to make similar choices in the future, and (ii) the circumstances surrounding the balance of terror will likely be different in thirty years in any case, the present deter-or-disarm choice should not be treated as simply one in a series of like choices.[20] Seventh, the probabilities of U.S. nuclear disarmament leading to Soviet domination and U.S. minimum deterrence leading to war are not so small as to be disregarded. Eighth, the probability of U.S. minimum deterrence leading to war is not very large. Ninth, the probabilities of U.S. nuclear disarmament leading to Soviet domination and U.S. minimum deterrence leading to war are not very close to equal.

Some reasons for believing the second and ninth statements are given in Chapter 6. The eighth statement is highly plausible because superpower leaders appreciate the awful consequences of nuclear war and because the main risks of nuclear war under current policies would be largely avoided by a policy of minimum deterrence.[21] The other statements are minimally controversial, save for the fourth which claims that large-scale nuclear war would not be hundreds of times worse than Soviet world domination. In evaluating this statement, we should note that such domination (a) might itself involve significant nuclear attacks, (b) could be expected to be long-lasting in view of modern methods of gathering and controlling information, and (c) would likely be replaced by other authoritarian systems if and when it broke down. Also, while large-scale nuclear war would be an enormous calamity for humankind, it seems on current evidence that it would not be likely to lead to human extinction,[22] and humankind might well recover from most of the damaging effects of such a war in the very long run. In light of these considerations, it may be reasonable to accept the controversial fourth statement.

If the nine statements are true, or very nearly so, then the deter-or-disarm choice (faced by the United States) is one to which DAP can be applied with considerable plausibility. Such application yields the conclusion that, from a utilitarian point of view, minimum deterrence is more rational than unilateral disarmament, and hence is morally permissible.[23] To lend support to this conclusion, certain objections to DAP and its application that might be offered by advocates of EUP or MMP are considered in the next section.

IV. OBJECTIONS

A plausible minimum requirement for a principle of choice being satisfactory is that it guarantees transitivity.[24] One might contend that, because the concept "roughly the same order of magnitude" used in the fourth condition of application of DAP is intransitive, DAP will not satisfy this requirement. Consider a choice between disaster-risking acts A, B, and C, in which the other eight conditions are satisfied, and the probabilities and magnitudes of the disasters that may follow from each of the three acts rank in reverse order (with A being least likely and C most likely to lead to disaster). Suppose B risks a disaster that is of roughly the same order of magnitude as the disasters risked by A and by C, without the latter two disasters being of roughly the same order of magnitude. It may appear that transitivity breaks down in such a case. For while DAP ranks A above B, and B above C, it appears to stand mute on the comparison between A and C, because the fourth condition of its application fails to hold.

In response, it should first be noted that DAP itself is transitive and would imply that A is to be preferred to C. The transitivity problem arises only with respect to applications of DAP, when we restrict the conditions for such applications in order to ensure high plausibility. Further, this problem does not appear to be unique to DAP, and may be a general feature of ordinal principles of choice under uncertainty. MMP cannot plausibly be applied to all choices under uncertainty, and certain sensible restrictions on its application would lead to a similar breakdown of the guarantee of transitivity. (This would occur, e.g., if we refused to apply MMP to choices between two acts, whenever the act with the worse worst outcome has a median value – that is, a value halfway between its best and worst outcomes – that is n times larger than the median value of the act with the better worst outcome.)

While this observation might inhibit use of the transitivity objection by maximiners, supporters of EUP may conclude that it shows that ordinal principles in general are inadequate principles of choice under uncertainty. Such persons may be more tolerant of another way of dealing with DAP's transitivity problem: viewing DAP, under the given conditions of application, as an approximation of a more complex nonordinal principle of rational choice. My candidate for such a principle is a sort of weighted average of DAP and EUP that may be called the Compromise Principle (CP).[25] Suppose one must choose between various acts under conditions of two-dimensional uncertainty. One estimates as best one can the utilities and probabilities of the various outcomes, then regiments the utility scale so that the utilities of the outcomes vary between zero and one.[26] Let EUj be the expected utility of the jth act based on these probability and (suitably regimented) utility estimates, r be a measure ranging between zero and one that represents one's level of confidence in one's probability and utility estimates, and $PDAj$ be the probability that the jth act will *not* result in disaster. To each act Aj, assign an index $Cj = r(EUj) + (1 - r) (PDAj)$. The Compromise Principle says to perform the act with the highest index. When $r = 0$, we have no confidence in our quantitative estimates and CP is equivalent to DAP. As r increases from zero to one, CP diverges from DAP and more closely approximates EUP. When $r = 1$, we have a choice under risk, and CP is equivalent to EUP.

DAP may be viewed as an ordinal approximation of the nonordinal and transitive CP, in that the two are likely to yield the same choice in cases in which the special conditions for plausible application of DAP are satisfied. The satisfaction of condition one implies that r, the confidence index, is quite low. Conditions four and five imply that the EUj's are not likely to be too far apart, while condition nine says that the $PDAj$'s are not very close together. Under these conditions, the second term of the index is likely to dominate the first, and CP and DAP are likely to yield the same prescriptions.[27]

In summary, the transitivity objection does not seem to be a telling objection to DAP. DAP is transitive (though not necessarily always plausible) when applied across the board to all choices under two-dimensional uncertainty. While transitivity is not guaranteed when application of DAP is suitably restricted, this appears to be a general problem with ordinal principles of choice and not a characteristic flaw of DAP in particular. Further, it is possible to view DAP as an approximation of a nonordinal principle of choice that guarantees transitivity. Thus, DAP may plausibly be applied with assurance of transitivity when the nine conditions hold between the entire set of alternative acts. If they hold between some pairs of alternatives and not others, CP can be applied to transitively rank the alternatives.

Introduction of CP aids us also in dealing with another objection that might be voiced by expected utility maximizers: that DAP is plausible only because its application has been limited to cases in which it agrees with EUP. Now it is true that some of the conditions of application were introduced to ensure that DAP is not applied when there is too massive a divergence between it and EUP. But the two principles will not necessarily agree, even when the nine conditions are satisfied. Viewing DAP as an ordinal approximation to CP makes clear that the main idea behind DAP is to diverge from EUP, by hedging against disaster occurrence to the extent required by the unreliability of expected utility calculations. Thus DAP is not simply a disguised version of EUP. Supporters of EUP may feel that this amounts to an admission that the use of DAP is irrational, but I do not see why this should be so. The disaster avoidance approach embodied in DAP represents an attempt to deal with some choices under two-dimensional uncertainty rationally, from a utilitarian perspective, while avoiding both of two opposite mistakes: using quantitative methods without the necessary quantities, and ignoring utility altogether because of our inability to apply precise quantitative methods.

Consider, finally, an objection that a maximiner might offer:

"Generally, one has an obligation to act more conservatively with respect to imposing risks on others than with respect to taking risks oneself. Therefore, DAP has considerably less plausibility as a utilitarian principle of choice regarding imposing risks on others, than it does as a principle of rational prudence."[28] In reply, it may be noted that conservatism, as used in the principle cited in this objection, generally means an aversion to risking losses in hope of obtaining uncertain gains. DAP applies, though, only in situations in which there is no sure way to avoid the risk of disastrous losses, and the only question is whether to minimize the degree or the probability of such losses. In such cases the usual notion of conservatism does not apply. Once this is seen to be so, it becomes apparent that in choosing between potential disasters, it shouldn't matter whether the potential victim is oneself or another. Imagine, for example, that the patient described in section III is your ward and is unconscious. You must decide whether she is to receive the drug, knowing that while she prefers paralysis to death, she regards either as an unmitigated disaster compared to retaining her health. The rational promotion of your ward's interests in this case should not involve appeal to principles that are different from those you would use to decide if you were the patient deciding prudentially. If it is rational for you to take the drug if you are the patient, it is moral and rational for you to ask that the drug be given to your ward when she is the patient. Hence, the maximiner's objection is answerable.

V. COMPLICATIONS

Our basic analysis considered only two outcomes for each alternative. At first, it may seem this biases the analysis in favor of deterrence. For it means, in effect, ignoring the possibility that one's rival's domination of the world following one's unilateral disarmament might be incomplete, or that substantial change for the better in the rival's system might accompany his domination. Further, no account is taken of the fact that a deterrent policy could lead – without war – to one's rival being dominant, as a result of his decisively winning the arms race or the accompanying ideological-political struggle. These features of the choice problem are not reflected in the above analysis, and they place the disarmament alternative in a more favorable light compared with the deterrence alternative. However, consideration of a wider range of outcomes also reveals features of the choice situation favorable to the deterrence alternative. For, like domination of the world by one's rival, nuclear war admits of degrees: it would not necessarily be fought to the limits. Also, unilateral disarmament would no more constitute a guarantee against nuclear war than deterrence constitutes a guarantee against one's rival dominating the world. (Some, in fact, would consider unilateral disarmament a virtual invitation to nuclear attack by one's rival, an invitation that might be accepted.) Hence, it does not appear that simplifying our problem by considering only two outcomes for each alternative policy introduces a net bias in favor of a deterrence policy.

Another simplifying assumption – ignoring the existence of other nuclear powers – results in a substantially lower estimate of the likelihood of unilateral disarmament leading to nuclear war. In fact, once such third powers are taken into account it might be supposed that unilateral nuclear disarmament by one superpower (say the United States) would, by eradicating any semblance of strategic balance, produce a much greater risk of nuclear war (in some form or another) than would a policy of minimum deterrence. Hence, if anything, this assumption makes the deterrence option seem less attractive than it really is.

These last two observations may be brought together and amplified by considering an objection to our argument offered by Jefferson McMahan.[29] Once we acknowledge that both minimum deterrence and unilateral nuclear disarmament could produce either disastrous outcome (as well as the status quo), we cannot infer that the former policy is more likely to avoid disaster simply from the fact that its most likely disastrous outcome is less likely than the most likely disastrous outcomes of the latter policy. We need instead a comparison of the likelihood that minimum deterrence would produce *some disastrous outcome* (either large-scale nuclear war or domination) with the likelihood that unilateral nuclear disarmament would produce one of these outcomes. This objection is correct, but can be readily answered in either of two ways.

First, it is asserted in the ninth statement in section III (and argued in Chapter 6) that the probabilities of the single most likely disasters following from minimum deterrence and unilateral nuclear disarmament are *not very close*. At the same time, it is highly plausible to suppose that the probabilities of the less likely disasters occurring (i.e., of deterrence leading to domination or of unilateral disarmament leading to large-scale nuclear war) are quite small. Thus, even if the former were larger than the latter, the difference between them would be smaller than the substantial difference between the probabilities of the most likely disasters. It follows that a minimum deterrence policy is more likely to avoid disaster than is unilateral nuclear disarmament. Of course, this argument employs "semi-cardinal" judgments in describing the probabilities of the less likely disasters as "quite small" and the gap between the probabilities of the larger disasters as "substantial." But these judgments are both plausible and much weaker than the more precise cardinal assumptions needed to calculate expected utilities.

Second, using nothing but purely ordinal probability comparisons, we can reach the same conclusion about the superiority of minimum deterrence for disaster avoidance. This requires making the assumption that unilateral nuclear disarmament is more likely to lead to large-scale nuclear war than minimum deterrence is to lead to domination. Given, on the one hand, the likelihood that third nuclear powers (especially China) would remain armed (and increase their stockpiles) if the United States disarmed unilaterally, and, on the other hand, the grave dangers of (and lack of incentive for) attacking a minimum-deterring United States, this assumption seems highly plausible. If it is true, purely ordinal probability considerations favor minimum deterrence according to DAP. For then minimum deterrence is less likely (than unilateral nuclear disarmament) to produce both its more and less likely disastrous outcomes, and hence less likely to produce some disastrous outcome.

Our last simplifying assumption is the setting of a thirty-year period for the operation of the chosen policy. Does this bias the analysis in favor of deterrence, by making the risks of war seem less than they really are? Admittedly, making the policy period very short might introduce such a bias. Thus if we choose *one day* as the policy period, and argued on Monday that we should practice deterrence because the risks of this one-day use of the policy are negligible, then argued on Tuesday that we should continue deterrence for another day for the same reason, and so on, we would be engaging in sophistry. However, the period used in our analysis is not so short that the risk of war resulting from practicing deterrence throughout that period is negligible, and our analysis does not rely on ignoring this risk, but rather on recognizing it and balancing it against the risks of the alternative policy.

Even if the thirty-year policy period is long enough, wouldn't repeated applications of the analysis at the beginning of each period lead to the recommendation to continue deterrence indefinitely? If so, perhaps the risks of continuing the policy in the very long run (e.g., for hundreds of years) should be taken explicitly into account. To suppose, however, that the same analysis can be applied at the start of each future thirty-year period is a mistake. Changing conditions may render deterrence either unnecessary or too dangerous, so that it can no longer be justified, in accordance with DAP, as the lesser utilitarian evil. Further, the overall argument of this book suggests that each side should specifically aim at bringing about changes of the former sort by seeking bilateral disarmament. In essence, then, our analysis is not intended to apply to the very long run, or to justify continuing deterrence regardless of how conditions change. Rather, it seeks to answer the moral question that seems most appropriate in the present historical context: given its perceptions of the political-military situation, is it permissible for a superpower to practice minimum deterrence for a significant period of time, if it uses this time to attempt to alter the conditions that (seem to) make deterrence necessary? No bias is introduced into the analysis by setting a definite time horizon for the purpose of answering this limited question.

We may conclude that the central implication of our analysis – the permissibility of minimum deterrence – is not a product of the simplifying assumptions introduced to render the basic structure of the deter-or-disarm choice clear. It is rather, I think, a conclusion that follows plausibly from a utilitarian thinking about the central elements of the deterrence problem.

A final observation is in order. One view of the balance of terror is that it results from each side selfishly pursuing its national interests, rather than adopting a moral posture and seeking to promote the interests of humanity as a whole. However, the arguments of this chapter indicate that given each side's perceptions of the present political-military situation, rational promotion of the general interests of humanity would recommend that each side practice minimum deterrence, at least in the short run. If this is correct, a rather surprising conclusion follows. Even a miraculous conversion to a general humanitarian morality by the United States and the Soviet Union (or their governments) would not, in itself, suffice to liquidate the world's nuclear danger. Rather, a solution to the balance of terror must be achieved by a different process, one often advocated by conflict theorists: changing U.S. and Soviet perceptions of each other and gradually building mutual trust between the two nations and their governments, by means of a stage-by-stage bilateral nuclear disarmament process. In Chapter 10 it is argued that no structural features of their nuclear competition would prevent the superpowers from carrying out such a process, were they to act in a rational and farsighted manner.

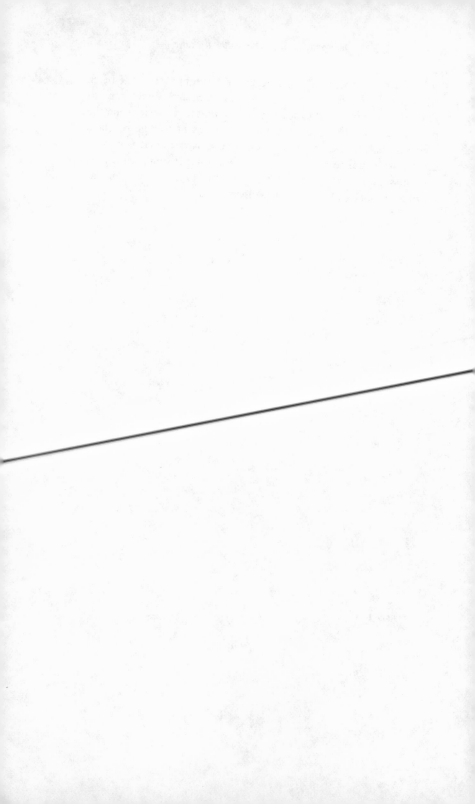

4. Nuclear deterrence: some moral perplexities

Is it morally permissible for the superpowers to practice nuclear deterrence, given that doing so could eventuate in large-scale nuclear war, an unprecedented disaster for humanity? This is a question not only of obvious moral (and political) importance, but also of great intellectual difficulty and complexity. In the last chapter, it was examined from a strictly utilitarian perspective. Here I shall discuss the application of certain deontological moral principles to this question. It is hoped that a potentially fruitful way of looking at the moral problem of nuclear deterrence will emerge from this discussion.

To get our minds churning on the subject, let us consider a fictional situation that parallels the nuclear balance of terror in certain key respects.[1] Hearing from a usually reliable source that a certain rival is out to get you, you begin to carry a gun when you go out. While you are so armed, an elevator you are riding in stops, apparently stuck, between floors. Looking up from your newspaper, you discover that the other occupants are a group of young children and your rival, who has noticed you and seems to be drawing a weapon. You immediately draw your gun and a standoff quickly ensues, with each of you pointing a gun at the other. You realize that firing could break out at any time and kill and injure the children as well as yourself and your rival. Yet you are afraid your rival will shoot you if you drop your gun, nor do you trust him to keep an agreement to drop guns simultaneously. In these circumstances, is it permissible for you to continue to point your gun at your rival? On

This chapter is a revised version of a paper I wrote while supported by a fellowship for independent study and research from the National Endowment for the Humanities.

the one hand, it appears clear that it is, since this reasonably seems necessary for self-defense. On the other hand, the act seems wrong because it seriously threatens the innocent youngsters with injury and death. Here we have a moral dilemma with no immediately evident solution.

Now, if we take you and your rival to be the governments and armed forces of the two superpowers, and the youngsters to be the rest of the population of these countries (and other countries that would suffer in a nuclear war), our elevator case can serve as a model of the nuclear balance of terror. The two situations possess many of the same morally relevant features and pose somewhat similar moral dilemmas. In fact, I propose viewing the moral problem of nuclear deterrence as, like the elevator case, essentially involving a tension between threatening innocent people and doing what appears necessary for self-defense.

This tension is best brought out by noting that the following three propositions form an inconsistent triad – that is, they cannot all three be true, though each pair of them is consistent.

(1) *Threat Principle:* It is impermissible to threaten and impose risks of death upon large numbers of innocent people.

(2) *National Defense Principle:* It is permissible for a nation to do whatever it reasonably believes is necessary for national self-defense.

(3) *Necessity Claim:* Practicing nuclear deterrence against the rival superpower in a way that involves threatening and imposing risks of death upon a large number of innocent civilians is necessary for the self-defense of each superpower and is reasonably believed to be so by its leaders and citizens.

Two of these propositions are absolutist moral principles. The Threat Principle is prohibitive; it says acts of a certain sort are wrong in any circumstances. The National Defense Principle is permissive; it says acts of a particular kind are permissible in any circumstances. The Necessity Claim is an essentially factual proposition[2] that ascribes two properties to the practice of nuclear deterrence. The first of these – that it threatens the innocent – renders the practice impermissible according to the Threat Principle. The second – that it is necessary for national defense – ensures, by the National Defense Principle, that the practice is permissible. Hence the inconsistency, which is disturbing in view of the fact that each of the three propositions has a considerable degree of initial plausibility.

How should this inconsistency be resolved? Which of the three propositions should we reject? Considering them in turn, I shall suggest that none of the propositions is acceptable as it stands. Each must be modified and revised. Identifying the weaknesses of these propositions, and the nature of the modifications needed to correct them, suggests further areas of inquiry. And while it does not provide a direct solution to the moral problem of deterrence, it does shed some definite light on what the problem really is.

I. THREATS TO THE INNOCENT

In practicing nuclear deterrence, a superpower threatens the civilian population of its rival in two senses: it declares that it will kill them if their leaders behave in certain ways, and it actually puts them under some risk of death. That is, nuclear deterrence normally involves a *declarative threat* together with *risk imposition*. It is this combination, directed against large numbers of innocents, that is morally prohibited under all circumstances by the Threat Principle.

Is such an absolutist prohibition plausible? To answer this I propose considering the two elements separately, focusing on the declarative threat first. Let us ask then what is normally wrong with threats, aside from the actual risks they impose on those to whom they are addressed. Four things come immediately to mind: threats may be counterproductive and encourage the wrongful conduct they attempt to deter, they may be effective in deterring permissible conduct (thus restricting the threatened party's rightful liberty), they may cause fear and anxiety, and their use may damage relations between the parties in question. Yet none of these seems to be the sort of consideration that would support an absolute prohibition. Further, there is little reason to suppose that declarative threats should not be permitted when these features are largely absent. Suppose, for example, that a declarative threat will very probably be effective, is aimed at deterring clearly impermissible conduct, does not cause devastating anxiety (compared to alternative courses of action open to the threatener) because people are used to living with it, and damages but does not destroy relations between the parties because threats of this kind are considered a fairly normal element in those relations. It is doubtful that a declarative threat of this sort is wrong simply because it is a threat. Yet it is arguable that the declarative threat involved in nuclear deterrence is just of this kind.

But perhaps it is the specific nature of the nuclear threat, rather than simply its being a threat, that makes it wrong. It has been frequently noted, for example, that the balance of terror holds each side's civilian population hostage to the good behavior of its government. And at least one writer has suggested that nuclear deterrence is wrong because hostage taking is wrong.[3] But if civilians are hostages to an adversary nation's nuclear weapons, they are hostages in place, who may go on with their normal activities without physical restriction. Hence, two of the usual objections to taking hostages do not apply: the violation of their personal integrity in seizing them, and the subsequent imposition of substantial limits on their liberty.[4] In view of this, it seems unlikely that, risk imposition aside, nuclear deterrence must be wrong because, in a sense, it makes civilians hostages.

Does the content of the nuclear threat – to kill a large number of innocent people – render that threat impermissible under any circumstances? In particular, is that threat impermissible because of its close relation to the *intention* to kill innocent people in response to a nuclear attack? Suppose that we accept an absolute prohibition on killing the innocent and also accept the Wrongful Intentions Principle, which says that if an act is wrong, forming the intention to perform it is also wrong. Since threats of nuclear retaliation (unless they are bluffs) involve forming the intention to kill innocent people, it follows that they are wrong.

This reasoning is valid, but unsound. As I have argued in Chapters 1 and 2, the Wrongful Intentions Principle fails when applied to a conditional intention adopted solely to prevent the occurrence of the circumstances in which the intention would be acted upon. Thus, for example, if I know I can prevent you from thrashing me only by sincerely threatening to retaliate against your beloved and innocent brother, it may not be wrong for me to do so. Since the intentions behind the threats of those who practice nuclear deterrence are presumably of this sort, these threats are not necessarily wrong.

Alternatively, it might be argued that (sincere) nuclear threats are prohibited not because they involve forming wrongful intentions, but because they knowingly risk performing absolutely forbidden acts (i.e., killing of the innocent) intentionally.[5] But, even if we acknowledge that there are absolutely forbidden acts, an absolute prohibition on undertaking risks of intentionally performing them is seen to be highly implausible once we recognize its implications. For practically any action one takes that could significantly influence one's values, motives, or incentives, runs some risk of leading later to intentionally perform a forbidden act. If, for example, you enroll in a good university, you undertake some, albeit a quite small, risk of turning into a violent ideologue of the left or right who will later wrongfully kill for the cause. (Enlisting in the armed forces, changing jobs, moving to another city, reading works of political philosophy, and so on carry similar risks.) It is hardly plausible that those who are aware of this fact are thereby under an absolute obligation not to engage in such activities.

I conclude that the present absolutist form of the Threat Principle cannot be supported on the basis of the declarative threat element. But if we focus instead on the imposition of risks, we again find little reason to adopt an absolutist principle of this type.[6] For it is generally recognized that if we evaluate policies in terms of the risks involved, we must also consider and weigh up the benefits the policies bestow and the risks and benefits entailed by alternative policies. Might an absolute prohibition be justified by the combination of our two elements, though by neither alone? This seems highly doubtful in the absence of an explanation of how being a declarative threat and imposing risk are much worse in combination than in isolation. Being unaware of any special internal relation between these elements that would provide such an explanation,[7] I conclude that our Threat Principle must assume some modified and nonabsolutist form such as:

(1')   *Revised Threat Principle:* It is wrong to *disproportionately* threaten and impose risks of death upon large numbers of innocent people.[8]

This revised principle requires that threats to the innocent not be excessively harmful or risky, compared to available alternatives. But how, in principle, are we to determine whether relevant harms and risks are proportionate or excessive? The most natural initial suggestion is to apply a utilitarian standard and ask whether a policy of nuclear deterrence promotes worldwide human welfare better than would its abandonment. However, casting the problem in these terms confronts us with the dilemma of Chapter 3. For while we cannot reliably estimate the precise numerical probabilities, most of us (on the Western side) would endorse the following ordinal judgment: it is considerably more likely that the Soviets would attack and/or dominate the world by blackmail, if the United States practices unilateral nuclear disarmament for a given period of time, than it is that continued nuclear deterrence of the proper kind (during the same period) would lead to large-scale nuclear war. If we believe this, and disregard outcomes with insignificant likelihoods, then the choice we face, in utilitarian terms, is essentially between a smaller risk of a graver disaster for humanity (i.e., nuclear war), and a greater risk of a smaller disaster for humanity (i.e., Soviet attack and/or domination).

Perhaps we could avoid this utilitarian dilemma by assessing risks in another way, or solve it by applying the Disaster Avoidance Principle. In any case, evaluation of the prohibitory Threat Principle leads toward viewing the moral problem of deterrence as a problem of risk assessment under uncertainty. Does a similar view emerge if we approach the problem from the perspective of a permissive National Defense Principle?

II. NATIONAL DEFENSE

What is the moral basis on which we posit the existence of a right of national defense? For present purposes, I shall take it that such a right is derived from principles of individual self-defense in one of two ways: by analogy, with the reasoning being that a nation is like a person in morally significant respects, and therefore possesses a right of self-defense like that of a person; or by composition, with the right of national defense consisting in an authorized government's exercising, in a coordinated fashion, the combined individual rights of self-defense of its citizens. In either case, we may assume that the right of national defense has the same limitations as the right of individual self-defense, unless there are specific differences between the situations of nations and individuals that either cancel or extend those limitations. Then we may use our knowledge of the individual right of self-defense to discover what limits, if any, govern the moral right of national defense.

Richard Wasserstrom, in his discussion of the morality of war, notes four restrictions on the individual legal right of self-defense: there must be an actual attack; the defender (unless on her own property) must have been unable safely to retreat; the force used must have been reasonably necessary; and the harm inflicted must be comparable to (or less than) that which would otherwise have been suffered by the defender.[9] Suppose that we agree that these are all limitations on the moral, as well as legal, right of individual self-defense. Are they also limits on the right of national defense?

With the exception of the use of force being reasonably necessary (a conditional already reflected in the National Defense Principle), it is doubtful that they are. The other three limitations seem justified only because individuals generally can appeal to public authorities to protect themselves and vindicate their rights. Temporary retreat and acceptance of limited harm and/or risk to oneself are morally acceptable if actual and potential assailants can be punished and deterred through the legal system. But there is no effective system of international criminal law to punish and deter aggressor states. If nations retreat as far as possible, or wait until the other side attacks, they may gravely weaken their chances of defending themselves successfully, with no hope of having their losses restored. Further, if aggression is to be effectively deterred in the absence of an international police force to mete out punishments, successful defenders may have to inflict more than comparable harm on unsuccessful aggressors.[10] Hence, the legal limits on the right of individual self-defense do not point to any substantial limitations on the right of national defense, beyond those already contained in our National Defense Principle.

As Wasserstrom notes, nations do not die in the same sense as people do.[11] Does this imply any special restrictions on the right of national defense that might apply to nuclear deterrence? To answer this, we must first distinguish between two senses in which a nation can die. Its people can be physically annihilated ($death_1$), or the people can survive but lose their independence or have their basic institutions substantially and forcibly altered by outsiders ($death_2$). Now, it is doubtful that nuclear deterrence is the only way a nation can prevent its $death_1$. It is highly likely, for example, that either superpower could safeguard the lives of (at least almost all of) its citizens if it were willing to accept $death_2$ by simply surrendering to its rival.

However, consideration of the nature of the right of individual self-defense makes it plausible to suppose that nations have a strong right to defend themselves from $death_2$ as well as $death_1$. Suppose a gang goes around kidnapping people and then, without ever killing them, either locks them up in secret prisons for life, blinds them and amputates their limbs, destroys their higher faculties by brain operations, or brainwashes them so they come to love what they previously hated and hate what they previously loved. Clearly whatever people are justified in doing to save themselves from murderers, they would be equally justified in doing to prevent being kidnapped by this gang. The implication of this is that the right of self-defense applies to the preservation of the central values of one's life as well as to biological survival. This suggests that a nation's right of self-defense applies to its central values (including its independence and the structure of its basic institutions), as well as the biological survival of its members – especially if, as seems likely, the central values of many of those members (and the survival of some of them) are inextricably bound up with the survival of the nation and its central values.[12] So even if nuclear deterrence were reasonably necessary only to protect a nation from death$_2$, it could still be sanctioned by a legitimate right of national defense.

We have yet, however, to consider the most important limit on the right of individual self-defense: restrictions on the risks or harms one may impose on other innocent parties in attempting to protect oneself. Suppose, for example, that mobsters credibly threaten to kill you unless you murder several innocent people. You may reasonably believe that doing these killings is necessary to save your life. It would be wrong, nonetheless, to do them. The same is true even in some cases in which the risk or harm you impose is decidedly less than the harm you are defending against. Thus, if you need a new kidney to survive, you have no right to kidnap an appropriate donor and have your surgeon friend transplant one of his kidneys into you.[13]

The lesson of the kidney case seems to be that one can, at most, actively impose substantially lesser risks or harms on other innocent people to protect oneself. Can this lesson be applied to national as well as individual self-defense? One might contend that it cannot be, appealing for support to the hallowed ought-implies-can principle. According to that principle, agents, including nations, can only be obligated to act in ways they are capable of acting. But, it may be suggested, nations are literally incapable of refraining from taking steps believed to be necessary for national defense, even if these impose horrible risks or harms on outside innocents. For any government that failed to undertake the requisite defensive actions (e.g., any government that abandoned nuclear deterrence) would be quickly ousted and replaced by a government willing to undertake them.

This argument that nations may permissibly do anything to protect themselves, because they can do no other, is interesting but unconvincing. In the first place, history shows that not all governments that fail to take available courses of action necessary for national defense fall when this becomes apparent. Thus, Chamberlain's appeasement of Hitler led to his downfall, but Stalin's did not lead to his. This example suggests restricting the argument to democratic nations, where the people clearly have the power to replace unsatisfactory leaders.[14]

But there are further difficulties with the argument. If democratic governments are incapable, because of popular pressure, of refraining from necessary defensive actions, democratic nations are not. For the nation includes the people, and if they allowed a government to forgo elements of defense to protect third parties, the government could do so. Hence, for the argument to establish that democratic nations are permitted to do whatever is necessary for defense, it must claim that the people, or an effective majority of them, are collectively incapable of doing otherwise. But this would seem exceedingly difficult to establish, especially when – as in the case of nuclear deterrence – the acts thought necessary for defense themselves risk national and international destruction. No known principle of individual or group psychology indicates that an effective majority of an independent nation's people *must* prefer to risk their own deaths and those of countless other innocents to losing their political independence. They certainly may so prefer, but the argument in question succeeds only if the opposite preference is impossible.

Finally, suppose it were true that democratic nations, at least, could do no other than defend themselves, even at the cost of imposing serious harms or risks on innocent others. Can we appropriately apply the ought-implies-can principle to conclude that such nations act permissibly in imposing these harms and risks? Comparisons with the case of individuals suggests not. Neither law nor morality allows people to murder other innocents in self-defense. Even when there is genuine irresistible compulsion derived from self-preservation instincts, this at most excuses the murdering of innocent others, or mitigates the appropriate punishment; it does not justify the action.[15] The same presumably holds true of the imposition of lesser but still serious harms (e.g., the theft of a kidney) and serious risks (e.g., tossing someone out of a crowded lifeboat when he or she has some reasonable chance of swimming to shore.) The "ought" in the moral rule "One ought not to impose death, serious harms, or substantial risk thereof on innocent people" is apparently not strictly governed by the ought-implies-can principle. Hence an unlimited right of national defense would not follow even from a nation's incapacity to refrain from taking whatever measures seem necessary for defense.

Suppose then we accept the limit on the right of national defense suggested by the kidney case: nations, like individuals, can at most impose substantially lesser risks or harms on other innocent parties to protect themselves. We might be tempted to conclude that nuclear deterrence by superpower A is impermissible because it imposes on innocent citizens of superpower B risks as great as those from which it protects citizens of A. Before, however, we jump to that conclusion, we must look more closely at the concept of innocence.

III. INNOCENCE AND IMMUNITY

As used in such claims as "Nuclear deterrence is wrong because it imposes risks on innocent people" and "It is wrong to kill innocent people," the notion of innocence has two components. Those people described as innocent are asserted to be innocent of doing (or bringing about) certain things, in the sense of lacking moral responsibility for them. Also, a certain moral status is ascribed to these people: that of being immune from deliberately imposed harm or risk. Thus, this use of the concept of innocence contains within itself a substantive moral doctrine.

(4) *Immunity Thesis:* Persons have moral immunity, and it is impermissible to deliberately impose significant harms or risks on them, unless they are themselves morally responsible for creating relevant harms or dangers.[16]

The intended concept of moral responsibility may be explained as follows. An agent is morally responsible for certain harms or risks when two conditions hold. First, certain moral flaws or shortcomings of the agent are expressed in his acts (or omissions) and make a significant causal contribution to the existence of those harms or risks. Second, the agent possesses the general psychological capacities necessary for being responsible for one's actions. Applying punishment only to those who are morally responsible in this sense seems sensible. It ensures that people are punished only for things over which they had some significant degree of control. And those punished can reasonably be said to merit punishment, because their moral flaws have produced identifiable harms or dangers. However, the concept of immunity has a use in some contexts in which punishment is not what is at issue. In particular, the question of a person's moral immunity may arise in a dangerous situation, as one considers acting so as to redistribute risks among various parties.[17] Our intuitions about certain situations of this kind imply that the Immunity Thesis is not universally valid.

Imagine that a powerful man, whom I know to hate me and to be insane, rushes me with a knife. I can stop him either by shooting him or by shooting a third party who would fall in his path and delay him long enough for me to escape. It is clear that the former alternative is morally preferable, even though neither the lunatic nor the bystander is morally responsible for the danger to my life. Note also the standard belief that, in war, you are justified in shooting at enemy solders because they pose a threat to you, your comrades, and your country. An enemy soldier may not be morally responsible, in the sense described above, for the threat he poses. (He may reasonably believe that he is obligated to fight for his country, or he may have been coerced into fighting by threats of death.) Yet his lack of moral responsibility would not impose on you the obligation to treat him as you would a civilian bystander. Finally, consider an example involving nuclear deterrence. Compare deterring country Y from attack by threatening retaliation against its cities, with deterring it by threatening retaliation against the cities of uninvolved nation Z. Most of us believe that, questions of effectiveness aside, the latter practice is substantially more objectionable. Yet the vast majority of citizens of Y, as well as the citizens of Z, probably lack individual moral responsibility for the danger that Y creates.

The correct explanation of our reactions to these cases seems to be this. Our moral beliefs about dangerous situations are complex enough to take account of the fact that there are various kinds of connections an individual may have to a given danger, and that these may hold in various combinations and degrees. We regard the kind of connection set out in the usual conception of moral responsibility as sufficient to annul the agent's immunity. But other "looser" connections – creating danger out of madness or belonging to a group responsible for producing a harm – are also sometimes taken to weaken or annul that immunity.

It might be thought that one particular sort of connection – *causing the danger in question,* even in the absence of moral responsibility – has privileged standing here. Those who cause harm or impose risk on us, according to this view, lose immunity, while those having other connections to the harm (such as sharing collective responsibility for it) do not. If this were so, harming the mad attacker would be justified, but imposing nuclear risk on innocent enemy civilians would apparently not be.[18] It appears, however, that causality in itself does not possess the privileged status accorded to it by this view. This can be seen by comparing an Innocent Threat to an Innocent Shield.[19] The Innocent Threat threatens to cause harm through nonculpable ignorance, as by ringing your doorbell which, unbeknown to him, will set off the dynamite under the chair to which you are tied. The Innocent Shield is situated so that you can stop someone else's threat only by harming her in the process, as when your enemy holds her in front of him as he aims his gun at you. Whatever moral limits there are on harming Innocent Threats or Innocent Shields to protect oneself, it seems highly implausible that the limits are less strict in the case of the Innocent Threat simply because it would *cause* the harm you would suffer, while the Innocent Shield would not. This indicates that causation does not occupy the privileged position that the doctrine under consideration ascribes to it.

Returning to the Immunity Thesis, it is not hard to understand why we subject it to qualification. The basic purpose of holding people liable for risks and harms is to protect people, by deterring and preventing dangerous and harmful acts. It is generally most efficient to control such acts by holding liable those morally responsible for them. Further, so doing gives people the opportunity to avoid liability by refraining from performing dangerous or harmful acts. In certain cases, however, control of harmful behavior is attained much more efficiently if looser conditions of liability are used. When the penalties are not severe, and the efficiencies are relatively large, we are not greatly bothered by such loosening of liability conditions. When penalties are more serious, such as imprisonment, death, or risk of serious injury, we generally believe that tight standards of liability should be employed. Thus, we are less inclined to accept vicarious liability in criminal than in civil law. However, when there is a significant present danger, and control of that danger requires loosening the conditions of liability, our inclination is to regard some loosenings as justified. This does not mean that we break down all distinctions. We still hold that the uninvolved bystander retains his immunity. What happens is that we shift more agents with intermediate degrees of connection to the danger out of the immune category (where the bystander resides), into the nonimmune category (where the deliberate wrongdoer resides), or into an intermediate semi-immune category.

Our justification for doing so in the case of collective action by an organized group is evident. In cases of cooperative action involving large numbers of people, it would be silly to require for liability that an individual's contribution to the group act be significant and flow from a flaw in the individual's character. When large groups act, individual members' contributions are typically indirect and too small to have substantial impact. Further, organizational decision procedures and group pressures can often funnel individually blameless inputs into an immoral group output. Hence, to require a significant causal contribution flowing from a character defect as a precondition of liability in such cases would be to let too many people (in some cases perhaps everyone) off the hook and largely lose the ability to influence group acts by deterrence. This is especially so when the group in question is a sovereign nation. For then, usually, outsiders can do little to punish key leaders who bear individual moral responsibility for the group's misbehavior, except by imposing military, economic, or political sanctions that affect the entire nation.

If we accept this limited defense of applying some notion of collective responsibility to citizens of nations, the argument against nuclear deterrence offered at the end of the last section fails. Superpower civilians typically lack full individual moral responsibility for the nuclear threat their government and military pose to the rival superpower, but this does not render them fully immune to counterthreats. Like the mad attacker, they are partially responsible and hence partly liable. Mutual nuclear threats may even reciprocally justify each other.[20]

Taken together, considerations advanced in this section and the last suggest that a proper form of the National Defense Principle should be neither absolutely permissive nor absolutely prohibitory.

It should not permit *anything* reasonably necessary for national defense, for there must be limits on what may be done to the innocent or partially innocent. But, as the adversary's civilian population lacks full immunity, it should not forbid imposing any substantial risks or harms on them. Perhaps the principle should read as follows:

(2′)   *Revised National Defense Principle:* It is permissible for a nation to do whatever it reasonably believes is necessary for national self-defense, provided such measures do not impose disproportionate risks or harms on other parties.

The key term in this principle is "disproportionate." The appropriate criteria of proportionality take into account not only the relative sizes of the various risks and the risks that would be produced by alternative courses of action, but also the "degree" of innocence or immunity of the threatened parties. Considerations advanced in this section indicate that risks imposed on guilty parties count for much less than those imposed on the partially innocent (e.g., those only collectively responsible), which in turn count for less than those imposed on purely innocent bystanders. Reading backwards, we should also add this element to the interpretation of the term "disproportionately" in the Revised Threat Principle (1′).[21] This renders our two revised principles of one mind. Both forbid imposing disproportionate risks or harms on others, but allow all proportionate measures necessary for national defense.

We now see that the moral problem of deterrence is more complex, in at least one important way, than the utilitarian dilemma sketched in Chapter 3. It involves assessing the degrees of responsibility and liability for military threats to others of the various parties and groups involved in the balance of terror and appropriately integrating this information into one's (otherwise) utilitarian analysis of risks and benefits.[22] The difficulty of this task may make us wish to avoid it. We could surely do so if nuclear deterrence were unnecessary for national defense. But is it?

IV. IS DETERRENCE NECESSARY?

Must a superpower practice nuclear deterrence to adequately defend itself? In particular, is threatening Soviet civilians with nuclear retaliation necessary for the defense of the United States, given the

Soviets' possession of a vast nuclear arsenal? At least one recent writer has answered no, on the grounds that conventional arms alone would suffice to deter the Soviets from attack or successful nuclear blackmail,[23] but, for reasons to be discussed in Chapter 6, I shall make the usual assumption that this is wrong. A recent proposal of President Reagan's suggests a different basis for answering our question in the negative.[24] Deterrence by threat of nuclear retaliation might be replaced by an effective technological defense against nuclear missiles, a system of lasers, missiles, and/or particle beams that would destroy enemy missiles before they have reached their targets. Critics of this proposal have claimed that such a system would be enormously expensive, would not work well enough, would itself be vulnerable to attack, could be counteracted by the other side's building more missiles, and might conceivably tempt the other side to strike first before the system was completed. They are probably right about much of this, as we shall see in Chapter 8. But unless such systems are perfect (i.e., 100 percent reliable) shields, there is yet another powerful strategic and moral reason against building them: they provide increased incentives for each side to select the other's cities instead of its missile bases as its primary targets.[25]

One side's possession of an effective defensive system makes the other side's missiles relatively less attractive targets; since they can probably be destroyed once fired, if necessary, they need not be attacked on the ground. This is starkly apparent in the simplest imaginary case in which each side has one missile, and one side has a defensive system providing a 90 percent probability of intercepting the other's missile if it is fired. If it lacked this defensive system, the side now possessing it would have to target the other side's missile as its own first-strike target. But now it may target the other's capital, relying on the defensive system to protect it against retaliation. Though the mathematics are more complicated, the same principle would seem to apply to cases involving more missiles.

What of the side that lacks a defensive system but faces an opponent with one? To ensure being able to inflict enough retaliatory damage to deter a first strike by its defended opponent, it will be forced to target virtually all its missiles on its opponent's population centers. In the case of both sides having effective, but imperfect, defensive systems, these two effects reinforce each other. The other side's missiles are rendered relatively less attractive as first-strike targets by one's own possession of a missile defense. And one's opponent's cities are rendered even more attractive as targets of retaliation. So the cumulative protective effect for civilians of both sides having 90 percent effective antimissile defensive systems would be much less than that provided by a 90 percent reduction of missiles on both sides (with defenses forgone). For the retargeting incentives with effective but imperfect defensive systems are such as to render population centers relatively more attractive as both first- and second-strike targets.

For this reason, as well as the others mentioned, I do not feel that technological defenses provide much hope of rendering nuclear deterrence entirely obsolete. It does not follow, however, that the answer to our question about whether threatening civilians with nuclear destruction is necessary for national defense is a simple yes. For defense by deterrence is a matter of degree, or probability. Different nuclear policies may deter different possible moves by a nation's adversaries with various degrees of reliability. Speaking from the Western perspective, whether a given nuclear policy is "necessary" for defense depends on what we in the West seek to defend against and what probability of successful defense would satisfy us.

Nuclear deterrence policies vary along a number of dimensions. The one discussed above, targeting, has been frequently discussed in the literature. In particular, the issue of whether to target military bases and missiles, or cities, has been seen to have considerable moral as well as strategic significance.[26] I shall now focus on a less noted and analyzed dimension, that of our willingness to retaliate if attacked with nuclear weapons.

Different imaginable policies reflect varying degrees of likely response, and willingness to respond, to nuclear attack. At one end of the spectrum is the construction of an automatic retaliator (rather like the doomsday machine described in Stanley Kubrick's 1964 motion picture, *Dr. Strangelove*) that we could not turn off even if we wanted to, once we had been attacked. Convincing our adversaries that we had such a system in operation would provide maximum credibility of response to nuclear attack. Moving down the ladder of likely response, we might have a semi-automatic retaliatory system, a sincere and declared intention to retaliate, no announced policy about the use of our nuclear arsenal, or a bluff posture, that is, a public policy of retaliation conjoined with a private determination by our leaders not to retaliate if the occasion should actually arise. Finally, at the end of the scale, is the least threatening posture possible short of dismantling our nuclear weapons: a public policy of not retaliating even if attacked.[27] To emphasize that deterrence is a matter of degree, and to trace some moral implications of this fact, let us look more closely at the two extremes along this dimension, the no-retaliation policy and the automatic retaliator.

Even a no-retaliation policy would probably have considerable deterrent value. The Soviets probably would not believe that we really did not intend to retaliate and, if they did believe it, might with good reason fear that we would change our minds if actually attacked. In other words, there would probably be enough uncertainty about our response to provide us with a considerable degree of what McGeorge Bundy calls "existential deterrence."[28] Nonetheless, such a policy would probably make deterrence considerably less reliable than it is now. In any case, it would be a domestic political impossibility, for regardless of its strategic or moral merits and demerits, it would require the government to spend billions on weapons it was pledged not to use under any circumstances.

The no-retaliation policy would mainly seem attractive to moralists who wish to retain an element of deterrence, but believe that *intending* to retaliate against civilians under any circumstances is impermissible. In Chapters 1 and 2, I gave some reasons for rejecting this belief. It is worth noting, in addition, that a no-retaliation policy does not escape the main moral objection to the United State's practicing nuclear deterrence – that it imposes serious risks on many Soviet civilians. For, as just mentioned, a no-retaliation policy might well be abandoned in the heat of battle. Further, by decreasing the reliability of deterrence, such a policy might substantially raise the probability of Soviet nuclear attack. This could actually increase the net danger to Soviet civilians over that which they experience under present policies.[29]

What of the policy, on the other extreme, of building the automatic retaliator? Because of the dangers of mechanical breakdown and accidental war, and the problem of convincing an adversary that the system is nonrecallable, it is doubtful that this would ever, in practice, be a morally permissible alternative. But suppose we put these problems aside, by stipulation, and imagine a mistake-proof and perfectly credible automatic retaliation system. Would there be any convincing moral objection to building such a system to obtain maximal deterrence?

Some writers have suggested that it is wrong to create circumstances one knows could lead uncontrollably to disaster.[30] In turning deterrence over to an autoretaliator, we certainly would be doing this. But the principle that always forbids doing this is too strong. We cannot prohibit all acts that could uncontrollably lead to grave moral wrongs. If we applied this principle on a smaller scale, we would be much too restricted in our actions. We would not parole criminals, because this could lead to more serious crimes being committed. We could not give a political speech for disarmament, because this could cause a riot. More to the point, in the case of nuclear deterrence, any course of action we adopt *could* lead, in a way we could no longer control, to nuclear holocaust. If we built an autoretaliator, a Soviet version of (fictional) General Jack Ripper could set it off. But it also could be, for all we know, that if we do not build it, the Soviets will eventually attack us. Choices of this sort must be evaluated in terms of how grave and how likely the various possible outcomes are, and what the alternatives are. We cannot proceed simply on the basis of what *could* happen.

There is also a positive argument that suggests it might be permissible, in principle, to build an autoretaliator. Imagine that the United States invents a radio device that 50 percent of the time is able to deflect Soviet ballistic missiles in flight and send them to preset targets. For purposes of deterrence, the United States programs Soviet cities instead of the oceans as targets for the deflected missiles, and announces this openly. I think we would regard it as morally permissible to build and operate such a defensive system.[31] (Just as we would regard it as permissible for you to use a bullet-deflecting shield against your rival in the elevator, if you had one, even if the deflected bullets might strike the children as well as your rival.[32]) Yet the system seems like an autoretaliator in virtually all morally relevant respects. The primary purpose of each system is deterrence,[33] and each could be built to preclude our side striking first. Both ensure the truth of the conditional statement, addressed to the Soviets, "If you attack us, your cities will be destroyed," and take control of the fate of both countries out of our hands and put it into those of our potential adversaries. There is this difference: in our latest scenario, the Soviets, if they attacked, would be destroyed by missiles they built themselves.[34] But is this a morally significant difference? It does not seem so. After all, nuclear deterrence as now practiced would be no less problematic if we were pointing captured (or purchased) Soviet missiles at the USSR. I conclude that, in principle, an ideal automatic nuclear retaliator might be permissible to build. Though I reemphasize that I am not thereby endorsing dangerous launch-on-warning strategies or other similar strategies in the circumstances we actually face.

Our analysis of the no-retaliation and automatic retaliation policies illustrates that there are a variety of different nuclear deterrence policies, each with their own advantages, dangers, and moral characteristics. This reinforces the main conclusion that emerged from our consideration of the Threat and National Defense principles: no absolutist principle, either permissive or prohibitory, is going to provide us with an easy and satisfactory solution to the moral problems posed by nuclear deterrence. Our approach to these problems must be more complex, beginning with the development of ways of assessing, under uncertainty, the dangers and advantages, for all humanity, of the various alternative nuclear deterrence policies.

V. THE SHAPE OF THE PROBLEM

I have argued that a utilitarian balancing of risks and benefits, rather than a rigid application of absolutist principles, should be the starting point of a moral evaluation of nuclear deterrence. But a starting point is only that. There are nonutilitarian dimensions to our problem as well, only some of which have been hinted at above, and all of which require careful attention. We need to know more about such issues as the role of collective responsibility in diluting civilian immunity, the relevance of the fact that the nuclear threats that superpowers impose on one another are reciprocal, and how a right of national defense is created out of individual rights of self-defense. To deal with the risks imposed by the balance of terror on non-nuclear nations and their citizens, special moral analysis of indirect risks and unintended side effects is required. The moral significance of the motives of those who practice deterrence must also be considered; in particular, it is important to know which (if any) practitioners' motives must be purely defensive for a deterrent policy to be potentially morally permissible. Finally, there is the very special moral problem of how to take account of the risk of human extinction entailed by the practice of nuclear deterrence.[35]

Given the numerous unsolved difficulties just mentioned, one might wonder what conclusion can safely be drawn about our problem. One plausible conclusion has been suggested by the U.S. National Conference of Catholic Bishops: it is permissible for a superpower to practice nuclear deterrence, but only on the condition that this superpower vigorously and sincerely seeks to remove the circumstances that make this practice necessary for national defense – that is, actively pursues bilateral nuclear disarmament.[36] This initially seems an entirely reasonable compromise between the moral considerations reflected in the National Defense Principle and those underlying the Threat Principle. But there is a problem with this compromise conclusion that must be addressed.[37]

Consider an analogous case in which we may be tempted to draw a similar conclusion about conditional permissibility. A woman steals food to save her starving child. This is permissible, we might say, but only on the condition that she did her best to avoid having to steal (e.g., she sought work or charity or government aid). But on reflection, do we really want to say this? Suppose she did not try to avoid having to steal to keep her child alive. Then she has acted wrongly and is less than fully virtuous. But, having acted wrongly, she may still permissibly steal to save the child, if she has no alternative way of saving it. Instead of speaking of conditional permissibility here, we should instead say that (1) this woman has an obligation to vigorously seek alternative means of child support and (2) it is permissible for her to steal food only if she has no alternative means (whether this results from trying and failing to obtain other support or from her wrongfully not trying).

Something similar may be said in the case of nuclear deterrence. Suppose nuclear deterrence is, at the moment, the "lesser evil" because a superpower has no alternative means of effective national defense against its nuclear rival. Because of the risks to the innocent this policy entails, this superpower has a moral obligation to try to remove the conditions that make such deterrence necessary. (It also has an obligation to practice deterrence in the least risky way consistent with national defense.) Until such efforts succeed, however – if they ever do – it is permissible for the superpower to continue nuclear deterrence whether or not the lack of an alternative is due to

its own past failures and misconduct. Since nuclear deterrence is justified by forward-looking considerations (e.g., the need for national
defense), its permissibility is not strictly conditional on seeking to
overcome its necessity. This seeking is itself obligatory, but it is not a
condition of the permissibility of deterrence.

In conclusion then, the unsolved utilitarian core of the moral
problem of nuclear deterrence is itself surrounded by a number of
complex and unresolved moral issues. As a result, we possess only
one fairly obvious moral imperative concerning the balance of
terror, that we should seek unceasingly to dissolve it through
negotiations and bilateral (eventually multilateral) disarmament.
The rest is a series of perplexities as stubborn and difficult as the
plight of nervous armed rivals trapped together in a stalled
elevator.

5. Dilemmas of nuclear protest

In earlier chapters, I have discussed some of the perplexities that arise when we attempt to determine the moral status of nuclear deterrence. But even with these perplexities unresolved, we may be tempted to think that the practical issues surrounding nuclear deterrence should be easy for morally serious citizens to deal with. For the actual present nuclear defense policies of the superpowers seem so irrational and beyond the moral pale, that the clear injunction for thoughtful people in democratic societies is to support nuclear peace movements and push governments in the direction of political détente, weapons reductions, and eventual abolition of nuclear weapons. While I am fully in sympathy with this general injunction, I regard it as a serious mistake to conclude that the moral choices faced by democratic citizens in this area are at all easy ones. Even the democratic citizen who is fully convinced (with good reason) that her government's present nuclear policies are immoral may encounter a number of significant rational and moral dilemmas in deciding how to act responsibly in light of this. It is the aim of this chapter to describe and briefly discuss some of these dilemmas.

The dilemmas all arise out of the central practical question, "Is it morally obligatory, and rational, for individual citizens of democratic nuclear powers to protest nuclear defense policies of their governments that they regard as being beyond moral justification (i.e., as being immoral because too militaristic)?" This question may be clarified as follows. First, it is concerned with ordinary democratic citizens, not with government officials, missile crews, bomb builders, and so on, who have a special role to play in making or executing nuclear defense policies. There are interesting moral questions to raise about persons occupying these special roles, but they fall outside the scope of this chapter (and book). Second, I focus on citizens of democratic nations on the assumption that ordinary citizens of nondemocratic nuclear nations can protest government defense policies only ineffectively and at excessive personal cost or risk. Third, I do not consider the obligations of citizens who agree with government defense policies. To do so would involve us in extraneous issues about the possible immorality of holding certain beliefs, while our current concern is the rationality and morality of acting on one's beliefs in certain ways. (For similar reasons, I ignore hard-liners who believe government nuclear policies to be immoral because they are not militant enough.) Fourth, by "protest," I mean legal or quasi-legal activities (e.g., nonviolent civil disobedience) that go beyond simply voting for dovish candidates (or referenda) in elections; I mean such protest activities as organizing or participating in demonstrations, donating time or money to organizations that are educating and lobbying for peace, writing letters to political representatives, and so on. I focus on peaceful protest to avoid special moral issues concerning the justification of violence.

Together, these restrictions significantly narrow the potential scope of our central question. But we shall see that our philosophical plate is full even so. In particular, I shall discuss five distinct dilemmas that arise from this question, given its restricted interpretation. None of these dilemmas applies uniquely to the nuclear defense issue; each applies in some form to protests of wrongful policies outside the nuclear sphere. But immoral nuclear weapons policies do have certain characteristics that seem to make protest of them special. Much greater amounts of harm are risked by nuclear arms policies, such policies may involve special kinds of evils (e.g., holding innocent people hostage, threatening them, intending [conditionally] to kill them), and protests of such policies, if they are to be effective, must be made before the policies are put into practice in combat.[1] Hence, I will consider how the five dilemmas arise with respect to protest of nuclear arms policies, and will mention other situations in which they apply only for purposes of comparison or contrast.

I. THE DROP-IN-A-BUCKET PROBLEM

In a democratic nation, changing government policy by protest requires the combined efforts of many people. This is especially so when present policies are perceived as important, have a long history, and are supported by specialized institutions and organizations with a stake in their continuation. Clearly this is the case as regards nuclear defense policies in the Western democracies. Hence, those seeking to change present policies by protest face a classic problem of collective choice. The chances that an ordinary individual's participation will make the difference between success and failure of a nuclear protest campaign are minuscule; his efforts would only be a drop in a bucket.[2] But such participation will ordinarily entail some costs (in terms of time, money, or effort) for that individual. Hence, from the individual's point of view, the expected costs of participation will exceed the expected benefits to be generated (for himself and others), and participation would seem to be irrational.[3] Thus we have the potential nuclear protester's first dilemma: Should I participate at some cost when my contribution is virtually certain to be either ineffective (if not enough others join in) or superfluous (if enough others besides me protest)?

I can identify three possible solutions to this dilemma. The Symbolic Protest solution argues that one should protest significant moral wrongs – especially those carried out in one's name – whether or not one expects those protests to be effective. This "solution" is open to the objection that it is irrational to undergo significant costs unless someone is expected to benefit thereby.[4] Alternately, the Collective Reasoning solution argues that one should protest or not according to the expected consequences, not of one's own protests, but of the combined protest efforts of all those in a similar position (e.g., all of one's fellow citizens who agree that government nuclear policy is beyond moral justification).[5] The problem here is that one controls only one's own actions, and not those of other individuals. Hence, it seems that the proper standard of choice and evaluation for individual action should be the expected consequences of that action, rather than the expected consequences of a hypothetical ensemble of similar actions by similar parties. Though these problems for the Symbolic Protest and Collective Reasoning solutions may not be unsolvable, they are daunting enough to make the more detailed exploration of a third possible solution to the drop-in-a-bucket problem worthwhile.

This Individualist solution looks at all three elements of the relevant expected-value calculation – benefits, costs, and probabilities – and suggests that the expected payoffs of individual participation in nuclear protest will often be positive. Consider benefits first. If protest participation did make a difference in nuclear policy, this could prevent a large-scale nuclear war. This means that, unlike in many other collective action problems, the potential gains of nuclear protest are enormous. Hence, even if the probability of making a difference is tiny, the expected gains may be positive (if costs are not high).[6] For example, if large-scale nuclear war could be expected to produce half a billion fatalities, it would take only a probability of one in half a billion of being "the drop that overflows the bucket" to make your nuclear protest have an expected (gross) gain equivalent to the certain saving of one person's life. This would surely be worth some investment of time, effort, or money.

Turning to the *costs* of participation, nuclear protest in a democracy is clearly an intermediate case between two familiar drop-in-a-bucket cases: voting, which has tiny costs, and joining a rebellion against an established government, which entails large risks.[7] (In fact, voting for dovish candidates and referenda may be viewed as the limiting case of a nuclear "protest" – one with trivial costs to the protester.) However, nuclear protest is far enough over on the voting end of the scale for it to be evident that its costs to the individual are often overridden by the benefits it may provide her. These include psychological benefits such as pride in doing the right thing and pleasure in taking part in a useful joint enterprise; social benefits such as meeting interesting like-minded people; and self-development benefits such as experience in organizing group activities and dealing with a variety of people. With these benefits taken into account, there will be no net cost (but rather a net benefit) of nuclear protest for many democratic citizens who oppose government defense policies on moral grounds.

The probability of making a difference is the third element in the relevant expected-value calculation. And the point to notice here is that not all drops in the protest bucket are of exactly equal size. Some people, in virtue of their talents, training, occupations, social connections, energy levels, or organizational skills, are in a better position to influence their fellow citizens and public officials than are others. Admittedly, even those with more than average influence will have only a very small probability of making a vital difference. But given the enormous potential gain and often low (net) cost noted above it is highly likely that nuclear protests by these individuals will have a positive expected value.

We may summarize and clarify our results to this point by comparing the drop-in-a-bucket problem in the nuclear protest case with its manifestations in the more familiar cases of voting and rebellion. Given what is at stake, there is a much greater potential gain in the case of nuclear protest than in the voting or rebellion cases. The gross individual cost of protest is greater than that of voting, and much less than that of rebellion. But the individual benefits of nuclear protest may well exceed those of voting and, more importantly, will often exceed the cost of protest. Finally, as in the case of rebellion, some individuals will have considerably more than average influence, rendering their efforts much more likely to make a difference. So, in the nuclear protest case, we have a high potential gain, a low (or negative) net personal cost, and significant variation in influence among individuals. This means that the drop-in-a-bucket problem is less severe for nuclear protest than in many other collective action contexts. And, for many of those democratic citizens who oppose their government's nuclear defense policies on moral grounds, it will be rational (in terms of expected-value calculations) to protest these policies. Or, at least, the drop-in-a-bucket nature of the nuclear protest situation fails to show otherwise.

II. COUNTERPRODUCTIVE PROTEST

The drop-in-a-bucket problem suggests that individual political action may be irrational because it is individually costly but highly unlikely to have a significant impact. We have seen that this problem may be at least partially solved in the nuclear protest case because of the personal benefits of protest and the enormous potential payoffs of a better nuclear policy. However, even if we completely set aside this collective action problem, a further dilemma concerning effectiveness confronts potential nuclear protesters. For nuclear protest might be worse than ineffective, it might be counterproductive. This could happen in either of two ways. Nuclear protest might spark a domestic political backlash that leads to more militaristic, dangerous, and immoral nuclear defense policies being adopted by a democratic nation. Alternatively, we can imagine such protests being too effective and resulting in hasty or ill-conceived changes in nuclear defense policy that produce greater instability and risk of nuclear war in the international environment (e.g., a rush toward complete unilateral Western nuclear disarmament, a policy argued against in Chapter 6). If either of these outcomes of nuclear protest is too likely, it may render such protest both irrational and immoral, because it indirectly contributes to an increased risk of nuclear war.

One might respond to this concern about counterproductivity by another appeal to symbolic protest, noting that we should protest immoral policies irrespective of the likely consequences of such protests. But surely this is the sort of context in which the notion of symbolic protest is least attractive.[8] For we are not simply talking about ineffective protest, but counterproductive protest where the potential stakes are about the highest imaginable. With so much at stake, any values achieved by symbolic protest can hardly be expected to outweigh, on the moral scales, even a small increase in the risk of bringing about the worst outcomes.

A better way of dealing with the counterproductivity problem is to acknowledge that it exists in principle, but is probably not decisive in practice at the present time. The nuclear peace movement in democratic countries seems to have so far generated more beneficial pressure than harmful backlash. On the other hand, that movement has hardly had such an enormous impact that we should fear sudden, large, and potentially destabilizing effects on the international environment. In any case, nuclear armaments at present are probably quite far beyond prudentially and morally optimal levels, while present policies err significantly in the militaristic direction. Hence, it is most reasonable to expect marginal increases in nuclear protest to be helpful in pushing things in the right direction, rather than to be harmfully destabilizing either domestically or internationally.

In changed future circumstances, however, nuclear protest – at least of certain kinds – may become counterproductive. To determine how to prevent this, how to tell whether and when it is in danger of happening, and how to proceed if this danger is detected, are problems of political judgment like those that arise in any political movement. The dangers of counterproductivity can perhaps best be avoided by choosing wise leadership and adopting methods of protest that work effectively through existing social institutions. But the issue of methods of protest, once raised, confronts us with yet another dilemma of nuclear protest.

III. MISLEADING PROTEST

In politics, even more than in most other spheres of life, there is often a trade off between effectiveness and strict adherence to norms of truthfulness, openness, and rationality. In particular, success in political campaigns and movements often depends on use of oversimplified and misleading claims, flawed but persuasive arguments, direct appeals to emotions, papering over of factional differences with vague and ambiguous formulas, and so on. This poses a dilemma for morally serious nuclear protesters: should some of the strict norms of truthfulness and candor be violated in order to make protests of immoral nuclear defense policies more effective?

It will not do to deny this dilemma by simply asserting that honesty is always the most effective policy; this is not at all plausible in the political arena, if we take "honesty" to mean strictest adherence to norms of truthfulness, openness, and rationality. Experience shows that too much openness is sometimes damaging to a political campaign or political figure. Thus, for example, we find an intelligent and well-informed observer of political events saying of an especially outspoken political figure, "Her impolitic concern for intellectual clarity is one reason why she has her share (and, it sometimes seems, half a dozen other people's shares) of critics."[9]

It is quite possible then, that genuine conflicts between success and full truthfulness and candor could arise for nuclear protesters (either individually or collectively). How should these conflicts be resolved? Deception or concealment cannot be justified simply on the grounds that "the other side [in the defense debate] is doing it." For if nuclear protesters were to mislead and deceive, it would be their fellow citizens of good will that they would be wronging and mistreating, not just those "nuclear warriors" who are themselves practicing deception. On the other hand, it would be morally indefensible to abandon hope of successful nuclear protest on the grounds that this would require stretching or violating strict norms of intellectual honesty and openness. For such Kantian absolutism could lead to the abdication of nuclear politics by the morally concerned and leave the field open only to the unprincipled and the self-deceptive.

A better approach is to justify some departures from some of the strictest norms of truthfulness and openness on grounds of necessity. These norms should not be taken lightly, but the stakes of nuclear politics are so high that considerable stretching and bending of certain of these norms is appropriate if this can help achieve better outcomes. This is especially so since the primary "victims" of any oversimplifications, rhetorical excesses, or other expedients that might be employed – the members of the public – would themselves benefit from the changes of policy being urged.

But which norms might it be permissible to violate? I once heard a morally serious person say "If I had to lie or give bad arguments to preserve legal abortion in this country, I would do it." A similar view about nuclear protest would be that any violation of the norms of intellectual honesty – even outright lying – would be justified if it promised to be effective in improving nuclear policy. I am disinclined to accept this view for two reasons. I believe that because of the vital importance for human social life of trust and the reliable communication of information, the moral prohibition on lying, while not absolute, is nonetheless very strong. Further, the nuclear protest movement draws much of its effectiveness from its being morally inspired; hence lying for this cause is likely to be counterproductive and harmful to the movement over the long run, even if limited to cases in which the agents in question think their lies will be effective. But there are other violations of the norms of intellectual honesty besides outright lying – for example, withholding of information or arguments supporting conclusions one disagrees with, oversimplifying, and use of persuasive but unsound arguments. In honor of the Senate Watergate committee witness who said of his and his colleagues' responses to earlier investigations, "We weren't volunteering anything, Senator," let's henceforth use the term *not-volunteering* to refer to these lesser violations of the norms of truthfulness, openness, and rationality. Now in many contexts, not-volunteering is morally wrong. But we could plausibly hold that the end in question in nuclear protests – more rational nuclear policies and a correspondingly safer world – is so unusually important as to justify the use of normally prohibited means, such as not-volunteering, to obtain it.

The position under discussion may be simply summarized as a three-step argument as follows:

(1) If the stakes are extremely high, not-volunteering is justified in achieving better outcomes.
(2) The stakes involved in determining nuclear weapons policy are extremely high.

(3)   Therefore, not-volunteering is justified in achieving nuclear weapons policies with better outcomes.

This argument does not say anything about *how much* not-volunteering (i.e., violations of the norms of honesty short of lying) is justified. One plausible principle concerning this issue says:

(4)   The higher the level of the stakes, the more not-volunteering is justified.

A somewhat more controversial principle would say:

(5)   If not-volunteering is justified for one side in a competitive endeavor (e.g., politics, war, business, athletic contests), the level justified is at least as high as each of the following: (a) the level of deception (i.e., not-volunteering plus lying) engaged in by the other side in the particular competitive endeavor, and (b) the normal level of deception for competitive endeavors of this kind.

Unfortunately, the state of politics is such that (4) and (5) together imply that a rather high level of not-volunteering is justified (if needed) to make nuclear protests effective. One hopes that this much not-volunteering will not be needed. But if it were, morally serious nuclear protesters might have to consider compromising their strict adherence to some norms of openness, rationality, and intellectual honesty.

IV. THE SUPERMAN PROBLEM

As a child, I wondered why the cartoon character Superman, with his long-range vision and incredible capacity to rescue people from impending harm, spent most of his time disguised as a mild-mannered newspaper reporter instead of constantly racing around the globe preventing one human tragedy after another. The reason, no doubt, is that the Man of Steel has a right to a life of his own – bumbling around the Daily Planet building, flirting with Lois Lane, and so on – and while each individual act of rescue does not seem too much to ask or require of him, doing all of them (or as many as he could) would irretrievably eliminate the possibility of living such a life.

This conflict between preventing as much harm as possible and living a relatively normal life, which I call the Superman problem, generalizes beyond the fictional cartoon context. It applies, though to a lesser extent, to virtually all people with scarce abilities to prevent or alleviate significant suffering: physicians, drug counselors, police officers, and many others. And if we accepted act-utilitarianism, it might apply to us all. For it follows from that theory that we are morally required to make sacrifices of our own personal welfare whenever this promises to produce greater benefit for others. But this, as critics of utilitarianism have noted, would rob us of the freedom to live our own lives and pursue our own plans and projects, unless by happy chance these always turned out to be expected-utility-maximizing.[10] For this reason, if not others, most of us would reject act-utilitarianism.

With the exceptionally capable, the problem in question arises out of the individual's special capacities to prevent harm, together with the tension between determining a person's responsibilities on a case-by-case basis and over longer stretches of activity. Act-utilitarianism, by extending obligation to cover any situation in which net utility levels can be raised, extends the problem to those with more normal capacities. A new version of the problem arises in the nuclear protest case for three reasons. The stakes are so great that it seems important that even those with only a small or marginal ability to influence events in the right direction should exercise that ability. Also, many people do not recognize the immorality of present policies, so those who do must pick up others' shares of the protest load, while at the same time working to change these peoples' minds. Finally, because immoral nuclear policies are so entrenched, and nuclear-armed democracies are such large societies (with many millions of members), individual protesters may have to make extraordinary efforts (in terms of time, energy, or money) to have any chance of changing such policies for the better. Thus, the great potential benefits of nuclear protest, the minority status of moral protesters, and the high personal costs of "making a difference" combine to create a Superman problem for ordinary democratic citizens who regard their governments' nuclear arms policies as immoral.

Nor will our earlier observation about the benefits of protest easily solve this problem. For many of these benefits can be achieved at relatively low levels of personal investment in protest. The dilemma before us is that the importance and needs of the cause seem to justify personal sacrifice virtually beyond limits – just as do Superman's extraordinary powers of rescue.

To deal with this issue, we must face a general unsolved problem in moral philosophy: How much cost is an individual obligated to bear in attempts to prevent harm? Many views on this issue have some degree of plausibility, and I will simply list a few to illustrate their variety. The Pure Libertarian view says that one is not obligated to bear any costs to prevent harms unless one has caused or contributed to those harms. The Fixed Limit view says that to prevent greater harms, you are obligated to bear costs up to some fixed limit of "heavy" or "substantial" costs. The Ruin view says that one is not obligated to ruin one's life to prevent harm, so that the limit of sacrifice required is just below that point, and varies according to how much cost different individuals can bear without their lives being ruined. The Marginal Utility view says that individuals must bear costs up to the point where they would lose more by further sacrifices than beneficiaries of those sacrifices would gain.[11] (This is the standard one would expect an act-utilitarian to employ.) The Utility Ratio view is that one should bear costs up to the point at which the marginal benefit/cost ratio falls below some fixed number, x, where x is greater than 1. (This criterion says, in effect, to maximize overall utility with the agent's utility being given extra weight in the calculation.) Probably, combinations of these views are more plausible than any of them taken alone without qualification. For example, the Utility Ratio view combined with the Ruin view may produce a position that is more plausible than either alone. This view says that you are obligated to sacrifice more provided this produces at least a given ratio of "benefits to others"/"cost to you" and does not ruin your life. If the benefit-to-cost ratio were set high enough, even some conservatives might be sympathetic to this view.

Of course, there is another dimension of relevant variation here. It may matter whether the harms or risks to be prevented exist independently of us, or are the results of wrongful practices that we participate in or that are carried out in our name. Thus, for example, someone might hold the Libertarian view regarding harms in general, but adopt one of the other positions with regard to harms (wrongfully) produced (or risked) by one's own group. For the nuclear-weapons-protesting citizen we have been considering, the relevant view is the one that applies to the latter class of harms, not harms in general.

Without determining what view about the limits on the obligation to sacrifice is correct, which I shall not attempt to do, the Superman problem for nuclear weapons protesters cannot be definitively solved. But we may make three observations that are of some relevance. First, according to the Marginal Utility or Utility Ratio view, those who are in a special position to be effective in their protest efforts (or other useful activities in this area such as the education of students about the nuclear arms race) may be obligated to sacrifice more. Second, according to any of these views but the Libertarian, those who reap personal benefits from nuclear protest can do more before their net costs reach the appropriate limit of sacrifice. Finally, there seem to be no moral limits on how much one may permissibly sacrifice to protest nuclear immorality, if one chooses to. Beyond some point of sacrifice, such efforts are supererogatory (i.e., beyond the call of duty), but they hardly can be wrong. Unless, that is, they preclude or interfere with the performance of other morally obligatory or desirable actions. The possibility that they will do so brings us to our fifth and final dilemma of nuclear protest.

V. OTHER GOOD CAUSES

Our fifth dilemma arises from the fact that individuals have limited resources while there are multiple serious harms and evils in the world to be combated. And in a large democratic society, there are bound to be a number of immoral or unwise policies that contribute to these harms and evils. If we determined individual democratic citizens' obligations to protest (or otherwise oppose) these evils separately by the principles discussed in section IV, the total burden that a person would be obligated to bear would be unreasonable and excessive. Several bottomed pits, we may say, add up to a bottomless one. Hence a serious issue arises about how a morally serious individual should act in the face of multiple evils.[12]

It may be thought that nuclear immorality overshadows all other wrongs so clearly as to avoid this problem. Such apparently was the conviction of the woman who once told my wife, "I used to be an active feminist, but now opposing the nuclear arms race must be one's first, second, third, fourth, and fifth priorities." This belief might be supported by appeal to the special timing needs of nuclear protest (i.e., before war starts) and the magnitude of nuclear evil. But, on closer examination, neither of these considerations is entirely convincing.

Consider timing first. The timing of nuclear destruction can give us some reason to assign nuclear evil priority in allocating our protest efforts against various group evils. But the timing factor has another side to it as well. Other evil practices (e.g., racial discrimination, social injustice, inequitable food distribution patterns) have their human costs spread more evenly over time than nuclear evil. But this means that real people are suffering real harms that might be alleviated if we protested and changed these practices. Many of these individual losses are irreversible and uncompensable once they occur. So by giving priority to nuclear protests, we allow some preventable undeserved suffering. The costs of nuclear evil, by contrast, will either be suffered by humanity in a huge lump (i.e., if there is a nuclear war) or hardly at all.[13] What matters here is that our protests be soon enough and effective enough to prevent nuclear war; if they are, it matters relatively little whether they are effective in plenty of time (e.g., decades or centuries ahead of when war would otherwise have occurred) or at the last minute. So whether it is best to allocate our protest energies to stop the nuclear arms race or to prevent smaller but ongoing (and irreversible) suffering of other kinds, depends on how far in the future nuclear war is likely to be. Given the great uncertainties on this matter, it is probably not irrational to play it safe and give nuclear protest top priority now. But if one views nuclear war as less than imminent, it may be just as rational to give greater priority to protesting and stopping other evil practices such as social injustice, racial and sexual discrimination, and policies that lead to overpopulation and famine. Hence the timing factor, in and of itself, fails to establish anything like an absolute priority for the obligation to protest nuclear weapons policies as opposed to other group evils.

Let us turn next to the magnitude of nuclear evil. If a certain policy of nuclear deterrence is a much greater evil than any other group practice, group members who are aware of this do have more reason to actively oppose this policy than those other practices. But it is not clear that immoral nuclear policies are so much greater evils when one takes into account their moral benefits as well as their moral costs, and the alternatives that are available. To begin with, it will not really do to evaluate how evil a given national nuclear weapons policy is according to its worst possible outcome. For, as noted in Chapters 3 and 7, *any* such policy *could* lead to nuclear war and extinction: even unilateral nuclear disarmament might provoke a disastrous nuclear war (or series of nuclear wars) among remaining nuclear nations. If we are utilitarians, we might identify how evil a policy is with how much less expected utility it generates than the best available alternative. Serious difficulties with making meaningful estimates of expected utility in this area were discussed in Chapter 3. But aside from these difficulties, it is not clear that applying this utilitarian test would show nuclear evil to be far and away the greatest evil. For a given deterrence policy may be wrong by the utilitarian test because it runs a somewhat – but not enormously – higher risk of war than some alternative policy. Given the basic stability and effectiveness of the present mutual deterrence posture, some would argue that this is the case as regards actual policies. And even if, as I have suggested in Chapter 3, current policies are much inferior to minimum deterrence on utilitarian grounds, it does not follow that they are by far the most harmful of utilitarian evils. For certain other wrongful policies, such as selfish or foolish population and food policies, can have a very high probability of leading to starvation for millions of people. This being the case, it is not clear that wrongful nuclear policies produce much, if any, greater deficit in expected utility than do these other policies.[14] So while the expected utility method for measuring amounts of evil would surely assign a "high" rank to nuclear evil, it might not assign it the highest rank, and certainly would not justify giving the duty to oppose it anything like absolute priority over duties to oppose all other group evils.

If this is correct, the rational moral protester cannot simply assign absolute priority to protesting nuclear evil, and she faces an allocation problem. Actually, there are two related problems here: the size of the protest "budget" and its allocation among causes. On the size question, the various views described in Section IV could all be reinterpreted as views about limits of the obligation to protest (or otherwise oppose) all harms or evils (or all those done by one's group or in one's name). In fact, these views are generally much more plausible thus construed than when interpreted to apply to a single sort of protest, because of the above-mentioned bottomless pit issue.[15]

Aside from this, however, the questions about allocation remain. And here there are two extreme views that are each plausible, but hard to reconcile with one another. According to the Efficiency view, one is obligated to allocate protest resources (within the established limits) most effectively, so as to maximize overall expected benefits of protest.[16] According to the Options view, one is free to allocate one's protest resources however one sees fit, so long as they are used effectively to protest (or prevent) some significant harms or evils. I see no obvious way of refuting either view. Probably the most plausible view is some compromise that allows options, but only so long as the benefit/cost ratios for protests of different evils are close enough together. If this is not so (i.e., if protests of some evils would be very much more effective relative to costs), the more efficient protests must be made. While from this view it is likely that morally serious citizens should devote a considerable portion of their protest efforts to opposing nuclear defense policies that they regard as wrongful, it is highly doubtful that all of their protests should be focused on this issue.[17]

VI. CONCLUSION

Even if we assume that the nuclear deterrence policies of democratic nations are clearly "beyond the moral pale," morally serious citizens who recognize this face a number of difficult rational and moral dilemmas in deciding how to act politically. I have briefly discussed five such dilemmas, which may be posed in the following form as questions:

(1) Should I invest personal effort in protesting wrongful nuclear defense policies when my individual contribution will be only a drop in a bucket and is nearly certain to have no significant effect?

(2) Should I protest nuclear evil, given the risk that such protests may be counterproductive?

(3) If effective nuclear protest sometimes requires violations of the norms of truthfulness, openness, and rationality, should I take part in such activities?

(4) What, if any, limits are there on the personal sacrifices I am obligated to make in order to effectively protest nuclear evil?

(5) How should I allocate my limited resources between protesting immoral nuclear defense policies and combating other wrongs and evils?

Partial solutions to some of these dilemmas have been suggested. In other cases, the outlines of the difficulty have only been sketched. All remain, to a considerable extent, open questions. But I hope I have said enough to establish that acting in a morally responsible way in the face of acknowledged nuclear evil is no easy task.

PART II

Alternatives to nuclear deterrence

6. Unilateral nuclear disarmament

The main theme of Part I of this book is that the practice of nuclear deterrence is surrounded by serious moral perplexities, so that it is not easy to determine whether, or in what form, this practice is morally permissible. A second theme is that, despite these perplexities, some type of minimum deterrence policy like that described in the Introduction may well be morally justifiable as a lesser evil, at least in the short run. In Part II, I further develop this second theme by discussing the main alternatives to nuclear deterrence that have been proposed in the literature. Proceeding roughly from left to right across the political spectrum, I consider and reject unilateral nuclear disarmament, world government, strategic defense, and nuclear coercion, and end up in the center supporting mutual nuclear disarmament as the ultimate end and minimum deterrence as a morally permissible transitional strategy.

This chapter is concerned with the most pacifistic of the major alternatives to nuclear deterrence: unilateral nuclear disarmament, or, as some proponents prefer to call it, nonnuclear defense. Because the evaluation of this alternative involves making assessments of the motivations and likely behaviors of a nation's particular nuclear adversaries, I neither assume nor seek to demonstrate symmetry between the superpowers as regards this alternative. Instead, I consider unilateral nuclear disarmament as a proposed policy for the United States, and I leave entirely open the question as to which, if any, of the arguments discussed might apply to the adoption of such a policy by the Soviet Union.

The original article upon which this chapter is based was written while I was supported by a fellowship for independent study and research from the National Endowment for the Humanities.

The issue at hand has already been broached in Chapter 3, where it was argued that minimum deterrence may well be a lesser utilitarian evil than unilateral nuclear disarmament. But this conclusion rested on two key assumptions about probabilities. The first is the purley ordinal assumption that the probability of some disaster (e.g., Soviet world domination, Soviet nuclear attack, or a Soviet–Chinese nuclear war) following unilateral U.S. nuclear disarmament within thirty years is greater than the probability of some disaster (e.g., large-scale superpower nuclear war or Soviet world domination) following the U.S. practice of a policy of minimum deterrence for the same period of time. The second assumption is a rough quantitative one. It says that these two (conditional) probabilities are not close to equal – that is, the former is considerably higher than the latter. These assumptions accord, I think, with conventional wisdom in the West, which says that superpower nuclear war is unlikely because both sides appreciate its awful consequences, while unilateral nuclear disarmament by the United States would be highly dangerous because the Soviets would very likely take active advantage of the great preponderance of military power they would then possess.

But is conventional wisdom correct on this? Some accomplished philosophers who are quite knowledgeable about nuclear strategy – notably Douglas Lackey and Jefferson McMahan – have offered arguments for thinking otherwise.[1] This chapter attempts to defend conventional wisdom, and our two key probability assumptions of Chapter 3, against these arguments. Before turning to this task, however, it will be useful to clarify what the main differences are between the view defended here and the positions taken by Lackey and McMahan. As should be clear from Chapter 3, my analysis joins Lackey and McMahan in rejecting "better dead than Red" reasoning – it explicitly assumes that large-scale nuclear war would be worse than Soviet world domination.[2] And all three of us seem to agree that the probability of minimum deterrence leading to war over thirty years is small.[3] Where we crucially disagree is over the probability of Soviet domination, nuclear attack, or successful nuclear blackmail if the United States unilaterally disarmed itself of nuclear weapons. I believe this probability is high, or at least "not low." They give reasons for thinking it is low. If they are right, the argument of Chapter 3 that minimum deterrence is a lesser utilitarian evil than unilateral nuclear disarmament would fail. To save that argument, Lackey and McMahan must be answered.

In my Introduction, the issue at hand was pictured as a disagreement about which of two models more accurately depicts deterrence of potential Soviet aggression by U.S. nuclear threats. Lackey and McMahan would presumably favor the elephant-dance model, which views Western nuclear deterrence as probably superfluous and unnecessary for deterring major (successful) Soviet aggression. I fear that the alternative bank-robber model, which is presented below as a response to one of Lackey's arguments, is more likely to be accurate. In arguing for this, and against McMahan and Lackey, my remarks are often brief, general, and – inevitably, given the nature of the subject matter – speculative. I hope that nonetheless many will find them persuasive.

I. PAST SUPERPOWER BEHAVIOR

The relatively cautious nuclear-era military behavior of each superpower is sometimes cited as evidence of the low risks involved in unilateral nuclear disarmament by the United States. The essentially nonaggressive foreign policy of the United States when it possessed nuclear predominance provides unilateral disarmament supporters with a hopeful model of how a world under Soviet nuclear predominance might look. Lackey, for example, lays much emphasis on the fact that the United States did not use its early atomic monopoly (1945 – 49) for blackmail or attack.[4] But there are too many differences between that situation and the one the Soviets would be in now after U.S. nuclear disarmament to rely on this precedent. The United States was a democratic nation whose people had just experienced a substantial war and that was recently allied with the nation it might have employed its weapons against – the USSR. Technologically, nuclear weapons were much less powerful, many fewer, and much less well tested than they are at present, and the instruments for delivering them were more vulnerable to defensive measures. Militarily, the Soviets had a massive, mobilized, and well-positioned land army that could have readily been used to conquer Western Europe. This to some degree counterbalanced the military power of early nuclear weapons. Nor was there sufficient appreciation of the power of nuclear weapons to allow leaders to use them most effectively as political-strategic weapons. None of these political, technological, military, and intellectual constraints (except for vivid memories of World War II losses) would apply in the same way to the Soviet Union now, if the United States dismantled its nuclear arsenal.

Might the Soviets' own generally cautious military behavior (for example, directly invading only nations on their geographic periphery) be taken as evidence that they would not exploit nuclear predominance if they had it? Lackey suggests so with regard to at least one instance – the Soviets' failure to attack Chinese nuclear facilities in 1969–70.[5] But the moral of that story is not what Lackey takes it to be. Memoirs from the Nixon administration suggest that the Soviets might have refrained from such an attack largely out of concern about the response of the United States, its only equal in nuclear power.[6] From this and other instances of relatively cautious international behavior we may not infer how the Soviets would act in the absence of any nuclear equal (or near equal). To do so would be to follow the lead of the apocryphal banker who, upon observing that the bank had never been robbed, did away with locks and guards as unnecessary.

Lackey fails to fully appreciate the force of this point. He writes,

> the Soviet Union has never made the conquest of the United States or a change in its form of government an announced policy goal, and . . . there is no scenario short of fantasy in which it could become a Soviet policy goal.[7]

This may be true, as there is no scenario short of fantasy in which the United States will adopt unilateral nuclear disarmament. But it does not follow that we would be safe from Soviet conquest if we practiced unilateral nuclear disarmament, as Lackey seems to suppose. Consider a potential robber's side of our bank case. Lefty may want money and be willing to rob to get it. But as the bank is well guarded and well locked, she never adopts robbing the bank as a goal.[8] But should our bank become unlocked and unguarded, we can predict that Lefty will be there with her hands in the till.

The bank case reveals a dual danger in inferring future behavior *under significantly changed circumstances* from past behavior. Not only may past behavior poorly reflect underlying motivations, but changed circumstances and opportunities may actually change motives. Thus, even if Lefty was initially unwilling to rob for profit, the temptations of a completely unguarded bank might alter her inclinations in this regard. Motives being changed by altered circumstances is especially likely in the case of political groups, where new opportunities may well increase the influence of members wanting to take advantage of these opportunities.

Even as astute a reasoner as McMahan overlooks this point about changed motives when he writes, "If, as is arguable, Soviet military policies are motivated primarily by defensive concerns, then the abandonment of nuclear deterrence would not significantly increase the probability of nuclear blackmail or Soviet domination."[9] This is true only on the assumption that Soviet motives – if defensive – would not change in the face of unilateral nuclear disarmament by the United States. Indeed, Lackey seems to rely on this assumption when he argues that after U.S. unilateral disarmament the Soviets would probably refrain from using nuclear weapons out of fear of world opinion.[10] But it seems to me unwarranted to assume that the Soviet leaders' views of the importance of world opinion would not significantly change after unilateral U.S. nuclear disarmament. One can readily imagine these leaders caring much more whether other nations like them in a world in which they are competing for influence with a militarily equal (and economically superior) United States, than in a world in which they possessed overwhelming military superiority. Indeed, in the latter world, if it ever came about, they might care more about other nations fearing them than liking them. Such priorities would not inhibit nuclear threats or nuclear use.

II. NUCLEAR BLACKMAIL AND CONVENTIONAL DEFENSE

McMahan and Lackey believe Soviet leaders are unlikely to attack a nuclear-disarmed United States because they would not have any good reason to attack in the absence of a U.S. nuclear threat.[11] But, notoriously, the mere expansion of one's power has seemed to numerous political leaders throughout history a good enough reason to undertake aggressive military action. And the Soviets might conceivably attack or employ nuclear blackmail out of loftier motives – for example, to impose lasting peace through world government or to prevent later U.S. nuclear rearmament and possible two-sided nuclear war.[12] After all, even so peace-loving and rational a person as Bertrand Russell advocated, during the time of the U.S. nuclear monopoly, that it adopt such a course toward the Soviet Union for essentially these very reasons.[13] And the Eisenhower administration at one time apparently contemplated taking such action.[14]

Lackey and McMahan make a case for conventional armament as an effective substitute for nuclear deterrence.[15] This may well have been plausible in the early days of atomic weaponry, but not today, given the enormous nuclear arsenals of the superpowers. If a modern superpower were willing to use nuclear attack on a nuclear-disarmed foe to obtain concessions or capitulation, resistance with conventional forces would be quite ineffectual. For even putting aside the potential vulnerability of conventional forces to tactical nuclear weapons, it is clear that such forces could not defend cities or military bases from nuclear strikes ordered to force compliance with political demands.

This last observation raises the issue of nuclear blackmail. Supporters of unilateral nuclear disarmament apparently feel that even if nuclear blackmail were attempted by the Soviets, it could be successfully resisted by a nation that practiced nonnuclear defense and refused to capitulate.[16] But if the Soviets were ruthless enough and cared more about frightening the rest of the world into submission than winning friends, this would not be so.[17] They could back up any political demands with actual nuclear strikes on selected American targets, including cities, and credible threats to carry out more strikes if their demands were not met. Soviet leaders would then be like airplane hijackers who execute hostages one by one until their demands are met, save for two factors that would give them enormously more bargaining strength: they would themselves be essentially invulnerable to attacks designed to stop their execution of hostages, and they would directly control the fate of the constituencies of the leaders who would have to decide whether to give in to their threats. It is hard to believe that, under such circumstances, an undefended U.S. population would hold out long against nuclear threats made credible by actual nuclear strikes.

III. OTHER NUCLEAR POWERS

So far we have largely ignored the fact that there are other nuclear powers besides the United States and the Soviet Union. When we take this into account, our estimate of the likelihood of disaster following U.S. unilateral nuclear disarmament must increase substantially. For if the United States adopted unilateral nuclear disarmament, it is unlikely that all other nuclear powers – especially

China – would follow suit. Their nuclear arsenals would then be tempting targets for Soviet preemptive attack, especially if these countries began to expand their nuclear weaponry to compensate for the removal of the American nuclear counterbalance. Lackey, citing a theoretical result of Lewis Richardson, suggests that the fewer the nations armed with nuclear weapons, the smaller the chance of nuclear war.[18] But U.S. nuclear disarmament might lead to more nations joining the nuclear club, as they sought alternative means of national defense. In any case, it seems reasonable to give considerable weight to the specific historical evidence that suggests, as noted above, that U.S. nuclear weapons may have prevented the Soviets from striking the Chinese. Are we not safer relying on our recent experience that mutual deterrence by nearly equal nuclear powers works, than laying humankind open to the uncertainties and instabilities of a world of vastly unequal nuclear powers, with the Soviets having nuclear forces much greater than all the others combined?

In sum, a number of considerations indicate that Lackey and McMahan have seriously underestimated the probability of nuclear attack or nuclear blackmail if the United States should adopt unilateral nuclear disarmament: (1) the general historical tendency of great powers and their leaders to exploit military advantages, (2) disanalogies between past U.S. nuclear dominance and (hypothetical) future Soviet nuclear dominance, (3) the significance of the distinction between current Soviet policy and behavior and what that policy and behavior might become after U.S. unilateral nuclear disarmament, (4) the existence of plausible prudential and "moral" motives for Soviet use of nuclear weapons in such circumstances, (5) the ineffectiveness of conventional defense against a vast nuclear arsenal, and (6) the instabilities of a world with multiple unequal nuclear powers. In light of these considerations, it seems reasonable to conclude that the probability of Soviet nuclear attack or blackmail following U.S. unilateral nuclear disarmament is not low. This vindicates the two assumptions about probability discussed at the start of this chapter, which underlie the argument of Chapter 3 that minimum deterrence is a lesser evil than unilateral nuclear disarmament.[19] (The present analysis leaves open the question as to whether unilateral nuclear disarmament would be a lesser evil than current deterrent policies.) It remains to consider, in later chapters, whether other alternatives to minimum deterrence might be superior to it.

7. World government

In the last chapter it was argued that unilateral nuclear disarmament runs risks that are too grave to qualify it as a lesser evil than minimum nuclear deterrence. By contrast, world government, at least of the right kind, might be a lesser evil than a regime of minimum deterrence, if it could be established.[1] However, this possibility calls into question the permissibility of minimum deterrence only if world government is a genuine or feasible alternative. But there are good reasons for thinking that it is not, even in the remotely foreseeable future. The system of independent sovereign states is well established, and it is hard to see what reasons might persuade the leaders and citizens of these states to surrender their sovereignty to a world government. Unless, that is, our nuclear danger itself clearly constitutes a rationally compelling reason for such surrender. And, indeed, some have suggested that it does. More specifically, a number of recent writers have suggested that, in a nuclear-armed world, an international analogue of Hobbes's famous argument against anarchy demonstrates the rational necessity of establishing a world government.[2] For convenience, I shall henceforth refer to the general argument underlying this claim as the Nuclear World Government Argument.

My aim in this chapter is to understand and evaluate the Nuclear World Government Argument and certain related arguments.[3] I begin by sketching Hobbes's actual argument against anarchy and his views on international relations. Then the supposedly analogous argument for world government is presented and analyzed in some

The paper this chapter is based on was written while I was supported by a fellowship for independent study and research from the National Endowment for the Humanities.

detail. In the course of this analysis, it emerges that there are several different versions and variants of the Nuclear World Government Argument, and that none of them succeeds in demonstrating the rational necessity of powerful nations surrendering their sovereignty to a world government. This, together with the current solidity of the international system of sovereign nations, justifies viewing world government, however desirable it might be in theory, as not being a genuine alternative to a regime of nuclear deterrence. I conclude by suggesting that we cease our fruitless longing for world government as the solution of humankind's nuclear danger, and concentrate instead on developing alternative ways of dealing with our nuclear problem.

I. HOBBES ON ANARCHY

In *Leviathan,* Hobbes presents a two-part argument designed to show that government is necessary for our security and well-being.[4] He imagines people living in a state of nature in which there is no common power over them to make and enforce laws. In the first part of his argument, he contends that *individuals* in such a condition will end up in a war of each against every other in which life is, in his famous phrase, "solitary, poor, nasty, brutish, and short."[5] The second part of the argument attempts to establish that the formation of *groups* does not solve the security problem, unless those groups have government and amount to sovereign states.

The argument concerning individuals starts from the assumption that people are forward-looking (in the sense of being concerned with their long-run as well as short-run survival and well-being), predominanty self-interested, and roughly equal in their natural powers (equal enough, in any case, so that each is vulnerable to death at the hands of others). Such individuals will often come into conflict with one another as they compete for scarce goods, disagree over their individual reputations, and seek safety against the potential aggressions of others. In addition, some individuals – who cannot always be readily identified – seek conquest or power over others for its own sake. In these circumstances, without a common power to enforce common rules of conduct, cooperation would be unreliable, since one party could not count on another carrying out his part of any agreement. More importantly, without such enforcement of rules, and without gross inequalities among individuals that would make the winners of violent conflict evident ahead of time, the most rational strategy for an individual to follow is one of anticipation. That is, attacking others and attempting to conquer them before one can be conquered by them, or building up one's coercive power so as to be in a position to prevail when the inevitable violent conflict comes. The result then, of a state-of-nature situation, is a general willingness on the part of individuals to fight each other, frequent violent conflicts, and a lack of reliable cooperation. According to Hobbes's definition, this general willingness to fight constitutes a state of war.[6] When this is combined with frequent actual violence and a general lack of cooperation, we have a war of all against all in which both security and the material benefits of social cooperation are absent.

The second part of Hobbes's argument, which concerns groups, is shorter and simpler. Cooperation can perhaps be achieved within small groups, but such groups cannot effectively deter outside aggression since somewhat larger groups could confidently expect to defeat them in violent conflict. Large groups may effectively deter outside aggression because of the uncertainty of the results of conflicts between larger groups. However, unless there is a concentration of power within such groups, irreconcilable differences of opinion about external defense needs and conflicts of interest among group members will lead to a breakdown of both external and internal security. But a large group with such a concentration of power simply *is* a state with a government. Hence, people can count on security and cooperation only within the state, and not in a condition of anarchy.

On the basis of this analysis, Hobbes recommends certain rules of rational prudence (and morality), which he calls "laws of nature," and applies these rules to the hypothetical situation of people living in a state of nature.[7] The first two laws of nature state that:

(1) *[E]very man, ought to endeavor peace, as far as he has hope of obtaining it; and when he cannot obtain it, that he may seek, and use, all helps, and advantages of war.*[8]
(2) *[A] man be willing, when others are so too, as far-forth, as for peace, and defence of himself he shall think it necessary, to lay down this right to all things; and be contented with so much liberty against other men, as he would allow other men against himself.*[9]

From these two laws, and the considerations advanced above,

Hobbes concludes that people in a state of nature should seek to establish peace by a mutual surrender of their natural rights and liberties to a common sovereign power, thus creating a state by means of an original agreement or social contract.

It is important for our purposes to notice two points about this Hobbesian justification of the state. First, the function of this argument in Hobbes's philosophy is to *retrospectively* justify obedience to existing states. In effect, Hobbes is warning dissatisfied citizens of existing states that (1) disobedience risks civil war or the collapse of the state, and (2) these are conditions that resemble the anarchical state of nature, and have a similar undesirable effect on people's lives. For this reason, objections based on the question "How do we safely get from the state of nature to the sovereign state?" are not germane to Hobbes's actual use of the social contract argument. Second, if interpreted *prospectively* as providing a rational justification for state-of-nature parties establishing a common sovereign, Hobbes's argument does not provide an unconditional endorsement of state formation. Collectively it is most rational for the parties in Hobbes's state of nature to enter into a state-creating social contract. But individually, it is only conditionally rational for a party to make and keep such an agreement – with the condition being, as the first two laws of nature make clear, the willingness of others to do likewise. This means that problems concerning the unreliability of one's potential fellow contractors, and the dangers of unilateral measures, are relevant to the use of Hobbes's argument to prospectively justify the establishment of a common sovereign power.

Before attempting, in the next section, to apply this prospective form of Hobbes's argument to the international sphere, it will be useful to note briefly Hobbes's own views about international relations. With no international common power over them, nations are in a state of nature with respect to one another. In consequence, according to Hobbes, they are in a posture of war, "having their weapons pointing, and their eyes fixed on one another."[10] But for two reasons that Hobbes notes, and two that he doesn't, the consequences of this war of all states generally are not nearly as bad as the consequences of a war among all individuals (or small groups) would be. Hobbes observes that nations are large enough to provide sufficient opportunities for productive cooperation among their own members, and that military deterrence is usually effective among nations because of the great uncertainties inherent in violent conflict among large groups. He might have added that there are many fewer agents on the international scene to start an escalatory cycle of violence, and that aggressor nations are more readily identifiable (than individual assailants) so that retaliation and punishment by other nations is at least possible.[11] For all these reasons, a state of war among all nations (which can involve much readiness for war but little actual fighting) may be tolerable, while a state of war among all individuals is not.

II. THE NUCLEAR WORLD GOVERNMENT ARGUMENT

The Nuclear World Government Argument attempts to apply Hobbes's argument against anarchy to the situation of sovereign states in a world armed with nuclear weapons. However, unlike Hobbes who stresses the economic as well as security problems of anarchy, the Nuclear World Government Argument focuses solely on the security issue. This is fully justified since even rival nuclear nations can carry on trade relations, and as noted above, large-scale economic cooperation within nations is possible even when nations are in a state of war (in Hobbes's sense) with respect to one another.[12]

With this qualification in mind, the Nuclear World Government Argument may be set forth as follows. Nations, like Hobbes's individuals, are forward-looking and predominantly self-interested. That is, especially in foreign affairs, they strongly tend to act in ways that their leaders feel best promote the present and future well-being and security of their members, regardless of the impact of these actions on the well-being of those outside the nation in question.[13] And nuclear-armed nations are equal, in Hobbes's sense, in that they are all vulnerable to destruction (i.e., death of population, loss of resources, collapse of national institutions and social structure) at one another's hands. Furthermore, nations will be subject to all the causes of conflict that Hobbes mentions and more. They will quarrel over scarce resources, national reputations, and security. Some nations, like some of Hobbes's individuals, may be especially prone to aggression and conquest. And nations can be propelled to war without any real national interest at stake, as the result of internal politics or the perceived interests of ruling groups (for example, when national leaders scapegoat a foreign power to deflect citizens' anger away from the leaders themselves). Finally, in international as well as individual conflict, anticipation – striking first or building up one's coercive power – increases one's chances of success. This is especially true with respect to nuclear armaments, against which there are no technically feasible means of defense except for destroying them before they can be used, or deterring their use by possessing a powerful retaliatory force.

Given the presence of these perpetual causes of quarrel among effectively equal nations, the great military advantages of striking first, and the absence of effective legal constraints on aggression, we can expect a nuclear-armed state of nature among nations to eventually end up just as a state of nature among individuals would: in a condition of active and violent war. But the destructive effects of nuclear weapons are so great that we cannot, prudentially or morally, allow such a nuclear war to occur. Hence, the only rational course for nations in a nuclear-armed state of nature to follow is to obey the first two laws of nature and establish an international government, or sovereign, with sufficient power to make and enforce international laws and prevent violent conflicts among nations.

Examination of this presentation of the Nuclear World Government Argument reveals two crucial features of the argument that shall be the focus of my criticisms of it. First, looking at the assumption of equality among nations reveals that there are at least three distinct versions of the argument along one important dimension. A nonnuclear version of the argument could be given, but it obviously founders on the vast inequality of nations in a nonnuclear world.[14] Nuclear weapons are supposed to eliminate this inequality, hence rendering the argument plausible. But nuclear weapons establish, at most, equality among nations possessing such weapons. Hence, there will be significant differences between two versions of the Nuclear World Government Argument: a *present-world* version applying to our current condition in which only a few nations possess nuclear weapons, and a *proliferated-world* version applying to possible futures in which all (or very many) nations possess nuclear weapons.[15] These versions of the argument, and the general meaning and signficance of equality among nations, will be discussed in the next section. Second, it is clear that the Nuclear World Government Argument is an attempt at prospective rather than retrospective justification. That is, the argument purports to establish the rationality of forming a world government, not simply the rationality of remaining subject to one that already exists and is effectively operating. This means that problems concerning the formation and nature of a world government are relevent to the evaluation of the Nuclear World Government Argument and similar arguments. Some of these problems will be discussed in section IV.

III. EQUALITY AND ANTICIPATION

In an anarchical nonnuclear world, the most powerful states may rationally resist and prevent formation of a world government, since their power may make them relatively invulnerable and provide them with significant economic and political advantages. According to the Nuclear World Government Argument, nuclear weapons are the great equalizer. By making the great powers more vulnerable, they establish effective equality among nations, and make it rational for all nations to prefer a world sovereign to world anarchy.

But this is clearly false. In the real world, nuclear weapons make for even greater inequality between the great powers, who possess them, and other nations who generally do not. In the present world, major nuclear powers are militarily vulnerable, at most, to the other nuclear powers, of which there are only a few. Since there are few potential sources of nuclear violence, and major nuclear powers can reasonably hope to protect themselves against these sources by watching other nuclear powers carefully, forming alliances, and threatening nuclear counterattack, present nuclear powers are not in the desperately bad security situation of individuals in Hobbes's state of nature. Though they run some risk of nuclear destruction, it is not evident that the risk is grave enough to outweigh the potential costs and dangers associated with the attempt to form a world government. Hence, the present world version of the Nuclear World Government Argument is unpersuasive.

On the surface, at least, the proliferated-world version of that argument is much more persuasive. It begins by imagining a future world in which very many nations possess nuclear weapons. Now even the greatest powers are vulnerable to death at the hands of many other nations, and many national leaders – some of whom may be unstable or irrationally aggressive – have the capacity to begin a nuclear war. And we seem to be approaching that condition of effective equality that Hobbes describes in which "the weakest has strength enough to kill the strongest."[16] Given the relative advantage to be gained by striking first in a nuclear war, aren't the dangers of escalating nuclear violence under these circumstances so great as to make the mutual surrender of sovereignty the only rational course of action for all nations? Given the effective equality and large numbers of the parties in the proliferated world, it would seem that the logic of Hobbes's argument against anarchy forces us to this conclusion. Further, the argument may be taken to imply the need to establish a world sovereign *now,* since it will become progressively more difficult to do so as more nations acquire nuclear weapons and the corresponding power to resist or prevent the formation of an effective world government. If this is correct, the proliferated-world version of the Nuclear World Government Argument leads us to the conclusion of the present-world version by an alternate, and more plausible, path.

But there is a serious problem with the proliferated-world version of the argument. It concerns the kind of effective equality that makes it rational for parties in a state of nature to attack one another. Mutual vulnerability to death at one another's hands is the criterion of such equality for Hobbes. But, in the most likely proliferated worlds, such mutual vulnerability is unlikely to exist between major and minor nuclear powers. Smaller nuclear powers are unlikely to have enough weapons or delivery vehicles to destroy major nuclear powers, at least the geographically largest ones, as functioning societies. Furthermore, by the time there are very many nuclear powers the major nuclear powers may have developed defensive systems that are quite effective against the small nuclear attacks that minor nuclear powers are capable of launching.[17] So minor nuclear powers may not be able to "kill" major ones after all.

More importantly, in claiming that mutual vulnerability creates effective equality, Hobbes presupposes a context in which killers can expect to survive their victims. It is this expectation that anticipatory violence will be nonsuicidal and advantageous (in that it removes a potential threat to one's security, obtains resources, or promotes one's reputation) that creates the likelihood of an escalatory cycle of anticipatory violence in the state of nature. Absent this expectation, the only deadly violence to be feared in the state of nature would be due to occasional outbursts of extreme irrationality. Now in a world of nuclear proliferation, major and minor nuclear powers are likely to be unequal in the crucial capacity to *nonsuicidally* attack other nuclear powers. Major powers will likely possess a first-strike capacity against (most) minor nuclear powers; that is, the ability to disarm or destroy the other power with a coordinated surprise first strike without suffering unacceptable retaliatory damage. But minor nuclear powers will surely not have a reciprocal ability to nonsuicidally attack major nuclear powers, since the latter will possess a second-strike capacity (i.e., an ability to inflict unacceptable retaliatory damage if struck first) against them (and against many or all major nuclear powers as well). This means that even in the proliferated nuclear world there is not effective equality among nations, nor are there the same general rational incentives for nations to attack one another as there are for individuals to attack one another in Hobbes's state of nature.

In a nuclear-armed world, present or proliferated, there is a plausible rational alternative to violent anticipation or formation of a world government. This is a policy of alliance and nuclear deterrence, the general sort of policy currently practiced by most of the world's nuclear powers. Nuclear deterrence seeks to render an attack, at least a nuclear attack, on one's nation predictably suicidal, hence highly irrational and unlikely.

Alliances serve several useful functions in a nuclear world. By joining in alliances, nuclear powers reduce the likelihood of deadly conflict with their partners and increase the difficulty of an outsider obtaining a first-strike capacity against them. Alliances also allow nonnuclear powers to obtain protection under the "nuclear umbrellas" of nuclear-armed allies, in a manner like that in which Hobbes saw weaker individuals seeking and obtaining the protection of more powerful ones.[18] In addition, to the extent that alliances among nuclear powers centralize nuclear decision making, they reduce the number of independent actors capable of starting a nuclear war. Nor are nuclear alliances subject to Hobbes's primary objection against small defensive groups in the state of nature – namely, that somewhat larger groups can be sure enough of defeating them that they cannot effectively deter attacks. For the size of nations, the tremendous destructive power of nuclear weapons, and the vast uncertainties about what a nuclear war would be like if it occurred should be enough to deter nuclear attack by a rational opponent on any nuclear alliance of significant size, certainly on any containing a major nuclear power as a member.

The above considerations suggest that nuclear deterrence and alliance may be a rational strategy to follow even in a proliferated nuclear world. Another way of reaching the same conclusion is to notice the signficance of the ambiguity of two key concepts that appear in Hobbes's argument against anarchy – "anticipation" and "state of war." Hobbes contends that it is rational for parties in a state of nature to "anticipate" against one another in a way that leads to a state of war of all against all. But, as noted above, anticipation is a disjunctive concept for Hobbes; it can refer either to attack, which may be called active anticipation, or to gathering coercive power in other ways (e.g., assembling armaments, making alliances), which may be called passive anticipation. Similarly, a state of war, for Hobbes, merely consists in a (known) mutual willingness to fight among parties, and may be either active, in the sense of involving actual fighting, or passive, in the sense of not involving actual fighting.[19]

Now, in a context of potential conflict among nuclear nations, it is vitally important *which sorts* of anticipation and war are rational and likely. Admittedly, the nuclear arms race involves substantial costs even if the weapons are never used: diversion of resources from welfare needs, accrual of domestic political advantages to militaristic leaders and parties, anxieties suffered by the peoples of the world, and so on. Nonetheless, these costs of passive anticipation and a passive state of war among nations (or alliances of nations) are very small compared to the likely cost of large-scale nuclear war. Hence, even if the Nuclear World Government Argument establishes the rationality and likelihood of anticipation and war if there is no world government, it would not establish the need for such a government unless the "anticipation" and "war" in question are active. But the considerations offered above – especially the suicidal (or at least highly risky and uncertain) nature of almost all nuclear attacks – indicates that it is passive anticipation and a passive state of war that most likely characterizes even the proliferated nuclear world. If this is so, the case for fleeing such a world for the uncertainties of world government may not be compelling; at least it is not established by analogy with Hobbes's argument against anarchy.

Are there other features of the nuclear world that mighty firmly establish the need for world government? This question is too wide-ranging to be effectively addressed here. But I would like to briefly consider, and reject, two simple arguments that are sometimes thought to supply an affirmative answer to the question. Then, in the next section, I shall take up a different sort of problem facing the Nuclear World Government Argument.

The first argument may be dubbed the Eventual Certainty Argument.[20] According to it, even if, without world government, there is only a small probability p of a major nuclear war in each given year, and the probability does not grow with time, it is a statistical certainty that eventually there will be a major nuclear war. For the probability of no major nuclear war within n years will be given by $(1-p)$ raised to the power n, a value that approaches zero as n increases toward infinity.

The problem with this argument is that the probability of major nuclear war (in a given time period) may *decrease* over time, and if the pattern of decrease is right, the total risk can still be small. For example, if the risk were 5 percent the first year and decreased by half each succeeding year, the total risk would approach a limit of 10 percent. Admittedly, there is no reason to expect the probabilities to follow this particular pattern. But there are two good reasons to expect the probabilities to decline year by year, on average and other things being equal. First, what has happened before in a world of two or more nuclear powers is a significant piece of evidence about what is likely to happen in the future in such a world. The more years we go in such a world without major nuclear war, the more likely this makes it – other things being equal – that there will not be a major nuclear war the next year. Second, leaders' decisions to start a nuclear war are likely to be a positive function of their expectations that such a war is coming anyway. As more time passes without a war, this expectation is likely to decline, other things being equal. Now, of course, other things may not be equal, and may be such as to increase the risk of major nuclear war in future years. Whether or not this is so is known neither by you nor me nor proponents of the Eventual Certainty Argument. Nor do any of us know whether the yearly decline in probability, if there is one, is of the right sort to make the total risk out to year infinity converge on some figure less than one. But this is just the point. None of us knows; certainty, even probabilistically based certainty, is not available. Hence the Eventual Certainty Argument fails.

A variant of this first argument has been suggested by Mc-Mahan.[21] According to it, current trends in the superpower arms race suggest rising (or at least "not systematically falling") probabilities of nuclear war from year to year. Hence it would be a reasonable guess, looking ahead, that nuclear war is a near certainty in the long run without world government.

I appreciate McMahan's main point, but do not think this argument establishes the rational necessity of world government. At most it shows the rational necessity of *doing something* to reverse current trends in the superpower arms race. But a switch to minimum deterrence by either side, or the rational pursuit of bilateral disarmament by both sides (as advocated in Chapter 10) would very likely reverse these trends and reduce the long-run probability of nuclear war to levels far below near certainty. So the Near Certainty Argument, if I may call it that, does not demonstrate that world government should be viewed as a necessary means of nuclear war prevention.

The second argument to be considered may be called the Maximin Argument. It begins where the last argument collapsed – with the grave uncertainties involved in predicting the long-run outcomes of nuclear policies. Under such uncertainty and with so much at stake, it is claimed, rationality requires following a maximin rule. This means comparing the worst possible outcomes that might arise from the various alternative strategies and choosing the strategy that has the best (i.e., least bad) worst outcome.[22] While the deterrence – alliance strategy might, at worst, lead to a major nuclear war, the worst a world government strategy could lead to would be tyranny by the world government, which would not be as bad. Therefore, establishing a world government is the rationally preferable strategy.[23]

This argument fails by wrongly assuming that world government, or the attempt to establish one, precludes the possibility of nuclear war. It does not. Trying to establish the world government, and in particular attempts to disarm nuclear nations in the process, might lead to cheating, misunderstandings, and so forth, that culminate in nuclear war. Even if a world government is effectively established, nuclear civil war is a possibility over the long run, involving either weapons retained or built by the government itself, or weapons surreptitiously produced in violation of the government's ban. (Remember that consolidation of federal power over the continental United States required a bloody civil war in which the most powerful weapons available were used.) Furthermore, since even a medium-sized nuclear war could, according to current estimates, have devastating environmental impact and thereby threaten the survival of our species, we cannot rule out the possibility that following the world government strategy will lead to outcomes as bad as can be imagined.[24] Perhaps it is less likely than other strategies to lead to such outcomes. Even if true, this lends no support to the Maximin Argument, which by its very nature ignores probabilities and focuses entirely on worst possibilites.

In rejecting these two straightforward arguments for the world government, I am not claiming to have proved that trying to establish a world government is necessarily a riskier strategy, either in the present or the proliferated world, than continuing to rely on deterrence and alliance. It may or may not be. But an argument to establish one or the other will have to be complex and shrouded with much uncertainty. No argument as simple as the Eventual Certainty Argument or the Maximin Argument is likely to succeed. In the next section, I shall consider a somewhat stronger argument in support of world government.

IV. DISARMAMENT AND WORLD GOVERNMENT

The Nuclear World Government Argument emphasizes the similarities between a world with nuclear-armed nations and Hobbes's state of nature among individuals. I have already noted how some relevent dissimilarities seriously undermine this argument. A different sort of argument for world government – which may be called the Modified Nuclear World Government Argument – focuses instead on certain distinctive features of nuclear weapons and the nuclear world. The most important of these features is the awesome destructiveness of nuclear weapons, which together with their existence in very large numbers in the present world, poses a potential threat to the survival not only of particular nations, but of human civilization and perhaps the species as well. The size and power of nuclear arsenals might seem to render their use by major powers irrational and inconceivable. But a large-scale nuclear war need not start by rational decision. There are various other ways it could start. Computer errors combined with procedures designed to negate the advantages of striking first (e.g., automatic launch on warning) can lead to accidental nuclear war; while proliferation greatly increases the risk of the nuclear button coming within reach of wildly irrational leaders. The same alliances that promise certain security advantages can draw major nuclear powers into wars (e.g., in the Middle East or in Europe) that may escalate into major nuclear conflicts. And the apparent military advantages of striking first at an opponent's nuclear weapons before they can be used, renders it unlikely (or at least highly uncertain) that a nuclear war could be controlled or limited once it had begun. Given the horrible consequences of large-scale nuclear war and the genuine risk that it might occur, both prudence and morality seem to require abandoning the present system of defense by alliance and nuclear deterrence in favor of world government.

The main problem with this Modified Nuclear World Government Argument is that it must provide a *prospective* justification of world government. Perhaps it does provide such a justification to the collectivity of nations, taken together. But to be an argument with practical significance in a world of currently sovereign and independent nations, it must provide a justification that is compelling (or at least attractive) to individual nations, especially the great powers who must lead the way if an effective world government is to be established.

There are, however, a number of rational (or at least not demonstrably irrational) reasons why great powers might resist the surrender of their sovereignty to a world government. They might realistically fear being forced, by the majority of poorer nations in the world government, into large transfers of economic resources to other nations. They might be genuinely committed to an ideology that forbids surrender of power to any institution not subscribing to the same ideology. Leadership groups (or military groups whose support the leaders need to remain in power) may rightly perceive it to be against their group interest if a world government is formed. In addition, smaller nuclear powers (e.g., Israel in the present or near future) may have special historical reasons, based on their experience with the United Nations, for fearing that a world government would be hostile to them and might threaten their vital interests. Most important of all, nations will be distrustful of other nations, fearing that some of them are cheaters and aggressors who will exploit the world-government formation process to gain unilateral military or political advantages, or will manipulate the established world government so as to promote their own interests. (Nor will all those nations who believe this about other nations necessarily be mistaken or paranoid in so thinking.) Given all these possible reasons, it may not be irrational for major nuclear powers to prefer the dangers of nuclear deterrence to the risks and disadvantages of surrendering sovereignty under a specific proposed scheme of world government, even a well-designed one.

Further, whether or not it is rational to so resist *when it is assumed that others will not resist,* it may well be rational for a nation to hang back if it expects other nations to resist for these or other reasons. For carrying the torch of world government when others will not go along could have major political, economic, and military costs; it could even lead to a nuclear war started by a hostile nation that is pushed too hard to join, or that fears the adverse consequences of being left out. In view of these potent sources of rational resistance to world government, we should not be surprised at the failure of the predictions of optimists in the 1960s who saw the dangers of a nuclear world leading nations to establish a world government by the mid-1980s.[25]

The likelihood of rational resistance by some nations to the surrender of their national sovereignty can also be demonstrated in another way. There are certain general questions about the nature of a world government that must be satisfactorily answered before nations can find it reasonable to accept such a government, even in principle. And it is not clear that they can or will be. The central issue is what powers the world government is to have. Dealing with the analogous issue as regards national governments, Hobbes held that sovereigns must exercise undivided and unlimited power – including the specific powers of taxation, military command, censorship, making and enforcing laws, and establishing rules of property – if they are to be able to provide citizens with lasting security. But he is notorious for underestimating the dangers of tyranny under such a scheme. And national governments that were considering the formation of a world government would not be inclined to follow Hobbes into error on this point. They would surely limit the powers of world government and demand protection of their basic national rights in the new system before they would seriously consider surrendering their sovereignty.[26]

So any world government created by the voluntary rational actions of its member states would be a limited government, containing safeguards against tyranny by the government or blocs of nations that might use the government to exploit and dominate other nations. One of the best-known proposals for a limited world government is that of Grenville Clark and Louis B. Sohn,[27] and I shall use it as my model of such government in what follows. Clark and Sohn propose a progressive, ten-year, inspected, complete (nuclear and nonnuclear) disarmament of all nations, coinciding with the creation of a substantial international police force equipped with both conventional and nuclear weapons. This police force would be under the ultimate authority and control of an assembly of representatives of all nations, with the largest nations each having up to thirty times as many representatives as each of the smallest nations. Nations, whether or not they chose to join the world government, would remain in control of their own domestic affairs. But they would be subject to the enforcement of the disarmament procedures and the rulings on international disputes of world courts (set up under the authority of the world representative assembly). All member nations would also be required to collect and pay taxes to support the world government and developmental aid for poor nations. In cases of resistance, the world police would enforce these central obligations, using nuclear weapons to do so only if necessary in extreme cases.

Any scheme for world government must face up to the ultimate question of whether the world government is to have an effective monopoly on the use of coercive military power. Without such a capability, international institutions (such as the League of Nations and the United Nations) are likely to be relatively ineffectual. A world body that is a military oligopolist, possessing military power surpassing that of all but a few nations, might fare better. But since it could not enforce its decisions against those few influential and powerful nations, other nations might well be disinclined to accept or rely on its authority. Recognizing these difficulties, theorists such as Clark and Sohn opt for an effective military monopoly in the hands of the international government. But this raises problems of its own. To secure and maintain this monopoly against even one small nuclear power that refused to disarm might well require the actual use of nuclear weapons. More importantly, the danger of tyranny, either by the entrenched international bureaucracy that is likely to arise over time, or a majority coalition in the world assembly, is real if a single group or organization has a monopoly of coercive power available to it. Various procedural safeguards against this are suggested by Clark and Sohn, e.g., having members of the police force and key officials in the international government come from a wide variety of the smaller nations. But at best, these reduce rather than eliminate the danger of international tyranny.

In reply, it may be observed that absolute guarantees against tyranny can never be had, and should not be expected. We know from experience at the national level that the risks of tyranny can be minimized by various constitutional and procedural devices, as, for example, in the evolution of the federal system of government in the United States. Even if we allow that people will, and should, accept centralized authority and the corresponding graver risks of tyranny only in preference to a still greater threat, this does not undermine the case for world government. For the nuclear arms race and the threat of nuclear destruction constitutes such a greater threat.

Whether or not our present (and likely future) nuclear danger constitutes a greater risk to humanity, or to the citizens of particular nations, than would an effective monopoly of power in the hands of a world bureaucracy and assembly is an open question. One's answer to it depends on highly uncertain estimates about the nature and likelihood of nuclear war or world tyranny under various circumstances. For the moment, I would simply like to observe that the analogy between centralization of power in federated nation-states such as the United States and the hypothetical centralization of international power in a world government does not unambiguously support the position of world government proponents. For in some cases such national centralization of power did produce tyranny, and in others it could only be brought about by the most violent conflicts over economic, social, ideological, or religious issues (as, for example, the U.S. Civil War). This suggests that serious attempts to form a world government could actually lead to the outcomes its proponents most fear: nuclear war or tyranny over the peoples of the world.

In light of all this, I propose a different way of looking at the relationship between our nuclear danger and world government. According to the Nuclear World Government Argument and related arguments considered in this paper, elimination of the danger of nuclear war is our end, and world government is the necessary means to that end. But is this really the case? Let us ask, in particular, what additional motive or reason does the prospect of world government (say of the Clark-Sohn type) provide for nuclear powers to undertake nuclear disarmament? The primary motive, avoidance of nuclear war, is present without world government ever entering the picture.

At most, world government seems to provide three subsidiary incentives or reasons for nuclear disarmament that might otherwise not exist. First, it creates a neutral body for inspection during the disarmament process. But the nuclear powers, if they wished to do so, could create such a body without endowing it with any powers but inspection. Second, the simultaneous (nuclear) arming of the world police force allows the nuclear nations to dismantle all of their nuclear arms without fearing that undetectable small-scale cheating will allow other nations to gain a decisive military advantage. But this purpose could probably be served nearly as well by the maintenance of conventional armaments by the great powers, together with either a temporary stockpiling of some nuclear weapons in the hands of a specially created neutral body or the construction of strategic missile defense systems.[28] For these measures would make it likely that any small nuclear stockpile that a nation retained in violation of the disarmament agreement would not give that nation a decisive military advantage. Third, and probably most important, the nuclear-armed police force can continually enforce a zero level of national nuclear armaments to prevent a new nuclear arms race from springing up again in the future. No alternative arrangement is likely to perform this function as effectively, though it has recently been urged that fear of the dangers of a new nuclear arms race might well suffice to deter nations from rearming with nuclear weapons once the zero level had been reached initially.[29] I have left out a fourth important function of world government – the authoritative nonviolent settlement of international disputes – because this is simply the other side of the coin of surrender of national sovereignty, and many nations and their leaders will regard this as a cost rather than a benefit of world government. In fact, the point I am trying to make is that nations, especially great powers, are unlikely to find this cost worth paying to achieve the nuclear disarmament-related purposes of world government when there are alternative (though less reliable) ways of achieving these purposes that do not involve surrendering national sovereignty.

If I am right about this, it is misleading to regard world government as a necessary means of achieving nuclear disarmament. Nuclear disarmament is possible without world government, but world government may not be possible without nuclear disarmament. The rationale for nuclear disarmament – mutual protection from the threat of nuclear war – exists independently of the possibility of world government, and there are alternative means of obtaining that objective (Though none is without its own dangers and drawbacks.) A primary focus of those promoting world peace should be on exploring those alternative means, designing better ones, and letting the world's people and leaders know about their advantages. The great powers are very unlikely to accept the loss of sovereignty in the foreseeable future, even to achieve nuclear disarmament. But they might eventually accept nuclear disarmament itself, as a lesser risk, if the process is sufficiently safeguarded. And if nuclear disarmament is achieved, this may so transform the world of international relations that world government would then become both a feasible and unambiguously desirable goal for mankind.

8. Strategic defense

Nuclear deterrence, as I suggested in Chapter 1, is a parent of moral paradoxes. Perhaps strategic defense is the other parent. One sign of this is that in the political debate on strategic defense you cannot tell the players without a scorecard – most conservative "militarists" favor defensive measures, while many liberal "humanists" prefer threats of murderous retaliation. A related aspect of the matter is revealed by extending our genealogical metaphor. In the family of nuclear defense and deterrence, moral paradox is an unwanted child. Security is the intended and desired offspring. But security might be produced asexually (that is, by strategic defense alone) or sexually (that is, by a combination of strategic defense and deterrence by threat of retaliation). Though some may sincerely believe in security through strategic defense, much of the public discussion of strategic defense is Victorian, with a highly sexual reality hidden beneath a veneer of asexuality.

My purpose here, however, is not to question the motives of the participants in the strategic defense debate, but to provide the beginnings of a moral analysis of strategic defense. I do this by first discussing strategic defense from a consequentialist perspective (in section I) and then exploring a different moral approach to the problem.

I am grateful to John Ahrens, George Draper, Robert Goodin, Russell Hardin, Karl Hufbauer, Carey Joynt, Steven Lee, Christopher Morris, and Edward Regis, Jr., for helpful comments on earlier drafts of the articles this chapter is based on. The University of California's Institute on Global Conflict and Cooperation supported my research and stimulated my thinking on strategic defense at its summer seminar in June 1983. An earlier version of section I of this chapter was presented at the *Ethics* conference on the Ethics of Nuclear Deterrence and Disarmament, Aspen, Colorado, September 1984.

I. A CONSEQUENTIALIST ANALYSIS

My main concern will be whether the United States should pursue development and deployment of strategic defenses instead of seeking to achieve or sustain treaties with the Soviets that ban them. (Though my primary attention is on U.S. policy, most of what I say also applies to Soviet development and deployment of strategic defenses.) I will largely limit my analysis to the foreseeable future – say, the next twenty years. For beyond that, the technical and political factors on which the current consequentialist assessment is based may well have changed so much as to vitiate my reasoning and conclusions.

What goals should be posited in evaluating strategic defense from a consequentialist perspective? I propose three primary goals, of obvious moral importance, ordered in terms of their priority, as follows.

1. Nuclear war prevention.
2. Minimizing the damage suffered by humankind in a nuclear war, should one occur.
3. Preservation of economic resources for nonmilitary use.

Goals 1 and 2 are to be given priority over goal 3 because of the unprecedented amount of human death, suffering, and social disruption likely to result from any sort of nuclear war involving one or more superpower.[1] This does not mean, however, that goal 3 is a trivial moral consideration. Given the likely enormous costs of building space-based weapons systems, we have very good reasons not to build them unless they really contribute to the attainment of goals 1 or 2. Goal 1, nuclear war prevention, is given priority over goal 2, damage limitation in the event of nuclear war, based on the plausible assumptions that nuclear war is not highly probable (in the time period under consideration) if appropriate steps are taken to prevent it and that a nuclear war even with damage-limiting technology would likely cause many millions of casualties.[2] If nuclear war can be avoided, and would be a moral and human catastrophe if it occurred, our first moral priority must be the prevention of such a war.

A consequentialist analysis of strategic defense in terms of our three goals will be prudential as well as moral. For any risks of war engendered by a nation's pursuit of such weapons, and their economic costs, will be borne, in substantial part, by the citizens of that nation. The crux of my argument will be that for the United States to develop and deploy strategic defenses in the foreseeable future would be unwise because of the likely effects on ourselves as well as immoral because of the likely effects on all humanity. In developing this consequentialist argument against strategic defense, I leave aside for consideration in later sections an argument of a different sort in favor of strategic defense.

Scientists are currently researching strategic defense (SD) systems that would be able to destroy enemy ballistic missiles in flight using a variety of means, including orbiting launch detectors, space-based and ground-based interceptor missiles, and space-aimed laser and particle beams.[3] As first indicated in President Reagan's "Star Wars" speech of March 1983, the development of these new strategic defense systems has recently been looked on favorably at the highest political levels.

There are a number of arguments one might give for developing and deploying SD systems. They might protect us against nuclear attack by the Soviet Union and would likely be very effective protection against nuclear strikes from a third power or accidental Soviet launches of a small number of missiles. If the Soviets did not develop their own strategic defense system, our system – even if imperfect – would improve our "destruction inflicted/destruction suffered" ratio enough so that we would be more likely to prevail in a nuclear war if deterrence failed. And it would enhance deterrence by increasing Soviet uncertainties about the effectveness of any nuclear attack they might contemplate launching.[4] If, on the other hand, both superpowers developed such systems, they would no longer have to rely on the prospect of "mutual assured destruction" (MAD) for defense. This would be desirable because MAD may not deter war forever and because it involves each side in the apparently morally dubious practice of threatening (and risking the lives of) the civilian population of the other side. In addition to these familiar considerations, there is a game-theoretic argument in favor of SD systems which I shall now present.

Strategic defense systems, to the extent that they work, prevent enemy missiles from reaching their targets. Hence an SD system with a certain percentage of effectiveness is equivalent to a like percentage reduction in the other side's missile force, in terms of its effect on one's own vulnerability.[5] From this perspective, it seems that rather than reducing their mutual vulnerability a certain degree by building SD systems, the superpowers could achieve the same effect more cheaply and reliably by mutual reductions in offensive missile systems. This is true, but it requires cooperation and (at least tacit) agreement between the two sides because the incentives for unilateral action in an arms competition inhibit arms reductions. But when it comes to strategic defensive systems, incentives for unilateral action favor steps that will decrease vulnerability. Hence in a situation in which arms agreements are hard to come by, deploying SD systems might be the only feasible way of reducing mutual vulnerability.

Game matrices may be used to illustrate the substance of this argument. Figure 1 represents the choices each superpower faces in deciding whether to maintain its status quo arsenal (S.Q.) or disarm by dismantling a certain percentage of its missiles (Disarm). In each quadrant, left-hand numbers represent U.S. payoffs (in terms of preference order), and right-hand numbers represent Soviet Union payoffs. In the standard way, it is assumed that each side's ordering of outcomes from most to least preferred is: other's unilateral disarmament, bilateral disarmament, bilateral status quo, one's own unilateral disarmament.[6]

		USSR	
		S.Q.	Disarm
U.S.A.	S.Q.	3,3	1,4
	Disarm	4,1	2,2

Figure 1

The result is a familiar prisoner's dilemma matrix with S.Q. being the dominant move for each side, so that if each acts rationally and independently, the mutually preferred bilateral disarmament outcome is not achieved. Figure 2 represents the choice of each superpower between maintaining its status quo and defending itself by deploying an SD system in addition to its current arsenal (Defend). It is assumed that each side most prefers being the only side defended and least prefers only its adversary being defended.[7] Each, however, prefers bilateral defense to the bilateral status quo because of the reduced vulnerability entailed by bilateral defense. In Figure 2, Defend is the dominant move for each. Comparing the two matrices, we see that of two outcomes that may equivalently reduce mutual vulnerability – bilateral SD deployment and bilateral disarmament – one may be achieved by rational unilateral action while the other cannot be. This is the most powerful theoretical argument I know favoring development of SD systems.

		USSR	
		S.Q.	Defend
U.S.A.	S.Q.	3,3	4,1
	Defend	1,4	2,2

Figure 2

Arguments against U.S. development of SD systems differ according to whether one considers unilateral development or cooperative development with the Soviets. Let us first discuss unilateral development. A major objection to SD systems is that they would not work very well. A number of major technical problems confront such systems: having enough weapons in orbit to have Soviet missiles always in target range, being able to destroy large numbers of fast-moving missiles in a very short time span, having very large energy sources to power laser components of an SD system, having large accurate mirrors in orbit to focus the laser beams, and having sufficient surveillance and computing capacity to identify and target missiles and to identify and retarget missiles that survive the first salvo.[8] In addition, such systems would be quite vulnerable to countermeasures such as coating of missiles to deflect laser energy, physical attacks on the components of the system, or overloading the system's capacity by deploying more offensive missiles.[9] In addition, a different system with different capabilities would probably be needed to protect against bombers and cruise missiles carrying nuclear weapons. And even if technological advances were able to solve the specific problems currently at hand, SD systems with (or without) substantial space-based components are unlikely to provide adequate defense of the United States for two reasons; very nearly 100 percent interception rates are needed for adequate defense (because of the enormous destructive power of nuclear weapons) and the Soviets are likely to find partly effective countermeasures to each advance we make.[10]

If, despite these considerations, the United States proceeded to develop and deploy SD systems, it would be enormously expensive.

Published estimates of the cost range from around 100 billion to 500 billion dollars, and it does not appear that these estimates take account of needed replies to all likely Soviet countermeasures.[11] There would also be the political cost of unilateral abrogation of the 1972 Antiballistic Missile (ABM) treaty, which would include worsened relations with the Soviets that might well increase the risks of war. Nor, if we maintained our strategic deterrent as a backup (which would be both likely and prudent, given that the SD system would be untested in combat and unlikely to work perfectly), would we be escaping whatever moral opprobrium might attach to our threatening Soviet civilians with nuclear destruction. Finally, even if an SD system were unlikely to be fully effective, it might seem to be effective enough to place its sole possessor in a position to neutralize his adversary's nuclear arsenal and practice nuclear blackmail. Fear of this situation might lead the other side to race to deploy its own SD system first, to increase its nuclear forces massively, to issue an ultimatum against deployment of the system, or even to make a preemptive strike before the system is able to go into operation.[12]

But what of the game-theoretic argument that SD systems are desirable precisely because they allow reductions of mutual vulnerability by rational unilateral actions? We are now in a position to see what was wrong with that argument: it considered too few options on each side, either doing nothing, deploying SD systems, or disarming. But even putting aside the drastic alternatives of making a strike or an ultimatum, there is still the option of building more offensive nuclear systems and/or taking countermeasures against the other side's actual or potential SD systems. This new option is represented by the strategy choice "Arm" in the matrix depicted in Figure 3.

This matrix was constructed on the basis of certain plausible technical-strategic and motivational assumptions. The technical-strategic assumptions are:

(T1)   The status quo, both Defending, and both Arming are all conditions of strategic equality.

(T2)   If one side Defends (deploys SD systems) and the other Arms (spends an equivalent amount on offensive systems and countermeasures), the Arming side gains a relative advantage.[13]

(T3)   If one side remains at the status quo, the other gains a greater relative advantage by Defending (deploying SD systems) than by Arming.

(T4) If one side Arms, it gains a greater relative advantage if the other remains at the status quo rather than Defending.

Assumption T2 is plausible because of the great expense of SD systems compared to the expense of building more offensive systems and taking countermeasures (e.g., coating missiles). Assumption T3 is plausible because the prospect of preventing your opponent from being able to retaliate effectively yields a greater strategic advantage than does an extra margin of offensive overkill capacity.[14]

The three motivational assumptions are:

(M1) Each side prefers relative strategic advantage, equality, and relative disadvantage, in that order.

(M2) Each side prefers a greater relative advantage to a lesser one and a lesser relative disadvantage to a greater one.

(M3) Among equal outcomes, each side prefers lesser mutual vulnerability to greater.

Combining all seven assumptions leads to the matrix in Figure 3.[15] There is no dominant strategy in this matrix, in contrast to those in Figures 1 and 2. (Arming is not dominant because, if the other side remains at the status quo, one would prefer to Defend.) But the Arm – Arm outcome is the only equilibrium – that is, the only outcome such that neither party would prefer to depart from it unilaterally. Therefore if we think of the parties to the situation monitoring one another's behavior over time and switching their moves to obtain more preferred positions, then (in the absence of explicit or implicit cooperation) the long-run tendency will be for them to move from the other sections of the matrix to the bottom right-hand corner. (For example, if each initially plans to Defend and perceives that the other so plans, either can gain [i.e., move from a fourth preference to a third] by switching to Arm. But the other then gains [i.e., moves from a seventh preference to a sixth] by Arming as well.) And they would remain there in the bottom right corner at the point of maximum mutual vulnerability, despite the outcomes being merely the sixth preference of each.

		USSR		
		S.Q.	Defend	Arm
	S.Q.	5,5	9,1	8,2
U.S.A.	Defend	1,9	4,4	7,3
	Arm	2,8	3,7	6,6

Figure 3

Lest it be thought that this game-theoretic reasoning is only of theoretical interest, it is worth noting that it accurately reflects the outcome of an earlier stage of the nuclear arms race. In the 1960s and early 1970s, the superpowers faced an essentially similar choice between the status quo, building ABM systems (Defending), and proceeding with the development of newer and more effective offensive weapons, especially multiple-warhead missiles (Arming). The result was bilateral abandonment of the more expensive and less reliable defensive systems and continuation of the race in offensive arms – or, in terms of Figure 3, a move to the lower right-hand corner.[16]

That the Soviets, at least, are aware of the possibility of moving toward the lower right-hand corner again, in the present context, is suggested by this comment on space-based SD systems by the director of Moscow's Institute of Space Research: "It will always be possible to create less expensive countermeasures for such a system or to increase the number of attackers."[17] This comment also reveals the fatal flaw in the argument – mentioned earlier – that unilateral SD development would improve our destruction capacities, relative to our opponent, in the event of nuclear war. Once we take into account likely Soviet countermeasures, it is doubtful that even unilateral development of an SD system would significantly improve our chances of prevailing (in any meaningful sense) in a nuclear war. What might happen, however, is that unilateral development of an SD system would make it possessors mistakenly feel invulnerable. And this could lead to a nuclear war in which neither side prevails, or survives.

Admittedly, the possibility of overloading or building countermeasures to an SD system does not refute the argument that such a system would enhance deterrence by introducing additional uncertainties into Soviet strategic plans and calculations. For the Soviets would not know, ahead of time, how well their extra missiles and countermeasures would fare against a U.S. SD system. But given the high survivability of U.S. strategic forces at present and in the foreseeable future, it is doubtful that we need these extra uncertainties to deter Soviet strategic attack. Thus any marginal increase in effective deterrence by uncertainty that an SD system might provide would likely be outweighed by the increased dangers of war that it would engender: possible Soviet preemption against the defense system or its possessors, war emerging from increased political tensions created by an accelerated arms race, and so on.

In summary then, there are numerous dangers inherent in the United States's attempting unilaterally to develop and deploy a strategic defense system. One possibility is a highly dangerous and costly race between the United States and the Soviet Union to assemble the first such system. Another possibility is that unilateral development will produce a false sense of invulnerability that could result in war. Perhaps the most likely outcome of all is that pursuit of such systems will never result in deployment of an effective strategic defense but will instead stir the development of yet greater and more sophisticated offensive arsenals on both sides, thus wasting valuable resources while actually increasing mutual vulnerability to nuclear destruction. It seems highly unlikely that protection against improbable third-power or small accidental attacks is sufficiently important to outweigh these great costs and dangers.

What of the possibility of U.S. – Soviet cooperation in developing space-based SD systems, as hinted at by President Reagan in an interview with reporters soon after his "Star Wars" speech? This would seem to avoid the political and competitive problems associated with unilateral development while promising to result in decreased mutual vulnerability and protection against third-party and accidental attacks. And surely it would be a much less objectionable approach than is unilateral development and its attendant risks. But even bilateral cooperative development of space-based defenses has its disadvantages. There is always the danger of cooperation breaking down during the process and resulting in a highly dangerous race with each side attempting to finish and deploy its own SD system first. Also, for the bilateral approach to work effectively, each side must expect that the other will not engage in secret parallel research to develop counters to the system or to enable a unilateral "breakout" leading to first deployment of an effective system. These expectations could be based either on a belief in the other side's reliability and trustworthiness or on a belief that the other side is farsighted and rational enough to see that seeking short-run unilateral advantage in this manner is likely to yield bad consequences (e.g., a fiercer and more dangerous arms race) for both sides in the long run. But if the two sides have, or can develop, this much faith in each other's reliability or rational farsightedness, they can probably decrease mutual danger and vulnerability more cheaply by bilateral reductions in offensive systems and improved political relations.

Supporters of cooperative bilateral SD development might reply in two ways. They could claim that offensive reductions beyond a certain point may decrease strategic stability by leaving each side without an "assured destruction" second-strike capacity.[18] Also, successful bilateral SD development would provide protection against third-party and accidental launches that would not be provided by offensive reductions. But the point about strategic stability applies to SD systems as well. A first strike on one's SD system and offensive strategic systems might well leave one without sufficient assets to penetrate significantly the striker's own intact SD system. So each side possessing an SD system that was highly effective but vulnerable to attack could actually increase strategic instability. The point about third-party and accidental launches is well taken. But given the massive costs of SD systems, it seems likely that equal or greater protection against these contingencies could be attained by spending these funds instead on improving warning and command and control systems to prevent accidents and on nonproliferation and third world aid measures to decrease the likelihood of third-party attacks.

All things considered then, it seems best in the real world to stick by the 1972 ABM treaty for the foreseeable future and to pursue cooperation with the Soviets in the direction of reducing mutual vulnerability by reducing offensive arms. If such reductions are obtained and political relations are improved enough to make a cooperative SD development program feasible, then it might be permissible to proceed with such a program, for example, if the third-party attack danger has grown more serious or if domestic politics make cooperative SD development – but not further offensive reductions – achievable. What we must be extremely wary of, however, is that the vague prospect of cooperative SD development will function, in public debate, to justify unilateral pursuit of SD systems "in the meantime." Given the severe dangers of attempted unilateral SD development discussed above, it would be neither prudent nor moral to proceed with such an attempt, either as a means of gaining a unilateral strategic advantage or as a means of encouraging Soviet participation in a cooperative development program.

But what of using strategic defense programs as a bargaining chip? In principle, this is fine *if it works;* that is, if it encourages one's opponent to accept reasonable and desirable bilateral disarmament measures and if one is willing to use the chip for this admirable purpose. But all too often, bargaining chips fail to be effective in either or both of these ways. They either scare opponents into arming instead of disarming, or they develop political constituencies or ideological justifications that prevent them from being traded off and cashed in. The danger of the latter sort of failure in the case of strategic defense is highlighted by the results of the October 1986 superpower summit in Iceland. While fear of the potential of U.S. strategic defense programs led to unprecedented willingness by the new Soviet leadership to accept serious bilateral nuclear disarmament measures, the refusal of the U.S. side to accept a ten-year ban on nonlaboratory testing of SD weaponry apparently prevented any agreements from being reached. Further progress would seem to depend on the willingness of U.S. leaders to trade off part or all of their SD programs for mutually beneficial measures of nuclear disarmament.

II. PURE DEFENSE

Supporters of strategic defense sometimes appeal (often implicitly) to a simple but highly attractive argument: strategic defense must be morally permissible because it is defensive rather than offensive.[19] Since purely defensive acts are never wrong, there can be no decisive moral objection to strategic defense. It is this Pure Defense Argument that I wish to examine and refute.

The Pure Defense Argument infers the permissibility of strategic defense directly from a general normative principle concerning the moral status of things that are purely defensive. Let us call this principle the Pure Defense Principle and initially formulate it as follows:

(PD1) If an act, object, institution, or policy is purely defensive, then it is morally permissible.

Though strategic defense is not a single act, but rather a complex of various objects, institutions, and acts, I will – to avoid unnecessary complications – discuss the Pure Defense Principle largely as it applies to acts. In the absence of arguments to the contrary, I assume that any problems that the principle encounters as regards acts will also arise in the case of policies.

Before the plausibility of (PD1) can be assessed, I must say something about when an act is purely defensive. Two distinct criteria are involved: one involving motive and the other involving the physical nature of the act itself. An act is purely defensive according to the motivational criterion if and only if the predominant motive of the agent is the prevention of possible harm to herself or some other person(s).[20] The intuitive idea behind the physical criterion is that purely defensive acts work by physically repelling a harmful force or by appearing to be able to physically repel it – they do not involve attacks on, or threats to attack, those who create or direct that force. According to this criterion, an act is purely defensive if and only if it tries to prevent harm by *deflecting* or *redirecting* the potentially harmful force or attack. The notions of deflection or redirection employed here are technical ones. "Deflection" means avoiding the harmful effects of a force by changing the path of the objects embodying it, by destroying those objects before they reach the protected objects, or by moving the protected objects out of the way. "Redirection" is short for "redirection by threat of deflection" and refers to changing a potential attacker's target by appearing to have the capacity to deflect an attack on the original target. Both natural forces (e.g., floods) and attacks directed by people can be deflected, but since the former cannot choose their targets, only the latter can be redirected.

Neither the motivational nor the physical criterion seems restrictive enough, by itself, to capture the notion of a purely defensive action. The former would be satisfied, for example, by the shooting down of a number of poor teenagers in order to prevent the violent crimes that some of them are likely to commit eventually, according to demographic statistics. (More generally, the motivational criterion classifies many preventive attacks as purely defensive.) The physical criterion would allow that one was acting purely defensively if one deliberately constructed a wall to deflect mudslides away from an unused corner of one's property and a flood control channel, and into a hated neighbor's hot tub.

To avoid these counterexamples, I propose a more restrictive account of pure defense – one that regards the stated motivational and physical criteria as individually necessary, and jointly sufficient, conditions of an act being purely defensive. Doing so has three additional advantages. First, it is plausible to claim that if an act is both defensively motivated and operates by deflecting rather than initiating force, then it is purely defensive. Second, this restrictive account of pure defense is fair to supporters of the Pure Defense

Principle – by narrowing the scope of what they have to justify, I make their job of justification easier and mine of criticism harder. Third, this account is broad enough to allow that SD (and the U.S. Strategic Defense Initiative) is purely defensive, provided that we are willing to stipulate (at least for the sake of argument) that the prevention of some of the harms of nuclear attack is the governing motive of those who are planning to create strategic defenses. In the sequel, then, purely defensive acts will be those that satisfy both the motivational and physical criteria.

Are all such acts morally permissable as implied by (PD1)? Remembering that the guilty can be defended as well as the innocent, we see that this is not so. If one is rightfully convicted of a serious crime, it is not permissible to resist just punishment even if one does so only to avoid harm and by "deflecting" the physical force of arresting officers. So (PD1) must be revised. Let us define a technical sense of "innocence" according to which one party is innocent with respect to a harm that might be imposed by another party if and only if it would not be morally proper for the latter to impose that harm on the former. Further, an act (object, etc.) is "purely defensive of an innocent party" when the party is innocent, in the above-defined sense, with respect to the harms he is "purely defended" against by that act (object, etc.). Then the revised Pure Defense Principle may be stated as follows:

(PD2)   If an act, object, institution, or policy is purely defensive of innocent parties, it is morally permissible.

This principle seems, on the surface, quite plausible. How could one criticize an act that tries to protect the innocent from harm by deflecting or redirecting potential attacks on them? We shall see that, surprisingly, there are a number of cogent ways of doing so.

III. CRITIQUE

How could an act of pure defense of the innocent be morally defective? There are at least four ways. Such an act could protect the guilty, deflect harm onto other innocents, make aggression by the defended party safer and more likely, or be ineffective as a means of defense. Let us consider these four possbilities in turn.

Protection of the guilty

Acts or policies that defend the innocent often save some of the guilty from deserved punishment. A nation, for example, may refuse to extradite any of its citizens accused of committing crimes in other countries, in order to protect its nationals from being wrongfully punished by foreign legal systems. It will thereby prevent the just punishment of some citizens who commit crimes elsewhere and flee back to its territory.

Believing that protecting the innocent from undeserved harm is more important than punishing the guilty, we are often willing to endorse such acts or policies. But there are limits to how much punishment of the guilty we are willing to forgo to protect the innocent. If the crimes are great enough, we may judge that defense of neither the innocent nor the guilty would be morally preferable to defense of both. Imagine, for example, that an official must decide whether to prosecute or to cover up a mass murder by members of a certain battalion, and that he is tempted not to prosecute because he realizes that the reputations and careers of members of the battalion who did nothing wrong would be damaged by prosecution of the wrongdoers. Most of us think that he should prosecute. For the punishment of mass murder is a stronger moral imperative than the protection of some careers and reputations from undeserved tarnishing. In any case, the fact that an act would protect the guilty from deserved punishment can carry considerable weight in the moral assessment of that act, especially if the crime in question is a horrible one.

Deflecting or redirecting harm onto the innocent

Sometimes when we defend against harm, the harm is deflected or redirected onto others who do not deserve to suffer it. The defensive act may still be permissible, as when I surround my home with conspicuous security devices that redirect burglars' attention to my neighbors' less well-guarded homes. But sometimes such deflection (or redirection) of harm is wrong. This would seem to be so, for example, if the new victims are as innocent as those protected, if the harm they suffer is as great or greater, if their suffering this harm is probable enough, and if they are less able to defend themselves by alternative means. Thus I should not protect my yard from mudslides by building a wall that deflects them onto an impoverished orphanage. There is no simple general rule indicating precisely when redirection or deflection of harm is, and is not, permissible. But surely if an act of pure defense would deflect or redirect harm or risk onto other innocent parties, this must, to some degree, count against its permissibility.

Aggression made safer

Pure defense can make aggression more probable. The danger of suffering harm from defensive acts during an attack (or retaliatory acts after) is often a deterrent to undertaking aggression. Defense of an agent may, by reducing this danger, make him more likely to commit acts of aggression. Thus, a criminal with a bulletproof vest may feel safer committing crimes, and therefore commit more of them.

It may be objected that the possibility of defense making aggression safer cannot count against the morality of pure defense. For purely defensive acts are, by definition, not (predominantly) motivated by aggressive designs, and hence are not subject to this criticism. However, even if we ignore the possibility of aggression as a secondary motive, this objection errs by confusing the motives and effects of defensive acts.[21] The criminal's motive in obtaining the bulletproof vest might be purely defensive – to protect himself from gunfire while practicing his trade. But the predictable effect of his having it may be that he is willing to commit more crimes and is less likely to abandon his trade out of fear. Note also that the offensive acts that defensive measures make more likely need not even be deliberate. For instance, a man may know that he often starts brawls impulsively when drunk, and that aversion to the pain of being hit in the stomach sometimes prevents him from doing so. While sober, he may consider strengthening his stomach by exercise so as to lessen his pain when punched there during brawls. The act in question satisfies both criteria of being purely defensive, yet it may be wrong to do if its predictable effect is to make the man likely to start more barroom brawls.

By making aggression safer, pure defense may also make capitulation to unjust demands of aggressors more likely. For some potential victims, perceiving the futility of repelling or retaliating against the well-defended aggressor, will simply give in. Bodyguards, for example, will be less likely to defend their clients against armed kidnappers if the latter are wearing bulletproof vests. This example, and those of the vested criminal and the barroom brawler, illustrates the same general point: acts of self-protection, even if they work by deflection (or redirection) and are defensively motivated, can lead to aggression (or capitulation) by changing the payoff structure of situations faced by potential aggressors and victims.

Ineffectiveness

A purely defensive act aimed at protecting someone from harm may be ineffective and make it more likely that he will suffer harm. This can happen in at least two ways. Others may not perceive the defensive motive behind the act and may be provoked into aggressive or preemptive action. For example, a drug dealer who wears a bulletproof vest to all his meetings with other dealers may provoke suspicions that lead to violence against him. Defensive acts may also lead to overconfidence and recklessness on the agent's part. Our vested criminal may undertake one too many dangerous crimes, and our hard-stomached drinker may start a brawl that leaves him with a broken jaw.

But is the ineffectiveness of a defensive act a *moral* failing of that act? There are at least three ways in which it can be. First, if there are duties to oneself, defending oneself from wrongful attack is probably one of them. One may be violating such a duty if one chooses ineffective means of defense when other and better means are available. Second, some agents (e.g., governments) may have duties to defend other agents (e.g., their citizens). If they choose certain means of defense, when available evidence indicates that such means are ineffective or counterproductive, they may be acting irresponsibly. Third, ineffective defensive measures can provoke conflicts in which innocent third parties are harmed. Thus, the ineffectiveness of an act of pure defense, like the other features discussed in this section, can have direct bearing on the moral status of that act.

IV. STRATEGIC DEFENSE

We have seen that, from a moral perspective, pure defense is not always as pure as the driven snow (or even as pure as Ivory Snow).

Acts of pure defense with one or more of the four features discussed in section III may not be morally permissible, despite what (PD2) says. What are the implications of this with respect to strategic defense? This depends upon whether any of these four features characterize strategic defense. If none does, the Pure Defense Argument for SD can be saved by simply inserting into it a new version of the Pure Defense Principle that takes account of the four features. One such version is:

(PD3)   If an act is purely defensive of the innocent only, and is effective without deflecting (or redirecting) harm onto other innocent parties and without making aggression by the agent (or other protected parties) more likely, then it is permissible.

But this plausible normative principle fails to apply, and tells us nothing about the moral status of SD, if SD possesses some of our four features, as we now proceed to show that it does.

Consider first protection of the guilty. An SD system that effectively protects nuclear command and control centers would, in the event of a nuclear war wrongfully started by the nation possessing it, protect the guilty war-starters from retaliation. Furthermore, these people who launched a nuclear first strike out of malice, ambition, or recklessness would be killers on a scale unapproached in human history. Of course, it seems highly unlikely that deploying SD systems would lead to a nuclear attack by the side possessing them (especially if that is "our side"). Still, the future is uncertain. And once SD systems that protect those whose fingers are on the nuclear trigger are deployed, there will be some risk of some such people committing unpunished mass murder.

Strategic defenses may also redirect some of the danger of nuclear attack onto other innocent parties. If a nation deploys SD, it may well be rational for its nuclear opponents to retarget some of their strategic weapons in either of two ways. They may aim some weapons once pointed at military targets at cities to ensure that they maintain a credible second-strike assured destruction capability.[22] Or opponents may retarget weapons onto allies of the strategically defended nation, either to maximize efficiency in the face of apparently effective defenses or to use the innocent civilians of these allied nations as nuclear hostages now that the civilians of the strategically defended nation no longer serve that purpose as well as they once did.

Strategic defenses, if those who possess them believe they are effective (or believe that others will so regard them), could lead to aggression. Just as the West's possession of a nuclear monopoly led even Bertrand Russell to contemplate preventive war,[23] unilateral deployment of SD by a superpower might make its leaders feel safer and more prone to foreign military adventures. Or if both superpowers deployed SD systems, it could well make them more aggressive in their dealings with lesser nuclear powers. It is imaginable, for example, that a strategically defended Soviet Union might launch a strike against China's nuclear arsenal.[24]

Finally, deploying strategic defenses – at least in the foreseeable future – is probably an ineffective, indeed counterproductive, means of a superpower defending itself. As argued in section I, either superpower pursuing SD would be a bad prudential gamble because the defense achievable would be highly imperfect, it would produce distrust and dangerous countermeasures by the other side, and it might lead to overconfidence and reckless action on the part of the leaders of the strategically defended nation. Overall, SD would most likely diminish, rather than augment, the security of those whom it was intended to protect. And it would also increase the nuclear risks borne by those living outside the defended area – friends, foes, and neutrals alike.

The upshot of all this is that SD possesses, to some degree at least, each of the four features that render acts of pure defense morally questionable. As a result, the Pure Defense Argument for SD collapses: that argument must either appeal to a faulty normative premise, (PD2), or a defensible normative premise, (PD3), that does not apply to SD. This, in itself, does not prove SD to be morally wrong. There may be other and better moral arguments for it. But such arguments should be considered and evaluated on their own merits. Proponents of these arguments and of strategic defense should no longer be allowed to maintain the pretense of occupying the moral high ground simply because the programs they favor are purely defensive.

9. Nuclear coercion

Nuclear weapons function as a deterrent when the threat of their use prevents another nation from undertaking certain undesirable courses of action. Put bluntly, nuclear deterrence keeps your enemies from starting trouble. But nuclear weapons can also be used coercively. That is, they can be used to force another nation to do something it was not already doing (e.g., remove troops from a certain area) or to cease an action it is already engaged in (e.g., stop an invasion in progress). Nuclear coercion stops trouble after it has started or induces positive actions. While many believe that deterrence is the only rational use for nuclear weapons, some strategists advocate nuclear coercion under certain circumstances,[1] and it has been suggested that the United States has actually employed nuclear coercion on several occasions.[2] Furthermore, looked at from a purely logical point of view, nuclear coercion seems to make as much sense as nuclear deterrence. After all, if it is really undesirable for your enemies to do X, why shouldn't you try to stop their doing X by nuclear threats once they have begun as well as before they have started?

Actually, there is a very good reason for being much more circumspect about practicing nuclear coercion than about practicing nuclear deterrence. Nuclear deterrence is much more likely to work and is therefore considerably less dangerous. This is because of the now well-documented tendency of human individuals and groups to take greater risks to prevent losses than to achieve gains.[3] As a result of this tendency, people and nations are much more easily deterred

The first version of this chapter was written while I was supported by a fellowship for independent study and research from the National Endowment for the Humanities. I am grateful to the Endowment for its support, and to Steven Lee for his very helpful comments on an earlier draft.

than coerced and, other things being equal, nuclear deterrence is likely to be much less risky than nuclear coercion.

This chapter considers the most famous example of nuclear coercion: the incident in which the United States forced the Soviet Union to withdraw its nuclear-capable missiles from Cuba in October 1962. The placement of these missiles might have been the first stage in a Soviet attempt at nuclear coercion. In any case, the actions of both sides constituted the gravest crisis of the nuclear era, and exposed humankind to perhaps the greatest risks we have experienced in recorded history. Here I shall briefly discuss whether, in light of this, the U.S. government was morally justified in employing nuclear coercion as it did in the missile crisis.[4] Then I shall seek to explain why nuclear coercion was practiced in the absence of a valid moral justification and speculate about what this implies concerning the role of morality in nuclear politics.

I. MORALITY AND NUCLEAR DECISION MAKING

Decisions about the development, placement, and use of nuclear weapons (and other weapons whose employment may lead to the use of nuclear weapons) have potentially enormous effects on the well-being of humanity. Wrong decisions in this area could even lead to the extinction of our species. Such facts tempt those of us trained in moral philosophy to view the formulation and execution of nuclear arms policies as essentially moral problems. But nuclear weapons decisions are typically made by political leaders, who are greatly influenced by a variety of nonmoral (e.g., political, military, and personal) factors. This prompts a number of questions about the role of morality in nuclear decision making. Have moral considerations had any influence on nuclear weapons policy? If so, in what way? What factors, if any, have interfered with or restricted this influence? Might moral factors come to play a greater role in nuclear politics, and if so, how can moralists – philosophers, theologians, and others – contribute to their doing so?

To obtain tentative answers to some of these questions, I shall use an illustrative case study, the U.S. government's decision making during the Cuban Missile Crisis of October 1962. This incident has been selected for a number of reasons. Ample documentation of the decision process in this crisis, and even some theoretical studies of that process, are available. Also, it is clear that the decision makers in this situation were cognizant of the presence of the factor that renders all nuclear weapons decisions of great signficance: the attendant risks of nuclear war. There was also a public intervention by a prominent philosopher, Bertrand Russell, which might provide some lessons about moralists' direct influence on nuclear decisions. Finally, a variety of particular facts about the missile crisis decisions suggest some interesting hypotheses about nuclear politics in general.

The missile crisis was in many respects an atypical instance of nuclear-weapons decision making. It was unusually important (because of the risks and stakes involved), received extraordinary attention from high government officials, and involved the time pressures and psychological accompaniments of crisis (rather than routine) decision making. So we should be cautious in extrapolating its lessons to cover more "normal" decisions about nuclear weapons development and deployment. At the same time, it would be highly surprising if the tensions and pressures of the missile crisis completely altered the tendencies present in normal nuclear decision-making situations. For example, it is clear from the record that the general tendency of decision makers to reflect the attitudes and perspectives of their own units or departments carried over into the missile crisis: Secretary of Defense Robert S. McNamara initially viewed the Cuba-based missiles in purely strategic terms; the U.S. ambassador, to the United Nations, Adlai, E. Stevenson, recommended a diplomatic approach; and high military officials urged forceful military action.[5] For these reasons, it does not seem inappropriate to treat the missile crisis as a source of suggestive hypotheses about nuclear weapons decisions and the role played in their formulation by moral considerations.

I begin by briefly reviewing the events of the missile crisis, including incidents of particular relevance to our concern with moral influences. I then proceed to discuss what should most puzzle moralists about U.S. decision making: that avoidance of nuclear war (and risk thereof) was not given even greater priority and weight. A solution to this puzzle is then proposed, which rests on the claim that political decision makers and moralists typically approach decision situations with different "mind-sets" – classes of background assumptions, ways of conceptualizing alternatives, and so forth. A review of the significant role moral considerations did have in missile-crisis decision making follows, in which the deontological form of such considerations is emphasized and discussed. Finally, I attempt to distill from all this some useful lessons about the possibilities for, limits on, and means of, future moral influence on nuclear decision making.

II. EVENTS OF THE MISSILE CRISIS

Soon after taking office as president of the United States, John F. Kennedy approved a CIA-organized invasion of Castro's Cuba by armed exiles. The "Bay of Pigs" landing of April 1961 was quickly crushed by Cuban forces. This fiasco caused extreme domestic and international political embarrassment to the new administration; and at the June 1961 summit meeting in Vienna, although Kennedy admitted the incident had been a mistake, Soviet leader Nikita Khrushchev reportedly "bullied" him about it.[6]

As the congressional elections of November 1962 approached, Kennedy was continually attacked by Republicans for being soft on Cuba. One senator charged that the Soviets were installing missiles in Cuba, and while the available intelligence estimates and the assurances of Soviet diplomats indicated this was not so, the president made two public warnings in September 1961 that the introduction of "offensive ground-to-ground" missiles would not be tolerated by the United States.[7]

Nevertheless, photographs of Cuba taken by U-2 surveillance planes on October 14 and analyzed on October 15 revealed that the Soviets were lying: medium-and intermediate-range ballistic missile sites were under construction. The president was notified the morning of October 16 and immediately called a meeting of an ad hoc group of high-level advisers, an Executive Committee that continued to meet frequently throughout the crisis, at first in the strictest secrecy. They initially considered six categories of alternative responses: doing nothing, a private diplomatic approach to the Soviets, a private diplomatic approach to Castro, a naval blockade of Cuba, a "surgical" air strike against the missile bases, and a full-scale invasion of Cuba.[8] Soon they narrowed the choices to two, blockade or air strike. Despite initial leanings toward the latter, a consensus for blockade developed, and the president decided on this course on October 20. The main considerations that apparently influenced this decision were that (a) an air strike would kill Soviet military personnel and risk immediate Soviet escalation, (b) an air strike would – as Under Secretary of State George Ball and Attorney General Robert

Kennedy (the president's brother) emphasized – be a Pearl Harbor in reverse, and would go against American traditions, (c) an air strike would not certainly destroy all the missiles,[9] and (d) the blockade was a first step that could be followed by stronger action if necessary.[10] U.S. officials were well aware, however, that even the blockade was dangerous and could lead to nuclear war between the superpowers.

In preparation for public announcement of the blockade, the administration sent emissaries to major allies, prepared for a presentation to the U.N. Security Council, and made arrangements for an Organization of American States meeting to endorse the blockade, thus giving it a degree of legitimacy under international law.[11] In addition, military moves were made to enforce the blockade, to prepare for a possible attack on Cuba, and to increase strategic readiness. After informing, but not consulting with, key congressional leaders, the president announced the existence of the Cuban missiles and the naval "quarantine" of weapons shipments to Cuba in a national address.[12] He had communicated the same message to the Soviets by diplomatic channels an hour earlier.

Less than two days later, the blockade was officially put into effect. The Soviets' immediate public and private response was that they would defy the blockade which they considered illegal and provocative.[13] Both sides apparently put their strategic military forces on alert. Bertrand Russell sent telegrams to Kennedy and Khrushchev urging restraint by each, but condemning only the actions of the United States.[14] Chairman Khrushchev responded to Russell publicly, calling for a summit meeting and blaming the United States, which he compared to a robber that needed to be taught a lesson.[15] President Kennedy also answered Russell personally, claiming that "your attention might well be directed to the burglars rather than those who caught the burglars."[16] Meanwhile, the extreme anxiety of U.S. officials was eased somewhat when half the Soviet ships on their way to Cuba stopped outside the quarantine line. The president tried to manage the blockade carefully, drawing back its radius to give the Soviets more time to think, letting through a Soviet tanker, and first stopping and searching a chartered vessel of neutral registry. But U-2 photos showed the missile construction on Cuba proceeding even faster than before and indicated that some missiles would soon be operational. Tension grew again when a U-2 was downed over Cuba (Kennedy canceled previous orders for retaliation to such an occurrence), another strayed over the USSR as a result of navigational error, and pressure for an air strike grew within the administration.

Two letters from Khrushchev on October 26 and 27 offered different terms of settlement for inspected removal of the missiles. The first, a rambling personal message, called only for a U.S. pledge not to invade Cuba.[17] The second, more formal letter demanded the removal of U.S. missiles in Turkey as well.[18] (President Kennedy had earlier ordered the dismantling of these missiles, but diplomatic complications had prevented this from being done.) Robert Kennedy's suggestion to accept the more generous proposal of the first message, while ignoring the second, was adopted and carried out. In addition, the president's brother personally told the Soviet ambassador to the United States, Anatoly F. Dobrynin, on the night of October 27, that the United States would attack the missiles unless, by the next day, the Soviets agreed to remove them. He also indicated that the president had previously ordered the missiles in Turkey removed and expected they would be gone soon after the crisis.[19] The next day Chairman Khrushchev agreed to withdraw the missiles under U.N. inspection, given the U.S. pledge not to invade Cuba.[20]

The missiles were withdrawn but had to be inspected on exiting ships, as Castro would not allow inspection in Cuba. A further snag concerned Illyushin bombers given to Castro. The Cuban leader initially refused the Soviets' request to return them, but President Kennedy, who considered them covered by the U.S. – Soviet agreement, threatened to attack them if they were not removed. On November 19 Castro gave in to Soviet entreaties, and the last Illyushins left Cuba on December 6, ending the crisis.[21]

III. UNJUSTIFIED RISKS

The actions of the U.S. government during the Cuban Missile Crisis risked a large-scale nuclear war with the Soviet Union. Given the magnitude of such a possible disaster, how could the risk possibly be justified? This question later worried Robert Kennedy, a central participant in the crisis, as well as some critics of administration conduct during the crisis.[22] In particular, a moralist looking at the record of U.S. decision making is likely to wonder why more serious consideration was not given to the more pacific alternatives that might have avoided the risk of war, such as doing nothing or making a private diplomatic approach to Khrushchev.

We cannot dispel the moralist's puzzlement by dismissing the president and his advisers as evil or irrational men; it is evident from the record that they were conscious of their awesome moral responsibility, were greatly concerned with doing the right thing, and planned their actions with considerable deliberation, ingenuity, and care. Nor will it resolve the matter to claim that U.S. decision makers were concerned only about the American people, while the moralist is concerned about the well-being of all people.[23] For key officials did worry about the effects of their acts on non-Americans as well,[24] and, in any case, either concern would justify placing the highest priority on nuclear war avoidance.

With this in mind, we may restate the moralist's puzzle. Why, during the missile crisis, did the Kennedy administration – composed of rational, decent, and well-informed men, and acting after careful deliberation – undertake unjustified risks of nuclear war? In this section, I will consider four ways of seeking to dissolve this puzzle by arguing that the risks were, in the circumstances, morally justified. These are based on the respective claims that (a) the risks were not significant, (b) there was no alternative, (c) all alternatives involved worse risks, and (d) the government followed an appropriate rational principle for risk taking under uncertainty.

Was there significant risk?

Perhaps the imposition of the Cuban blockade would have been morally justified if it had entailed only a small or insignificant risk of nuclear war with the Soviets. But were the risks small? This is not the opinion that knowledgeable observers and participants expressed after the crisis. British Prime Minister Harold Macmillan later said, "the Cuban crisis . . . was the week of most strain I can ever remember in my long life."[25] Bertrand Russell similarly reported that "never before in the course of a long life have I experienced anything comparable to the tense anxiety of those crucial hours."[26] Khrushchev spoke of "our [the Kremlin leaders'] anxiety, which was intense."[27] This war anxiety was behaviorally reflected in preparations by Soviet diplomats in New York to burn secret papers.[28] Secretary of State Dean Rusk, a member of the Executive Committee, said to Under Secretary of State George Ball the morning after the president announced the blockade, "We have won a considerable victory. You and I are still alive."[29] Robert Kennedy wrote of a time during the crisis when "the feeling grew . . . that a direct military confrontation between the two great nuclear powers was inevitable,"[30] and of his brother, the president, that "the possibility of the destruction of mankind was always in his mind."[31] That the president viewed this possibility as genuine and of significant probability is evidenced by his having encouraged his wife to move closer to government war shelters,[32] and having later told his close adviser Theodore Sorensen that the odds of war had then seemed to him "somewhere between one out of three and even."[33]

It might be replied that the participants' perceptions of the risks of the missile crisis were wrong. Since both sides feared war and wished to avoid it, the likelihood of its actual outbreak was of necessity extremely low. But historical precedent suggests otherwise. World War I began, as President Kennedy was well aware, with neither side wanting it.[34] And there were a number of not implausible scenarios by which the Cuban events might get out of control and escalate into nuclear war. (The president was so concerned about one of these involving U.S. missiles in Turkey that he ordered those missiles defused at a key point in the crisis.)[35] In fact, certain incidents occurred that could well have set off escalation but for luck and caution on both sides – the U-2 downing over Cuba, another U-2 straying over Soviet territory, and U.S. Navy ships forcing Soviet submarines to surface (without the president's knowledge).[36] At the same time, at least one U.S. military leader was pressing for the use of nuclear weapons,[37] and it is not implausible to speculate that some of his Soviet counterparts may have been doing likewise. It thus seems clear that there was a real and substantial risk of escalation to nuclear war, had the Soviets rejected the ultimatum delivered to Dobrynin and had the United States carried out its planned attack in response.

A final piece of evidence concerning the real dangers of the missile crisis is the behavior of the superpowers in the more than two decades since then. Despite their continued political, ideological, and military rivalry, the United States and the Soviet Union have managed to avoid direct confrontations between their military forces in any part of the world, have generally taken great care to do so, and have sought a partial détente with one another. This cautious behavior is frequently attributed to a desire to avoid crises like that of 1962.[38] The powerful aversion to such crises on both sides is strong evidence that, even in hindsight and from the perspective of considerable temporal distance, the governments of both superpowers regard the missile crisis as having been fraught with extreme danger.

Perhaps President Kennedy's estimate of a one-third to one-half chance of war arising from the missile crisis was a considerable overestimate. Given, however, the testimony of decision makers on both sides, the cautious behavior of the superpowers since in avoiding military confrontations, the fact that historically there have been wars that neither side wanted, the fact that a high U.S. military official wanted to use nuclear weapons during the crisis, and the fact that some military events did get out of the leaders' control during the crisis, it is clear that the U.S. course of blockade followed by ultimatum and, if necessary, conventional attack, carried a not insignificant risk of resulting in nuclear war with the Soviet Union. What was it about the nature of the circumstances that might have justified pursuing a course of action that entailed such risks?

Were there alternatives?

One possible justification for pursuing a dangerous course of action is that there are no alternatives. And Executive Committee members often spoke in language suggesting that this was so during the missile crisis. For example, Robert Kennedy used modal phrases such as "action was *required*," "the U.S. *could not* accept what the Russians had done," and "he [the president] would *have to* do something."[39] And Sorensen said that Kennedy's previous "pledge to act was *unavoidable*" and "action was *imperative*."[40]

Yet it is clear that there were alternatives and that inaction was among them. In particular, at least two more pacific and initially less dangerous alternatives than blockade were proposed and considered at early meetings of the Executive Committee. Secretary of Defense McNamara initially took the view that no action was a viable alternative, since the missiles in Cuba did not really much alter the strategic balance.[41] And private diplomacy *might* have caused Khrushchev to remove the missiles without the risk of a public and military confrontation.

Perhaps, however, these alternatives were not within the power of the president and his advisers to pursue effectively, for, as the president and his brother once mused, the president might have been impeached and removed from office if he had not taken strong action.[42] This is a possibility, of course, but hardly a certainty since a

U.S. president had never been removed from office, and a less war-risking course might still have resulted in the removal of the missiles from Cuba. Hence, while alternatives more pacific than blockade may have carried their own risks and disadvantages, they were genuine alternatives.

Were the alternatives more dangerous?

The most plausible justification for the blockade of Cuba is that the more pacific alternatives of inaction and private diplomacy were, in the long run, even more risky. Forms of this justification are suggested by some of the U.S. decision makers and by knowledgeable analysts.[43] They appeal to two sources of long-run danger: changes in the international political situation and domestic political changes leading to more dangerous U.S. policies.

President Kennedy believed that if the United States did not act strongly in response to the Cuban missiles, U.S. prestige would suffer, the Atlantic Alliance would be in danger, and – most important – Soviet leaders would doubt our willingness to defend our interests and would engage in other aggressions even more likely to lead to war than a confrontation over Cuba.[44] But this belief derived from several questionable assumptions. First, Kennedy viewed the placement of missiles in Cuba as primarily a test of American will.[45] Thoughtful American analysts have suggested instead that stopgap defense of the USSR against a U.S. first strike strategic capacity and/or defense of Cuba were more likely motives.[46] Second, there is no evidence of any consideration of other ways of shoring up U.S. credibility that might have posed less of a direct challenge to the Soviets – for example, using the missiles in Cuba as a domestic justification for greatly increased defense spending, or sending more troops to Europe. Third is the assumption that private diplomacy would not get the missiles out of Cuba and would allow the Soviets to delay and play to world opinion. But, like the blockade, private diplomacy did not preclude stronger action later, and it would have allowed Khrushchev to yield more gracefully. It would thereby have minimized the danger of irrational action by an embarrassed adversary caught by surprise in public. Nor would private diplomacy have precluded offers and ultimata of the sort that eventually ended the crisis. Given the weaknesses in these three key assumptions, it seems highly doubtful that pursuing a more pacific path would have posed graver risk than did the blockade-ultimatum-attack strategy that was actually pursued.

Nuclear war could have resulted in another way from the administration following a more cautious policy. The president might have been politically weakened or even removed from office for being too "soft," or a Republican congress might have been elected that would apply irresistible pressures for future dangerous U.S. actions.[47] But removal from office would have resulted in a Democratic successor – Vice President Johnson. And a Republican congress, if elected, could not have forced Kennedy – if he stayed in office – to undertake foreign policy moves that he considered dangerous and provocative. So it is doubtful that this path would have led to a stronger probability of war than the risks encountered as a result of the blockade.

Finally, it may be worth noting that the blockade, too, may have carried long-range as well as short-run risks of war. Some believe that the Soviets' public retreat in Cuba led to their massive invest-ment of resources in a strategic buildup over the two decades since.[48] If this buildup has increased the risk of nuclear war, such increase might be charged partly to our failure to adopt a less challenging posture toward the missiles in Cuba.

In summary, the blockade (and threatened air strike) may con-ceivably have been less likely to lead to nuclear war than the more pacific alternatives. But the arguments for this are so weak that one must regard the quick dismissal of these alternatives as unjustified and hard to comprehend, if we view the decision makers as having been engaged in anything like rational, moral decision making.

Rational disaster avoidance

The Executive Committee was operating under what I have else-where called *two-dimensional uncertainty*:[49] not only did they not know the outcomes of the available courses of action, they did not even have reliable estimates of the probabilities and utilities of the various possible outcomes of each course of action. Further, they believed any alternative might have resulted in a disastrous out-come: doing nothing or warning the Soviets privately might have led to the missiles staying in Cuba with a consequent loss of prestige, credibility, and strategic advantage for the United States, while stronger actions (including blockade) might have led to nuclear war with the Soviets. But the probabilities were not the same. Severe political losses seemed likely to follow from choosing a pacific course, while the blockade may have risked nuclear war with a probability of one-third to one-half, or less. So their choice seemed to be between a greater likelihood of a lesser disaster (severe political-strategic losses) and a smaller risk of a greater disaster (nuclear war). In Chapter 3, I argued that for *some* choices of this form under two-dimensional uncertainty, it is rational (or, at least, not irrational) to choose the alternative that maximizes one's chances of avoiding disastrous outcomes.[50] Would it not follow that American decision makers acted in a purely rational and justified manner in running a smaller risk of nuclear war rather than a more probable risk of severe loss of U.S. prestige and credibility?

It does not follow, because there are restrictions on my principle that recommends maximizing one's chances of disaster avoidance under two-dimensional uncertainty. This principle can be plausibly applied only when the disasters risked are of roughly the same order of magnitude. (Otherwise the unknown but expected probability gains will not offset the risk of bringing about the more disastrous outcome.) But it is doubtful that a loss in U.S. prestige and credibility is a disaster of even roughly the same order of magnitude as large-scale nuclear war, whether we measure in terms of the welfare of the U.S. population or of the world population. Missile-crisis decision makers might, then, have (implicitly) followed the principle of minimizing the probability of a disastrous outcome. But, if they did so, it was a misuse of the principle, which could not appropriately serve to justify their choice.

Running unnecessary risks

The most plausible justifications of U.S. government actions during the missile crisis are that these minimized the risk of war and/or of other disastrous outcomes. In the last two subsections, I have pointed-ed out some glaring weaknesses in these justifications. Nevertheless, another fact clinches my case that we cannot plausibly view their deliberations as a process of moral decision making: the fact that the president ran *unnecessary* risks of nuclear war by prolonging the crisis to obtain marginally better terms of settlement. When it still looked as if the Soviets might challenge the blockade, he rejected the idea of an immediate summit meeting with Khrushchev, because "before a summit took place, . . . the President wanted to have some cards in our own hand."[51] Later, instead of accepting the formal Soviet offer of withdrawal of the missiles in return for a U.S. pledge not to invade Cuba and the removal of the missiles in Turkey, Kennedy chose the riskier course of an ultimatum combined with, at most, an implicit promise about the Turkey-based missiles. Finally, after the basic settlement he threatened to restart the crisis with military action to remove the Illyushin bombers, which before the crisis the administration had accepted as posing no significant danger to the United States.[52]

In the case of the bombers, Kennedy perhaps ran no significant risk of war, as it was clear that Khrushchev, who had already given in on the missiles, would not be inclined to resist.[53] But the rejection of the idea of a summit and the refusal of an explicit pledge on the missiles in Turkey came at the two points in the crisis when war fears were greatest on the American side.[54] Nor would Kennedy have risked or lost much by acting in a more conciliatory manner. He had already ordered the missiles in Turkey dismantled, and ended up making something very close to an implicit promise, through his brother, to remove them (which he did). Nor by holding out on this point was he establishing the principle that he would concede nothing under pressure from the Soviets; for, under pressure, he did pledge not to invade Cuba. We may conclude that by holding out on certain particular points – especially the missiles in Turkey – the president probably ran unnecessary risks of nuclear war.

The puzzle

We have seen that given their perception of the risks of nuclear war involved in blockade and military action, the missile-crisis decision makers should have selected – or at least given much more lengthy and serious consideration to – the more pacific alternatives. This seems the relatively straightforward conclusion of a moral analysis. Given that they were not evil or unintelligent persons, and that they appreciated the risks and consequences of nuclear war, why did American leaders act otherwise? This is the moralist's puzzle.

IV. MIND-SETS, MORALS, AND POLITICS

I have suggested that President Kennedy and his key advisers were wrong to reject, especially so quickly, the more pacific possible responses to the placement of Soviet missiles in Cuba.[55] Yet I believe that overall, Kennedy performed admirably in the situation, and that we were fortunate to have had him at the head of the U.S. government at the time.[56] This seeming paradox is understandable when we recall that Kennedy was a politician making a political decision. In such a position, he was atypically sensitive to the relevant moral issues and took extraordinary care in the formulation and execution of his policies, because of his perception of the enormous stakes involved and the dangers of the situation. In saying this, I am not simply adding a wrinkle to the old charge that Kennedy was just another calculating politician, making his decisions to help himself and his party in the next election.[57] (The added wrinkle would be that Kennedy was *less* like this than most politicians.) For in my view, international politics had as much, or more, to do with Kennedy's decisions than did domestic politics. And, even more important, in speaking of Kennedy's decisions as "political," I am not referring to the sort of ends he was deliberately trying to promote, but to the general *mind-set* with which he approached the decision.

This concept of a mind-set is the key to understanding the missile-crisis decision making. It refers to the general way of thinking and to the background assumptions about both the world and the making of decisions that decision makers bring to a problem situation. A decision maker's mind-set includes the ways in which she tends to (a) formulate and define a problem, (b) search for, define, select, and discard various alternatives for action or solution, (c) view certain constraints on action as absolute or nearly so, and (d) interpret the world, especially the acts and motives of other agents. It is obvious that people's mind-sets often influence the decisions they reach without the people themselves being aware that, or how, they do so. Individuals who are reflective and self-aware, and take the time and trouble to step back and think about their worldview and methods of decision making, may be able to discern certain features of their own mind-sets. But, more typically, we bring our mind-sets to our decisions without being aware of their existence or their natures, and they influence the way we structure and decide issues without our even being aware that this is occurring.

When individuals or groups with different mind-sets consider a given situation or problem, they are likely to reach different conclusions, and may well be puzzled, confused, or angered by the other party's stance. For each side's mind-set is so natural and leads so directly to its own conclusions that, in an important sense, one side cannot understand what the other side is thinking and doing. Defining the problem and steps to its solution in its own particular way, and implicitly assuming that the other party must see the same problem and solution, one party can only interpret the other party's resistance as a symptom of irrationality, craziness, or perversity.

An interesting example of this sort of tension between mind-sets arose at a conference on philosophy and psychoanalysis, the proceedings of which were subsequently published.[58] In one paper, a philosopher sympathetic to psychoanalysis struck a discordant note by analyzing the unconscious reasons that philosophers hold certain metaphysical positions.[59] (No doubt to many philosophers at the conference, this paper seemed at worst an *ad hominem* irrelevancy, and at best a gross instance of the genetic fallacy.)[60] But the interesting point, for our purposes, is that it was a clash between rather different mind-sets. Each side defined the question at issue and sought its solution in terms of the mind-set typical to its discipline. Hence, most of the philosophers applied logical analysis to the activities of the psychoanalyst, while their colleague adopted a psychoanalytic viewpoint and sought after the unconscious explanation of their activities. Each may have been right from his own point of view, but each portrayed the other's analysis as a piece of logical, or psychological, pathology. But (unconsciously) structuring the key issues differently and adopting different methodological approaches to them, each side was unable to understand fully and appreciate what the other was doing.

A less extreme, but nonetheless significant, clash of mind-sets creates the moralist's puzzle about the missile crisis. The moral analyst finds it difficult to understand or appreciate the actions of the Kennedy administration, because he does not share the mind-set of the political decision maker. This is the mind-set that determined the quick dismissal of the moralist's preferred pacific alternatives.

President Kennedy and most of the men around him shared a basic mind-set toward making foreign and military policy decisions. This mind-set was fundamentally "political" in the sense that it was in many ways typical of the mind-set of political actors, and its content and structure were largely determined by its usual function of guiding agents to the satisfactory solution of political problems. Three distinguishable elements of the Kennedy administration mind-set contributed to the way it dealt with the missile crisis, including, in particular, its quick rejection of the more pacific alternatives. These elements concern international politics, domestic politics, and personal politics.

International politics

The missile crisis was primarily an international political crisis; during it, President Kennedy's main concern, other than avoiding nuclear war, was to uphold the international political position of the United States.[61] The president and his advisers shared a certain mind-set about international politics as they approached the issue of Soviet missiles in Cuba. For our purposes, the most important features of that mind-set were certain norms concerning how great powers should or must act in international affairs, and certain beliefs about the motives of adversary nations.

The norms of great-power behavior that seem to have greatly influenced American decision makers were that great powers (a) should not suddenly upset the status quo balance of power in the world, (b) should not launch surprise attacks on much smaller powers, and (c) should (even *must*) actively resist challenges to the balance of power and their own credibility. The first norm is reflected in the administration's view of what was, at bottom, wrong with the Soviet's surreptitious placing of missiles in Cuba. In his address announcing the blockade, the president described the Soviet's action as a "provocative and unjustified change in the status quo,"[62] and insiders reported that this was his private view as well.[63] The second norm lay at the heart of George Ball's and Robert Kennedy's arguments against an air strike on Cuba, which apparently had great influence on the president and others.[64] The third norm was accepted by the administration not only as a reason to respond forcefully to the Cuban missiles,[65] but also as a reason for avoiding actions that would pose a provocative challenge to the Soviets, such as military acts likely to produce Soviet casualties.[66]

Notice that these norms of international behavior restricted the administration's options on both ends of the scale of imaginable responses. The Soviets had blatantly attempted to violate the first norm, and – by virtue of the third norm – this called for a strong (i.e., more than diplomatic) response. But the second norm counted heavily against precipitate military action directed at tiny Cuba. United States action was also influenced by its leaders' perception of

Soviet motives. The president and his advisers saw the Cuban missiles as a political challenge and a test of American will.[67] Instead, Soviet motives may actually have been primarily defensive – against another invasion of Cuba and against the Americans' newly advertised first-strike capacity.[68] The Kennedy administration, not planning such an invasion or strategic attack, would naturally have been more inclined to see serious aggressiveness behind Khrushchev's move. The traditional pattern of viewing one's own international conduct as benign and one's adversary's as threatening doubtless contributed to the quick U.S. decision to go beyond acceptance or diplomacy in its reaction to the missiles in Cuba.

Domestic politics

Political leaders depend for their continued power and effectiveness on the support of key groups within their countries. This necessity of maintaining domestic political support is an accepted background assumption of decision making, so that political leaders are strongly disinclined to undertake actions that cannot command signficant domestic support or that would cause damaging criticism. And since staying in power and remaining an effective leader is generally a dominant personal goal as well as a necessary means for accomplishing one's policy aims, political leaders habitually and automatically tend to avoid loss of support and power.

Once we note this tendency, which is part of the ingrained mindset of politicians, we can recognize that the domestic political situation in the United States influenced and imposed constraints upon decision making in the missile crisis, even while we reject as misleading the charge that Kennedy manufactured the crisis – or exploited it – for domestic political reasons.[69] Domestic politics influenced the administration mainly in a negative way: rather than promising advantages or encouraging calculations of domestic gains and losses, it seems to have made administration officials perceive their options as more limited than they really were. In particular, it made the president and his advisers regard the more pacific alternatives as unfeasible, partly because they would not satisfy strong domestic audiences and their pressures.

Prior to the crisis there had been strong Republican criticisms of Kennedy for not taking action against Cuba, and the president had issued two public warnings against Soviet missiles in Cuba. When the missiles were discovered, the president's "pledge to act was unavoidable."[70] As one noted analyst put it,

> This is a classic illustration of the effect of the "backdrop" – in this instance, the opposition and congressional committees – on policymaking in a crisis. . . . [T]he administration was pinned down on a response to Soviet offensive missiles in Cuba, and the President's *options were narrowed.*[71]

Two other incidents demonstrate the administration's sense of having "no options" because of domestic politics. Another Executive Committee member passed Sorensen a note indicating that operable missiles in Cuba would produce Republican congressional gains that "would completely paralyze our ability to react sensibly and coherently to further Soviet advances."[72] And the Kennedy brothers felt the president had to act to avoid impeachment.[73]

Thus domestic politics did seem to affect missile-crisis decision making, but not in the way critics charge. Kennedy did not choose blockade to obtain domestic political gains or to avoid domestic political losses. Instead, domestic politics apparently influenced what the president and his advisers perceived to be their feasible options. They operated according to an axiom of the typical political mind-set, which says "alternatives are not real options and should be eliminated from consideration, if they lack domestic support and seriously risk loss of power." As a result, they set aside the moralist's favored options of no action and private diplomacy.

Personal politics

Political leaders are human beings. And insofar as they deal with other political leaders, there is bound to be a personal element in their official relationships and interactions. We all have certain ways of interpreting the behavior of those with whom we come in contact – ways of reading their motives, responding to their overtures, and influencing their subsequent behavior toward us. These tendencies, in political leaders, form part of their mind-set for "personal politics," interactions with other politicians. When the politicians in question are heads of states acting in official or semiofficial capacities, the personal interaction between them may well be expressed in and through governmental decisions and policies.

So it was, apparently, in the missile crisis. President Kennedy, who had tried to improve U.S. – Soviet relations and establish them on a rational and predictable basis, apparently felt personally betrayed by the clandestine introduction of Soviet missiles into Cuba.[74] He felt that he himself was being challenged and tested by Chairman Khrushchev, who had already bullied him at Vienna. In fact, his initial reaction upon learning of the missiles is reported to have been "He can't do this to *me*."[75] Thus, Kennedy's mind-set on the problem of the missiles included the tendency to see the issue partly in personal terms, as well as the belief that a personal challenge must be answered. As one commentator put it:

> Kennedy had worried, both after the Bay of Pigs and after the Vienna meeting with Khrushchev, that the Chairman might have misjudged his mettle. This time Kennedy determined to stand fast. . . . The nonforcible paths – avoiding military measures, resorting instead to diplomacy – could not have been more irrelevant to his problem.[76]

At the same time, the personal aspects of the situation may have constrained Kennedy from resorting to a more dangerous action than blockade. He was influenced by his brother's appeal that the United States should not suddenly attack a small nation and inevitably kill many of its innocent citizens.[77] Perhaps, to the extent he saw the issue in personal terms, the president was as determined to resist becoming a bully himself as he was to resist Khrushchev's apparent bullying.

Contrasting mind-sets

We have seen how elements of the mind-set of the president and his advisers involving international, domestic, and personal politics converged to bring about what puzzles the moralist – the early elimination of the nonmilitary options. The Soviets had violated the perceived norms of great-power behavior, and this demanded of the United States – as another great power – a forceful response. In addition, the domestic political atmosphere and the personal challenge by Khrushchev to Kennedy made an acquiescent or pacific response unthinkable.

As noted above, the possessors of a mind-set are typically unaware of it. It consists of precepts, rules, assumptions, and

schemas for interpreting reality that are generally useful or necessary for arriving at decisions. Since one sees the world through one's
mind-set, but usually does not see the mind-set itself, the rules and
assumptions constituting it are seldom questioned, analyzed, or
reexamined at the time of decision making. This is true even for
exceptionally important decisions. Thus, President Kennedy saw the
missile crisis as sufficiently important to call for special procedures
of decision and execution, such as formation of an ad hoc Executive
Committee and personal direction of military moves.[78] But he did
not think to call for a critical reexamination of the fundamental precepts and assumptions of the political mind-set that he shared with
his top advisers.[79] This oversight is understandable in view of the
time pressures of the crisis, the difficulty of even being aware of
having a mind-set, and so on. But it is also rightfully criticizable.
One wants to say that with so much at stake, decision makers should
exercise special care to take as little as possible for granted, to question all vital assumptions, and not to eliminate alternative courses of
action from consideration too soon.

Consider, for example, the Kennedy brothers' reaction to the
observation that the president might be impeached if he did not act
forcefully to remove the missiles. They had been worrying about the
dangers of military action, but possible impeachment served as a
final and clinching argument that settled the matter in their minds.[80]
They apparently accepted the simple rule that any option that leads
to (a substantial chance of) impeachment is to be rejected. It is
interesting that a similar but broader rule was invoked by another
Executive Committee member, McGeorge Bundy, in a recent discussion of Truman's decision to build the hydrogen bomb. After
acknowledging that the United States would not have lost significant
ground in the arms race if it had waited to see if the Soviets would
make the first move on the hydrogen bomb, Bundy wrote:

> No American president could have avoided the heaviest kind
> of political damage if a unilateral decision to stay out of the
> thermonuclear race had been followed by an apparent Soviet
> breakthrough. On the issue as presented, I think the president
> made the right choice.[81]

Thus, three members of the Executive Committee, the Kennedy
brothers and National Security Adviser Bundy, shared the assumption that an option that leads to the heaviest political damage, such as

serious risk of impeachment, is itself a decisive reason for rejecting it. This seems a reasonable assumption in normal circumstances, since a president or other politician suffering such damage is likely thereby to have his most important personal and political goals shattered. But when undergoing the risk of massive political damage would or might save humanity from tremendous danger – a substantial risk of holocaust during the missile crisis or the dangers of an ongoing nuclear arms race in the case of the H-bomb decision – it clearly seems wrong simply to follow the normal political rule, rather than seriously to weigh and compare the risks of the alternative courses of action.

Let us compare the more mundane situation of a college teacher who wants to keep her job. In normal circumstances, the fact that a certain action – for example, giving a student a much higher grade than deserved to improve chances of medical school admission – might well lead to loss of her job would count as a decisive reason for her not undertaking it. But suppose she had very good reason to believe that this student would kill himself if, and only if, he did not receive the higher grade. Then the danger of job loss would no longer be an obviously decisive consideration, and the teacher should open the matter up to serious moral deliberation (including, perhaps, searching for new alternatives that would preserve all the major values at stake). If she does not, but blindly follows the normal rule in this abnormal situation, she may rightly be accused of irrational "rule worship,"[82] as may the members of the Executive Committee who did not recognize humanity-risking decisions as abnormal enough to call for a reexamination of deep-seated political rules.

This moral criticism of the missile-crisis decision makers does not show that they were bad people. They were not. Instead it reflects the difference in the mind-sets of the moralist and the political decision maker. The moralist has an analytical-critical mind-set that includes the principle of pausing to reconsider carefully one's own presuppositions and assumptions when one is confronted by a decision situation carrying abnormally large stakes. Differences in mind-sets result from differences in experience and training, and also differences in function. Political decision makers are constantly making practical decisions, and hence they generally need a relatively simple, useful mind-set that can repeatedly and effectively aid them in that task.

It may be useful to draw an analogy between the moralist's relation to the political decision maker and the latter's relation to military subordinates. Robert Kennedy writes of the military advice given during the missile crisis:

> President Kennedy was disturbed by this inability [of representatives of the military] to look beyond the limited military field. When we talked about this later, he said we had to remember that they were trained to fight and wage war – that was their life. Perhaps we would feel even more concerned if they were always opposed to using arms or military means – for if they would not be willing, who would be? But this experience pointed out for us all the importance of civilian direction and control and the importance of raising probing questions to military recommendations.[83]

We have seen that the moralist looking at the missile crisis is likely to have a view of the political mind-set that is similar to President Kennedy's view of the military mind-set. To the moralist, since the politician often does not look enough beyond the political field to the wider (and moral) significance of his actions, "the importance of raising probing questions" about political decisions must be stressed.

We may use this analogy between the politician's attitude toward the military and the moralist's attitude toward the politician to clarify further our central claim about different parties possessing different mind-sets. One possible way to look at the relationship between mind-sets is to view them as nesting within one another. According to this view, the military mind-set is a simplified and specialized subset of the political mind-set, which is in turn a simplified and specialized subset of the moral mind-set. This means that the principles of decision embodied in the military mind-set are simplified rules of thumb guiding military decision makers toward correct or adequate decisions about "the right thing to do" in most situations they are likely to face, while the political mind-set embodies more complex rules containing various exception clauses and reflecting sensitivity to a wider range of relevant considerations. The moralists' mind-set is broader still, in the sense that it subsumes political rules of thumb under yet more complex systems of moral rules, pays attention to more relevant considerations (e.g., the well-being of humanity instead of the well-being of a nation), and employs the metaprinciples that prescribe adopting a critical stance toward one's own principles and assumptions. One implication of this view of the relationship of different mind-sets is that military, political, and moral decision makers are all really trying to decide the same thing – what it is morally right to do – and are simply using more or less sophisticated methods.

I believe, however, that the nesting view is misleading in certain respects and fails to convey accurately the relationship between moral and political mind-sets. It is better to think of different mind-sets as overlapping in the sense that only some of the various assumptions and principles embodied in them may appropriately be viewed as more complicated (or simpler) versions of one another. Three reasons make this overlapping view preferable to the nesting view. First, it allows for the fact that the moralists' mind-set embodies controversial substantive principles and assumptions as well as the unassailable metaprinciple of critical self-examination. It is not obvious that in a world of independent sovereign states, such substantive principles (e.g., those requiring substantial consideration of the interests of all affected) should govern the actions of national decision makers. But the nesting view, in treating the moralist's mind-set as the all-encompassing one at the top of the hierarchy, suggests that its components are beyond criticism from the viewpoint of other mind-sets.

The second disadvantage of the nesting view also flows from this suggestion. There is tension, in the nesting view, between the metaprinciple of critical self-examination and the nesting view's implication that the moral mind-set already contains whatever is of value in other mind-sets. By contrast, the overlapping view correctly suggests that moralists may have something to learn from studying and coming to understand other mind-sets. Third, and finally, it seems doubtful that – as implied by the nesting view – military leaders, politicians, and moralists mean precisely the same thing by the question "What is the right thing to do?" Of course, they are all seeking directives for action by posing the question; but the substantive criteria they apply in answering it may be so different as to ensure that they are not answering the *same* question in any sense beyond this very minimal, formal sense of "sameness." Thus, for example, it is hard to imagine that moralists mean the same thing by "doing the right thing" in the Cuban crisis situation, as did the U.S. general who apparently believed it would be "right" to use nuclear weapons in an attack on Cuba, since our adversaries would use such weapons if they attacked the United States.[84]

It is worth noting, further, that even if the nesting view were correct, moralists would not be in a position to impose on others the decisions flowing from their more encompassing mind-set, as President Kennedy was able to impose his more broadly based decisions on the military. Until there are philosopher kings, moralists, if they are to have any significant effect on policy, must try to understand the political mind-set and how to deal with it. Investigating the ways this mind-set does not fit within, or overlap with, the moralists' own mind-set is an important part of this task. This is not to say, however, that moral considerations do not as yet play any role in political decision making. They did play a role in the missile crisis, and before we reach any final conclusions, we must consider what that role was.

V. THE ROLE OF MORAL CONSIDERATIONS

The moralist's view of the American side of the crisis is that the U.S. government should have given even greater priority and heavier weight to the avoidance of nuclear war, and pursued (or at least more carefully considered) a more pacific diplomatic course. The substance of this view was implicit in a telegram to the president from the eminent philosopher Bertrand Russell. But instead of giving a clear and politically balanced statement of the moral case, Russell unfortunately hid it behind a harsh one-sided condemnation of U.S. actions.[85] Understandably, this provoked an angry response from the president and had no beneficial impact on U.S. thinking or action. But even had the message been clear and even-handed, it is unlikely to have had a significant effect. For example, no evidence exists that a balanced statement from Pope John XXIII, published in the *New York Times* on October 26 and calling on "all rulers" to "save peace" and "accept negotiations, at all levels," had any impact within the administration.[86] And while Russell's much friendlier telegram to Khrushchev did receive a favorable public response from the Soviet leader, who exercised caution in challenging the blockade as the philosopher urged, Russell himself later doubted that he had any real influence on Soviet actions.[87]

However little effect Russell's moral intervention may have had, we have seen already that moral considerations did play a significant role in the deliberations of the Executive Committee. George Ball and Robert Kennedy argued that a surprise attack by a large nation on a small one, entailing many civilian casualties, would go against American traditions.[88] This may reasonably be viewed as an appeal to such moral principles as the immunity of noncombatants from attack and the unfairness of the strong attacking the weak. Certainly, though, most moralists would regard exclusive concentration on these deontological principles as misguided, in a context in which a serious risk of nuclear holocaust is present. The primary moral concern, in such situations, should be the avoidance of the horrible consequences of nuclear war, with adherence to ordinary deontological principles being, at most, a second priority.

Thus, to the trained moralist, it was an oversimplified and misguided conception of morality – involving simple, general, prohibitory rules – with which the missile-crisis decision makers operated. Yet, ironically, had they followed the theoretically correct procedure of giving more weight to *consequences* in such a context, they might have adopted a worse and more dangerous course of action. For they might not have estimated and evaluated consequences in the moralist's preferred manner; rather, they might have followed the lead of hard-line Executive Committee member Dean Acheson, who observed that "[Robert] Kennedy seemed . . . to have been moved by emotional or intuitive responses more than by the trained lawyer's analysis of the dangers threatened and of the relevance of these to the various actions proposed."[89] Acheson seems to have advocated acting according to a consequentialist risks-versus-gains analysis, rather than by appeal to intuitively based deontological principles. But his consequentialist analysis, unlike the moralist's, led him to favor vehemently an air strike against the Cuban missiles.[90]

It is worth noting in passing that the Kennedy – Acheson disagreement provides some confirmation for a seemingly paradoxical claim sometimes made by consequentialist moral theorists; namely, that it may have better consequences if people generally believe and try to act as deontologists rather than as straightforward consequentialists. This is because simple deontic rules are easier to learn and apply, lead to fewer coordination problems, and are less open to self-interested or self-deceptive manipulation than are consequentialist calculations.[91] The missile-crisis deliberations lend support to this "paradox," because Robert Kennedy's deontological principles and arguments appear to have led to a safer course of action and a better outcome than the consequentialist cost – benefit analysis of Dean Acheson would likely have led to. If this was not purely accidental, the consequentialist paradox is sustained.

We may now draw some general conclusions about the role of moral considerations in the missile-crisis decision making. Moral intervention by outside "experts," such as Bertrand Russell and the pope, had little, if any, influence. Moral considerations advanced by Executive Committee members themselves apparently had substantial impact, but primarily in the form of oversimplified and rigid deontological constraints, which were perhaps given greater weight than they deserved. On the other hand, the *really important* moral consideration – the avoidance of nuclear war – while given substantial weight, probably received much less than it should have been given, or else the pacific alternatives would certainly have received greater consideration.

VI. MORALISTS AND NUCLEAR POLITICS

What do our observations about missile-crisis decision making suggest about the possible future influence of morality, and moralists, on nuclear weapons policy? The main lesson, I think, is that the differences between the mind-sets of moralists and political leaders are substantial and are likely to limit the manner and extent to which the former can influence the latter. Direct moral intervention by outsiders, even if packaged more diplomatically than Russell's messages to President Kennedy, is highly unlikely to have any impact. This is not only because unsolicited advice is generally disregarded, but also because outsiders with different mind-sets are unlikely to address the problems as the decision makers perceive them.

Nonetheless, moral considerations are likely to affect nuclear weapons decisions in two ways. First, they affect decisions when they are introduced by insiders who share the basic political mind-set, but are concerned with certain moral dimensions of the problem at hand (as, for example, Robert Kennedy was concerned about civilian casualties and the ethics of surprise attack). Second, moral considerations and arguments may influence the domestic (and even international) political background, in the context of which political leaders frame and decide nuclear weapons policy. We have seen how the domestic background during the missile crisis served to inhibit Kennedy and his advisers from following the courses of action moralists would likely have preferred. Similarly, a different sort of political climate could close off, for politicians seeking (as nearly all do) to retain political support, certain bellicose and immoral options as unfeasible. Perhaps, for example, the peace movement in certain countries of Western Europe is already exerting influence in this way.

So if moralists are going to influence nuclear weapons policy, it appears that they are going to have to do so primarily in two *indirect* ways: (1) through education, by which they can introduce future leaders and citizens to the moralists' method of analyzing problems (including adopting a critical attitude toward one's own assumptions), as well as to the substantive moral principles and issues relevant to nuclear weapons policy; and (2) by political action, in the form of support for groups adopting a morally enlightened position concerning disarmament, the arms race, and related matters.

At this point a difficulty emerges. As I have emphasized in Part I of this book, the moral issues surrounding nuclear weapons policy are exceedingly complex and difficult and pose a number of unsolved puzzles and paradoxes. Yet, for purposes of political action (and for some educational purposes at some levels), oversimplification, the papering over of relevant differences between positions, and the ignoring of significant objections are quite often required for effectiveness. Hence, for moralists dealing with nuclear weapons policy, there is a potential pragmatic conflict between the requirements for adequate analysis and the demands of successful politics. I close with a suggestion about how the community of moralists concerned about nuclear weapons policy might deal with this conflict. Perhaps rather than everyone trying in her own way to harmonize the conflicting elements, what is called for (and will be most effective) is some form of specialization. Thus some may devote their main energies in this area to moral analysis, some to education, and some to political persuasion, as their individual abilities and inclinations lead them.

10. Mutual nuclear disarmament

The chapters in Part I of this book explain why it is so difficult to determine the moral status of nuclear deterrence, while suggesting that some forms of nuclear deterrence may be morally permissible. If nuclear deterrence is permissible, it is mainly because there are no feasible and morally acceptable alternatives to it. And, in fact, a primary function of the earlier essays in Part II is to point out the fatal flaws of the major alternatives: unilateral nuclear disarmament, world government, strategic defense, and nuclear coercion (as practiced by both sides in the Cuban Missile Crisis). However, despite the practical and moral shortcomings of the alternatives, the risks of practicing nuclear deterrence for centuries would seem to be so grave as to deprive this practice of moral justification, even as the least of several evils. Hence, to the extent that I defend nuclear deterrence in this book, it is as a temporary measure to be employed to protect ourselves while we move humankind down the road toward the abolition of nuclear weapons. If it is to be a moral policy, deterrence must be accompanied by every reasonable attempt at achieving bilateral (or multilateral) nuclear disarmament, including unilateral initiatives and ventures entailing some risks.

But is not my favored solution to our nuclear peril – bilateral nuclear disarmament – as fatally flawed as the alternatives I have criticized in earlier essays? In particular, bilateral nuclear disarmament may be thought to be infeasible, as I have argued world government is, or destabilizing, as I have claimed strategic defenses would be. The remainder of this chapter is devoted to arguing that the usual reasons for thinking bilateral nuclear disarmament to be infeasible, or undesirable because destabilizing, are unconvincing. I hope thereby to render plausible my own conviction that we are obligated to pursue bilateral nuclear disarmament vigorously and steadfastly because it is the only long-run solution to our nuclear danger that is both possible and permissible.

I. IS BILATERAL NUCLEAR DISARMAMENT POSSIBLE?

Establishing bilateral nuclear disarmament would certainly be more feasible than establishing a world government, because it would not require nations (especially the great powers) to give up all military means of protecting their sovereignty and independence. Hence, if it were genuinely bilateral (eventually multilateral) and sufficiently verifiable, governments of the nuclear powers would not have the same overwhelming incentives to resist it as they have to resist world government. Still, bilateral nuclear disarmament might be thought to be impossible for any of a variety of reasons: the structure of the superpower arms competition, bureaucracy and internal politics, the uncooperative nature of the Soviet regime, or because our experience up to now with the nuclear arms competition shows it simply cannot happen. I have relatively little to say about the last two alleged reasons. The Soviets have been difficult but businesslike negotiators on nuclear arms in recent decades, and it is arguable that they are, as of this writing (1987), less intransigent in this area than current U.S. leaders. Furthermore, the most intolerable danger of the nuclear arms race is over the long run, as small yearly probabilities of nuclear war may aggregate to substantial overall risks. During the long time that we may well have to liquidate our nuclear arsenals, the Soviets might become considerably more cooperative. Nor may we conclude by simple induction that our frustrating experience with nuclear disarmament over the last forty years will continue indefinitely. The parties may learn something, or may change, or the "right" farsighted leaders may emerge simultaneously on both sides simply by chance.[1]

But time and learning, and even good luck, will not help us much if there are general structural features of international or domestic politics that preclude bilateral nuclear disarmament. It is the claim that there are such features that I wish to examine in more detail in this section. I begin by considering whether the logical structure of· nuclear competition renders bilateral nuclear disarmament irrational for each superpower, and hence impossible to attain. I then turn to the question of whether certain general features of domestic politics make bilateral nuclear disarmament impossible.

Superpower competition

The Structural Argument for the impossibility of bilateral nuclear disarmament goes as follows. The superpower nuclear arms race may be portrayed as a two-party prisoner's dilemma. Figure 4 (with numbers 1 through 4 reflecting preference order among outcomes, with U.S. preferences listed first) illustrates this. As reflected in this matrix, each superpower is supposed to prefer unilateral armament, bilateral disarmament, bilateral armament, and unilateral disarmament, in that order. Each, therefore, if rational, will choose to Arm, since this is a dominant move; that is, it yields one a more preferred outcome whichever move the other makes. (Unilateral armament is preferred to bilateral disarmament, and bilateral armament is preferred to unilateral disarmament.) If each acts in this individually rational way, however, they both end up with a less preferred outcome – bilateral armament – than the outcome – bilateral disarmament – they could have reached if both had acted otherwise. Thus, the rationality of the superpowers, and the unfortunate prisoner's dilemma structure of the situation they find themselves in, seems to doom them both to a continuing arms buildup that each would prefer to avoid.

		USSR	
		Disarm (some)	Arm (some)
	Disarm (some)	(2,2)	(4,1)
U.S.A.			
	Arm (some)	(1,4)	(3,3)

Figure 4

Given, however, that each can achieve a more preferred outcome if they act together to Disarm, couldn't rational adversaries solve their problem very simply by making a disarmament pact? Unfortunately not. For in deciding whether to comply with such a pact, they would each face another prisoner's dilemma situation as depicted in Figure 5. Because there is no outside party (e.g., a world government) to punish violations of an arms control pact, so long as each side's underlying preferences stay the same, making such pacts cannot, in itself, change the fundamental prisoner's dilemma structure of the superpower arms competition. Realizing this, the superpowers, as rational agents, will either avoid such pacts or violate them if they are made. Barring extreme irrationality on both sides, they can never achieve bilateral disarmament because of the logic of the situation in which they find themselves. This completes the Structural Argument.

		USSR	
		Comply	Don't Comply
U.S.A.	Comply	(2,2)	(1,4)
	Don't Comply	(4,1)	(3,3)

Figure 5

The Structural Argument fails, however, because the superpower arms race is a dynamic process that takes place over time and allows each side to respond to earlier moves by the other side. As a result, to the extent that it is modeled by the game-theoretic prisoner's dilemma, it is modeled by iterated, rather than single-play, prisoner's dilemma. In iterated prisoner's dilemma, it can be rational to cooperate with your adversary in order to induce further cooperative behavior on his part. Indeed, recent work by Robert Axelrod suggests that the best general strategy to use, when playing iterated two-party prisoner's dilemma of indefinite length against rational opponents, is tit-for-tat.[2] This is the strategy of cooperating initially and then mimicking your opponent's last move – punishing her when she defects with a defection of your own on the next move, and rewarding her when she cooperates with your cooperation on the next move. If Axelrod is right, the prisoner's dilemma structure of the superpower arms competition does not preclude rational cooperation – in particular, bilateral nuclear disarmament – on the part of the participants. Indeed, if those participants were rational and far sighted, and chose new strategies starting from the present, they would follow the tit-for-tat strategy and would achieve bilateral nuclear disarmament.[3] Thus, the Structural Argument for the impossibility of bilateral nuclear disarmament fails in virtue of the iterated structure of the superpower arms competition.

Domestic politics

Even if it is rational for each superpower, taken as a single collective entity, to cooperate in bilateral nuclear disarmament, this cannot happen unless it is rational for the key decision makers in the two countries to follow such policies. And, according to the Domestic Politics Argument, it is not rational for them to do so. Opposition parties or candidates in the United States and opposition factions in party and government in both the United States and the USSR would be able to gain domestic political advantages by attacking prodisarmament moves by their own national leader. Hence, the leaders of each side would be constrained from taking effective measures that would bring about, or constitute, mutual nuclear disarmament.

To evaluate this Domestic Politics Argument for the impossibility of bilateral nuclear disarmament, it will be helpful to view the interaction (from the perspective of one superpower) as a game with three players: the domestic Opposition, the domestic Leader, and the Adversary nation. With respect to a given measure implementing bilateral nuclear disarmament, each player must choose to cooperate (C) or defect (D), that is, support or oppose that measure. From the point of view of each of the domestic players, they must make their moves (i.e., commit themselves to supporting or opposing the given measure) without knowing what the other two players will do. In this game there are 8 (i.e. 2 × 2 × 2) possible outcomes defined as combinations of moves by each of the three players. Let us analyze the game from the perspectives of the Opposition and the Leader, in turn.

We assume that Opposition's goals, in strict lexical order of importance, are (1) gaining domestic political advantage, (2) avoiding unilateral disadvantage for his country, and (3) promoting cooperation between his nation and the Adversary nation.[4] This ordering reflects the main idea of the Domestic Politics Argument – that domestic political incentives are primarily what motivates the Opposition. It also realistically portrays the political point of view of many who oppose concrete disarmament proposals: they favor bilateral disarmament in principle, but are more concerned with avoiding unilateral disadvantage for their nation. We also assume that if Opposition and Leader make the same move, neither gains a domestic political advantage, while if they make different moves, the one whose move is duplicated by Adversary gains a domestic political advantage. (In simpler terms, the odd man out suffers domestically for passing up an opportunity for international cooperation that is there or seeking one that is not there.) Finally, the odd man out suffers greater political disadvantage if he alone chooses C than if he alone chooses D. Those suckered by the Adversary nation suffer worse politically than those who miss opportunities for international cooperation.

Given these assumptions, we can determine Opposition's preference order for the eight possible combinations of moves by the three players. With Opposition's move listed first, then Leader's, then Adversary's, this ranking is given below, accompanied in each case by a brief explanation of the ranking.

(1) D–C–D   Larger domestic political advantage for Opposition.
(2) C–D–C   Smaller domestic political advantage for Opposition.
(3) C–C–C   No domestic political effect; international cooperation.
(4) D–D–D   No domestic political effect.
(5) D–D–C   No domestic political effect; Opposition misses an opportunity for political advantage.
(6) C–C–D   No domestic political effect; international disadvantage.
(7) D–C–C   Smaller domestic political disadvantage for Opposition.
(8) C–D–D   Larger domestic political disadvantage for Opposition.

These preferences of Opposition can be readily diagrammed in two dimensions by two matrices (see Figure 6), one representing the outcomes when Adversary cooperates and the other representing the outcomes when Adversary defects. Inspection of the left matrix taken in isolation reveals that C is a dominant move for Opposition. Inspection of the right matrix taken in isolation reveals that D is a dominant move for Opposition. What this means is that *regardless of what Leader does,* Opposition does best by doing whatever Adversary will do. Therefore, if rational, Opposition will support the disarmament measure if and only if he expects Adversary will cooperate. If he guesses right about Adversary's eventual move, he gains politically if Leader guesses wrong and avoids losing politically if Leader guesses right.

This conclusion is important because it partially undermines the Domestic Politics Argument. It shows that domestic political considerations will not necessarily lead rational domestic opposition actors to oppose bilateral nuclear disarmament, given reasonable assumptions about the priorities of such actors and the way disagreements about disarmament affect domestic politics.[5] Of course, the analysis shows that rational opposition actors will support bilateral disarmament only if they expect Adversary to be cooperative. Further, this support would be effective in bringing about disarmament only if their Leader cooperates. Thus, to complete our evaluation of the Domestic Politics Argument we must also analyze the three-player game from Leader's perspective.

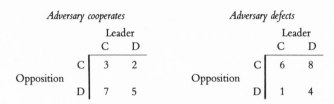

Figure 6

Leader, we will assume, has different priorities from Opposition's. She has, in our model, the power to actually decide what foreign policy course the nation will pursue. Her sense of responsibility will correspondingly be greater and she will look to history as her ultimate judge. The Opposition may rationalize giving domestic political gains priority by saying "to promote the national interest, we must first attain power." Leaders will think differently, and may be supposed to have as lexically ordered priorities: (1) achieving international cooperation, (2) avoiding unilateral disadvantage for the nation, (3) gaining domestic political advantages.[6] Given these priorities and our earlier assumptions about how domestic political advantages are generated, Leader will rank the eight possible outcomes (in which Opposition's move is listed first, then Leader's, then Adversary's) as follows:

(1) D-C-C   International cooperation; domestic political advantage for Leader.
(2) C-C-C   International cooperation.
(3) C-D-D   Domestic political advantage for Leader.
(4) D-D-D   No international cooperation or domestic political effect.
(5) D-D-C   Like (4) plus missed opportunity for cooperation.
(6) C-D-C   Domestic political disadvantage for Leader.

(7)   C-C-D   Unilateral disadvantage for nation.
(8)   D-C-D   Unilateral disadvantage for nation; domestic political disadvantage for Leader.

As with Opposition, we can represent Leader's preferences with a pair of matrices (Figure 7). Inspection of these matrices yields a conclusion like that in the case of Opposition. Cooperating dominates in the left matrix and defecting dominantes in the right matrix. Thus, *regardless of what Opposition does,* Leader does best by cooperating if and only if Adversary cooperates. If rational, Leader will act based on what she expects Adversary to do. Further, as in the case of Opposition, this is a rather robust result that comes out the same under a variety of assumptions – for example, if the priorities of avoiding international disadvantage and gaining domestic political advantage are switched in Leader's preferences.

		Adversary cooperates				*Adversary defects*	
		Leader				Leader	
		C	D			C	D
Opposition	C	2	6	Opposition	C	7	3
	D	1	5		D	8	4

Figure 7

The upshot of all this is that inserting domestic considerations into our analysis does not, as the Domestic Politics Argument suggests, show the rationality – and hence inevitability – of either superpower leaders or their domestic political oppositions opposing bilateral nuclear disarmament. Given plausible assumptions about how domestic advantages are gained, and the relative priorities such considerations have for leaders and their oppositions, both should find it rational to support bilateral nuclear disarmament if they expect the adversary superpower to be cooperative. But our earlier iterated prisoner's dilemma analysis indicated that rational adversaries would (or at least might) cooperate. Hence, we have found no support for the view that there are general structural features of international or domestic politics that preclude the possibility of bilateral nuclear disarmament.

However, we have so far assumed that national leaders have the power to pursue mutual disarmament even in the face of domestic opposition (if they are willing to accept the political risks involved).

This will not always be the case. Indeed, according to the Hard-liner's Veto Argument, it will never be the case. This argument says that military officers, ideological hard-liners, weapons makers, government bureaucrats, and others having ideologicial, economic, or career interests in keeping the nuclear arms race going will always have sufficient power to prevent significant steps toward nuclear disarmament from being taken by each side. There is a valid insight behind this argument. There are, and will doubtless continue to be, powerful groups on both sides resisting mutual disarmament for a variety of reasons ranging from the most selfish to the most idealistic. But must they always have veto power over nuclear policy? Both superpowers, after all, have strong traditions of civilian political leadership. And, as I have argued, bilateral nuclear disarmament is, overall, a rational policy. As more people become aware of the dangers of the nuclear arms race and the rational necessity of ending it, this could over time lead to overwhelming pressures for bilateral disarmament from both the top of the political pyramid – a new generation of presidents and general secretaries – and the bottom – ordinary citizens.[7] Such favorable developments may not be likely, but in the absence of arguments to the contrary, they certainly seem to be possible.

Are there plausible arguments to the contrary? One possible argument – the Incompatible Demands Argument – begins from the assumption that most citizens, especially leaders, on each side will have the following preference ranking with respect to any mutual disarmament agreement (explicit or tacit):

(1) An agreement favorable to our side.
(2) No agreement.
(3) An agreement unfavorable to our side.

The argument continues by noting that each side will therefore demand terms favorable to itself, and hence no agreement will be reached.

This Incompatible Demands Argument is fallacious. It is based on the false assumption that nuclear weapons competition is a purely conflictual situation in which security gains for one side must be security losses for the other. But in reality, many agreements (e.g., bilateral abandonment of first-strike weapons) would be favorable to both sides in the sense of increasing the security of both sides. Since it is a favorable agreement in this security-increasing sense that most citizens may be presumed to demand (rather than an agreement that is "favorable" in the sense of giving your side a short-term military advantage over the other side), the stated preferences are entirely consistent with reaching agreement on nuclear disarmament.

The argument may be revised, however, to avoid simple fallacy. This new argument, which may be called the Distorted Perceptions Argument, goes as follows. The great majority of leaders and citizens will not support a disarmament agreement unless it seems *fair* in the sense of providing their side with security advantages at least roughly equal to those provided the other side. But no trade-off will be perceived as fair by both sides because of systematic perceptual distortions. In particular, a given increment of military capacity will be more salient when it belongs to the other side (than when it belongs to one's own side) because it is threatening and frightening. Also there are information asymmetries: each side knows more about its military liabilities and its own nonmalevolent intentions than the other side does. (The former because of military secrecy and the latter because of the difficulty of credibly communicating benign intentions in an atmosphere of distrust.) These information asymmetries lead to worst-case reasoning on each side – assessing what our side needs to balance their side in terms of the worst they could do to us, given our present information. Such systematic distortions as these ensure that no significant disarmament agreement will be perceived as fair by enough influential people on both sides to be feasible.

This argument pinpoints some central difficulties on the road to achieving nuclear disarmament. But it shows that achievement to be impossible only if we assume we are collectively unable to deal with these perceptual problems now that they have been identified. But there are ways to deal with them. Early agreements could focus on especially salient equivalences to meet demands of fairness (e.g., a nuclear test ban, a freeze of weapons levels, a ban on space weapons). If these early agreements proved successful, later, more complex agreements would be politically easier to reach. Also, public education about the existence of these perceptual distortions might limit and contain their effects. The valid point that in nuclear disarmament agreements strict equality is less important than mutual benefit (since inequalities are unlikely to be exploitable or exploited) could be emphasized in public political discourse. These political-educational tactics might well fail. But they could succeed, and given what is at stake and the absence of any morally promising alternatives, they should be tried. Otherwise, we risk turning the claim that nuclear disarmament is impossible into a self-fulfilling prophecy.

A final argument for the impossibility of nuclear disarmament derives from the existence of multiple nuclear powers. According to this argument, the superpowers would never accept strategic inferiority with respect to the lesser nuclear powers, and hence would not disarm themselves of nuclear weapons while France, China, and other powers retained their nuclear arsenals. This may well be true. But all it shows is that the lesser nuclear powers would have to be brought into the nuclear disarmament process along the way. Once the superpowers showed their sincerity by substantially reducing their gigantic nuclear arsenals, the process could be broadened to include proportionate reduction by all nuclear powers. There would, no doubt, be complications and difficulties in carrying out multilateral negotiations on such vital security matters. But since the basic interests of all parties would be served by reaching agreement, there is no good reason to think such difficulties are insurmountable. If bilateral superpower nuclear disarmament is possible, so is multilateral nuclear disarmament.

II. IS BILATERAL NUCLEAR DISARMAMENT DESIRABLE?

In the last section it was argued that bilateral nuclear disarmament is possible, or at least that there is no compelling argument to the contrary. But some have questioned whether such disarmament would be a good thing for the world.[8] Their position may be supported by two sorts of arguments: those that emphasize the disadvantages of a state of nuclear disarmament, once achieved; and those that emphasize the dangers of the process of disarmament itself. Here, representative arguments of each sort will be briefly considered.

The strongest argument that a nuclear-disarmed world would be undesirable is based on the idea that possession of nuclear weapons deters (or limits the extent of) conventional wars among great powers. With modern technology, even conventional wars can be horribly destructive. But the nuclear era has seen no major war in Europe despite intense ideological differences, a general avoidance of direct military confrontations among nuclear powers, and careful limits on such conflicts when they have occurred (as in the Soviet – Chinese border clashes). Fear of the destructive power of the nuclear weapons that could be brought into action by escalation of initially conventional wars is no doubt an important factor in the avoidance and limitation of such wars among major powers since World War II. If this fear were eliminated by the removal of nuclear arsenals, there would be more large-scale conventional conflicts and resultant human suffering.

This argument has some force but, for two reasons, is not convincing. First, however devastating modern conventional wars might be, they are likely to be less devastating than a major nuclear war by more than an order of magnitude. Thus, reductions in the probability of nuclear war brought about by nuclear disarmament are worthwhile (in expected value terms) even if the corresponding increase in the probability of conventional war is more than ten times as great. This condition will be satisifed unless the long-run risks of nuclear war, assuming nuclear armament, are very small, while the long-run risks of major conventional war, assuming nuclear disarmament, are very large.[9] In other words, even if disarmament opponents are right that nuclear disarmament would increase the risk of major conventional war, this does not show such disarmament to be undesirable once the magnitudes as well as the probabilities of the relevant possible outcomes are taken into account.[10]

Second, this argument for the undesirability of nuclear disarmament fails to take account of the effects that the disarmament process itself would have on the international climate and the risks of conventional war. Successful achievement of nuclear disarmament would both require and tend to produce improved overall relations among major nuclear powers. As the disarmament process proceeded step by step, each side would likely become less distrustful of the other as it saw the other keeping its part of the latest bargain. Under these conditions, explicit and tacit agreements to reduce the risks (and negative consequences) of conventional war would be easier to reach. This is not to say either that nuclear disarmament would eliminate all distrust and conflict of interest among major powers, or that there might not be some overall increase in risks of conventional war if nuclear disarmament were achieved. The point is rather that this increase (if it exists at all) will likely be much less than we are inclined to think when we imagine present nuclear powers with their current attitudes suddenly stripped of their nuclear arsenals. Recognizing this, and taking account of the order-of-magnitude difference in devastation to be expected in nuclear and conventional wars, leads directly to the conclusion that a condition of worldwide nuclear disarmament would be desirable, if it could be achieved.

But there could be serious dangers on the way to nuclear disarmament. In particular, strategic thinkers have noted that there might be more incentive for a first strike with small numbers of nuclear weapons on both sides. For the attacking nation could reasonably hope to survive retaliation from the very small number of weapons that might remain usable after such an attack. In addition, the final stage of disarmament in which all sides are supposed to dismantle their last nuclear weapons would be exceedingly dangerous. Concealing a few nuclear weapons at this stage could give one nation an enormous military advantage over those who completely denuclearize their arsenals. Since it would be relatively easy as well as advantageous to maintain such a secret nuclear stockpile, one or more parties might do so and attempt to gain political-military advantages by nuclear blackmail or nuclear attack.

In my opinion, there is a convincing response to this Dangers of Transition Argument against nuclear disarmament. The main dangers can be contained within acceptable limits if nuclear disarmament is carried out in the proper way. Incentives for first strikes can be minimized throughout the process by early elimination of weapons possessing first-strike characteristics (i.e., vulnerability, high accuracy, multiwarhead capabilities). As allowed numbers of nuclear weapons get very low at late stages in the process, various devices can be used to ensure a safe transition to a zero level. Simultaneous construction of strategic defense systems capable of dealing with low-volume attacks, together with extensive arrangements for on-site inspections, could minimize the likelihood and negative consequences of cheating.[11] Also, by this late stage, earlier compliance should reduce distrust among the parties and increase their expectations that mutually beneficial agreements would be adhered to. With nuclear disarmament so close, each nation would have strong incentives not to cheat, since cheating would alienate the other great powers and start a new nuclear arms race in which its small head start would probably not be exploitable or maintainable.[12]

And what if one or more nations did cheat at levels small enough to go undetected? Without publicizing their cheating, they could not use their nuclear weapons for intimidation or political gains. If, on the other hand, they did admit possessing such weapons, other nations could take remedial steps such as proportionate nuclear rearmament. The main danger would be that such weapons could be fired or used for blackmail during a war. But the same danger could occur after open nuclear rearmament during a war. To say this is to admit that there is no guarantee that even complete nuclear disarmament would be permanent. But a guarantee of permanency is not required; a sufficient likelihood of being long-lasting is enough to make the initial achievement of complete nuclear disarmament desirable. The considerations advanced in the last paragraph indicate that this sufficient likelihood would be attainable if the disarmament process were carried out in the right way.

Not everyone will be convinced by this reply to the Dangers of Transition Argument. But notice that even if the reply fails and the argument stands, the case for bilateral nuclear disarmament to the lowest level providing a secure second-strike capacity to each side (i.e., minimum deterrence) is unaffected. If reducing nuclear weapons below a certain fairly low number is too dangerous and destabilizing, it still makes great sense to reduce both the probability and expected destructiveness of nuclear war by mutually disarming to this level (while retaining only those weapons with greatest stability characteristics).[15] For the superpowers to do less than this is both immoral (because of the excessive and unnecessary risks they impose on others) and irrational (because of the excessive and unnecessary risks they undergo themselves).

The point of this concluding chapter has been to argue that there is a feasible and moral alternative to the practice of perpetual nuclear deterrence for national defense. This is the vigorous pursuit of bilateral – eventually multilateral – nuclear disarmament. It has been argued that neither the logical structure of international competition nor the logical structure of domestic defense politics renders bilateral nuclear disarmament impossible. There are serious difficulties, to be sure, and no guarantees of success even assuming best-faith efforts on the part of all those who appreciate the danger of the nuclear arms race. But there are no absolutely insurmountable obstacles as there would seem to be in the case of establishing world government or pursuing a policy of unilateral nuclear disarmament.

Further, bilateral nuclear disarmament is desirable as well as possible because, though by no means risk-free, it entails less overall risk than strategic defense, nuclear coercion, perpetual nuclear deterrence, or unilateral nuclear disarmament.

There are a number of concrete steps that our nation (and its superpower adversary) could each take in the very short run to start us along the road toward bilateral nuclear disarmament: endorsement in principle of a nuclear freeze, a comprehensive test ban, a ban on space weapons, a continued ban on strategic defenses (until the late stages of bilateral nuclear disarmament), large reductions of nuclear arsenals, elimination of strategic weapons with first-strike characteristics, and a pledge of no first use of nuclear weapons. Most of these endorsements could be quickly followed up with serious negotiations on mutually beneficial treaties that would put into practice the principles in question.[14] In such negotiations, the focus on each side should be on long-run security gains for both sides (and humanity) rather than short-run political, military, or strategic advantages for either side. If necessary to get the disarmament process started, each side should be willing to undertake limited but significant unilateral steps toward disarmament on its own, and to respond reciprocally to such acts on the part of its adversary. (More abstractly, each side should try to initiate or continue a series of cooperative moves in the iterated prisoner's dilemma game that the superpowers are playing.)

At any given time, we may despair at how far one or both superpowers are from acting in this sensible manner. But with patience, good luck, continued education of the world's leaders and population about the dangers of nuclear arms and the nuclear arms race, and wise action on the part of political groups favoring nuclear peace, things may turn around before it is too late. Achieving nuclear disarmament (even down to minimum deterrence levels) is not certain or perhaps even likely. It will not in any case be easy. But it is morally imperative. For the alternative is for us and our descendants, so long as we survive, to live constantly in grave physical and moral peril, a button push away from being both victims and perpetrators of mass murder.

Notes

1 On the contrasting views of philosophers and strategists, see Russell Hardin and John Mearsheimer, introduction to Russell Hardin et al. (eds.), *Nuclear Deterrence: Ethics and Strategy* (Chicago: University of Chicago Press, 1985).

2 See, e.g., The Harvard Nuclear Study Group, *Living with Nuclear Weapons* (New York: Bantam Books, 1983).

3 Briefly, for nonphilosophers, utilitarians evaluate actions or policies solely in terms of their effects on human well-being. Deontologists hold that other features of actions are directly relevant to their moral evaluation, and that certain kinds of actions are impermissible (e.g., lies, torture) or permissible (e.g., acts of self-defense) largely in virtue of the intrinsic nature of such actions.

4 Its adoption is, however, no guarantee against such a race, since some will always maintain that more and better nuclear weapons are necessary for adequate deterrence, given the opponent's ruthlessness, aggressiveness, and potential for improved capabilities.

5 See, e.g., Ground Zero, *Nuclear War: What's in It for You* (New York: Pocket Books, 1982), chap. 8.

6 Somewhat similar views are put forth in David Lewis, "Finite Counterforce," in Henry Shue (ed.), *The Shadow of the Bomb: Extended Deterrence and Moral Constraint* (forthcoming); and Robert Art, "Between Mutual Assured Destruction and Nuclear Victory: The Case for the 'Mad-plus' Posture," in Hardin, *Nuclear Deterrence*. I differ from Art in being doubtful of the propriety of extended deterrence. I differ from Lewis in being less confident of the reliability of "existential deterrence" (see Chapter 2), in doubting that anything approaching the size of current nuclear arsenals would be needed to carry out the described strategy, and in worrying about the propriety of large-scale second-strike counterforce attacks carried out in hopes of damage limitation. Lewis's slogan for his position is "Buy like a MADman [i.e., mutual assured destruction supporter], use like a NUT [i.e., nuclear use theorist.]" My slogan would be: Buy few; threaten and intend to use like a MADman; use, if at all, like a very scrupulous NUT." Under heavy pressure, I might concede that this is a less catchy slogan.

7 National Conference of Catholic Bishops, *The Challenge of Peace: God's Promise and Our Response* (Washington, D.C.: U.S. Catholic Conference, 1983).

8 The only conceivable exception would be if one had reliable and

conclusive evidence that one's opponent was about to launch a strategic first strike, and could not be dissuaded from doing so. The likelihood of this exception coming into play in the real world is, we may hope, very small. The danger that leaders on one side or the other may mistakenly *think* that the exception – or a less stringent version of it – has come into play is real, however, and will remain so as long as the nuclear arms race continues. This is a main reason that moving to the greater stability of minimum deterrence, and eventually to complete nuclear disarmament, is a moral imperative.

1. SOME PARADOXES OF DETERRENCE

1   *The Strategy of Conflict* (New York: Oxford University Press, 1960), chaps. 1 – 2; and *Arms and Influence* (New Haven, Conn.: Yale University Press, 1966), chap. 2.

2   To avoid problems concerning whether one can have genuine intentions regarding situations that one is *certain* will not arise, we assume that N's confidence falls short of certainty.

3   The rational utilitarian evaluation need not take the form of an expected utility calculation. See Chapter 3. A rational utilitarian evaluation *substantially* favors an act when it favors the act and "a great deal of utility is at stake" in the sense defined below in the text.

4   See e.g., Herman Kahn, *On Thermonuclear War,* 2nd ed. (Princeton, N.J.: Princeton University Press, 1960), p. 185; and Anthony Kenny, "Counterforce and Countervalue," in Walter Stein (ed.), *Nuclear Weapons: A Catholic Response* (London: Merlin Press, 1965), pp. 162-64.

5   See note 11 of this chapter and Chapter 2.

6   Nozick, *Anarchy, State, and Utopia* (New York: Basic Books, 1974), pp. 30–31,n.; Nagel, "War and Massacre," *Philosophy and Public Affairs* 1, no. 2 (Winter 1972): 123–44, esp. p. 126; Brandt, "Utilitarianism and the Rules of War," ibid., pp. 145–65, esp. p. 147, n. 3; Walzer, *Just and Unjust Wars* (New York: Basic Books, 1977), pp. 251–63.

7   Interpretations (or extensions) of Absolutism that would block some or all of the paradoxes include those which forbid intending to do what is wrong, deliberately making oneself less virtuous, or intentionally risking performing an inherently evil act. (An explanation of the relevant sense of "risking performing an act" will be offered in section IV.)

8   I assume henceforth that, if it would be wrong to do something, the agent knows this. (The agent discussed in section IV, who has become corrupt, may be an exception.) This keeps the discussion of

the paradoxes from getting tangled up with the separate problem of whether an agent's duty is to do what is actually right, or what he believes is right.

9   See *Peter Abelard's Ethics,* trans. D.E. Luscombe (New York: Oxford University Press, 1971), pp. 5–37; Thomas Aquinas, *Summa Theologica,* la2ae. 18–20; Joseph Bulter, "A Dissertation on the Nature of Virtue," in *Five Sermons* (Indianapolis: Bobbs-Merrill, 1950), p. 83; Immanuel Kant, *Foundations of the Metaphysics of Morals* (San Francisco: Harper & Row, 1964), sec. 1; Jeremy Bentham, *An Introduction to the Principles of Morals and Legislation* (New York: Macmillan, 1948), chap. 9, secs. 13–16; Henry Sidgwick, *The Methods of Ethics* (New York: Dover, 1907), pp. 60–61, 201–04; Kenny, "Counterforce and Countervalue," p. 159, 162; and Jan Narveson, *Morality and Utility* (Baltimore: Johns Hopkins University Press, 1967), pp. 106–08.

10   A qualification is necessary. Although having the intention involves only a small risk of applying the threatened sanction to innocent people, it follows, from points made in section IV, that forming the intention might also involve risks of performing other inherently evil acts. Hence, what really follows is that forming the intention is right in those SDSs in which the composite risk is small. This limitation in the scope of (P1′) is to be henceforth understood. It does not affect (P1), (P2), or (P3), since each is governed by an existential quantifier.

11   In *Nuclear Weapons,* Kenny and others use WIP to argue that nuclear deterrence is immoral because it involves having the conditional intention to kill innocent people. If, however, nuclear deterrence takes place in an SDS, the considerations advanced in this section suggest that this argument, at best, is inconclusive, since it presents only one side of a moral paradox. At worst, it is mistaken, since it applies WIP in just the sort of situation in which its applicability is most questionable.

12   "Rational and morally good" in this and later statements of the second and third paradoxes, means rational and moral in the given situation. A person who usually is rational and moral, but fails to be in the situation in question, could, of course, have the intention to apply the sanction. (P2′) is quite similar to a paradox concerning utilitarianism and deterrence developed by D.H. Hodgson in *Consequences of Utilitarianism* (Oxford: Clarendon Press, 1967), chap. 4.

13   See, e.g., S. Hampshire and H.L.A. Hart, "Decision, Intention and Certainty," *Mind* 67, no. 1 (January 1958): 1–12; and G.E.M. Anscombe, *Intention* (Ithaca, N.Y.: Cornell University Press, 1966). Some have taken the opposed position that the rationality of the intention is determined by reasons for *being disposed* to perform the

act, not reasons for performing it. Arguments against this are presented in my Chapter 2 discussion of the "Retaliator's" view.

14 Alternatively, the agent could undertake to make himself into an *irrational* person whose intentions are quite out of line with his reasons for action. However, trying to become irrational, in these circumstances, is less likely to succeed than trying to change one's moral beliefs, and, furthermore, might itself constitute self-corruption. Hence, this point does not affect the paradox stated below.

15 As Donald Regan has suggested to me, (P3) can be derived directly from our normative assumption: imagine a villain credibly threatening to kill very many hostages unless a certain good person corrupts himself. I prefer the indirect route to (P3) given in the text, because (P1) and (P2) are interesting in their own right and because viewing the three paradoxes together makes it easier to see what produces them.

16 Nagel, "War and Massacre," pp. 132–33.

17 Its supporters might, of course, allow exceptions to the principle in cases in which only the agent's feelings, and not his acts or dispositions to act, are corrupted. (For example, a doctor "corrupts himself" by suppressing normal sympathy for patients in unavoidable pain, in order to treat them more effectively.) Further, advocates of the doctrine of double-effect might consider self-corruption permissible when it is a "side effect" of action rather than a means to an end. For example, they might approve of a social worker's joining a gang to reform it, even though he expects to assimilate some of the gang's distorted values. Note, however, that neither of these possible exceptions to the Virtue Preservation Principle (brought to my attention by Robert Adams) applies to the agent in an SDS who corrupts his *intentions* as a chosen *means* of preventing an offense.

18 See Hodgson, *Consequences of Utilitarianism*. See also Robert M. Adams, "Motive Utilitarianism," *Journal of Philosophy* 73, no. 14 (Aug. 12, 1976): 467–81; and Bernard Williams, "A Critique of Utilitarianism," in J.J.C. Smart and Williams, *Utilitarianism: For and Against* (New York: Cambridge University Press, 1973), sec. 6.

2. A PARADOX OF DETERRENCE REVISITED

1 National Conference of Catholic Bishops, *The Challenge of Peace: God's Promise and Our Response* (Washington, D.C.: U.S. Catholic Conference, 1983).

2 This is pointed out in Susan Moller Okin, "Taking the Bishops

Seriously," *World Politics* 36 (July 1984): 527–84; and in George Sher, "The U.S. Bishops' Position on Nuclear Deterrence: A Moral Assessment," in Douglas MacLean (ed.), *The Security Gamble* (Totowa, N.J.: Rowman & Allanheld, 1984). The bishops' position could be rendered consistent by attributing to them the view that nuclear deterrence could and should work with the deterring nation having no intention to retaliate, or only the intention to retaliate in an extremely limited way against isolated military targets. Such views are discussed in section III of this chapter. Some knowledgeable writers attribute one or the other of such views to the bishops (see e.g., Joseph Nye, *Nuclear Ethics* [New York: Free Press, 1986], pp. 52–53), but I find no direct evidence for this in the Pastoral Letter itself. A useful review of recent Catholic writings on this subject is Richard A. McCormick, "Nuclear Deterrence and the Problem of Intention," in Philip J. Murnion (ed.), *Catholics and Nuclear War* (New York: Crossroad, 1983).

3 The prohibition on harming the innocent in the course of wreaking vengence on the guilty may not be absolute, but only strongly presumptive. See the discussion in Chapter 8.

4 See, for example, George Quester, *The Future of Nuclear Deterrence* (Lexington, Mass.: Lexington Books, 1986), pp. 76–77, 80, 83–84.

5 Here, and in the sequel, I use the notion of "forming an intention" in a broad sense that includes the various ways an agent can, on purpose, come to have an intention. Daniel Farrell argues (in "Intention, Reason, and Action," typescript, Ohio State University, 1986) for reserving this terminology for the case where one's intention results, in the normal fashion, from deliberations about reasons for and against the action in question. I agree that this is the paradigm case of *rational* intention formation. But normal intention formation is not always so rational – there are many intermediate cases between this and causing oneself to have an intention by purely external means (e.g., hypnosis). Hence, I am disinclined to follow Farrell in limiting the term "forming an intention" to the case of pure deliberative rationality.

6 I do not assume that the utilitarian balancing is carried out by a calculation of expected utilities. See Chapter 3.

7 Douglas Lackey, "The Intentions of Deterrence," in Avner Cohen and Steven Lee (eds.), *Nuclear Weapons and the Future of Humanity* (Totowa, N.J.: Rowman & Allanheld, 1986), p. 312. I have replaced Lackey's "C"s with "O"s to fit our terminology.

8 Introduction to James P. Sterba (ed.), *The Ethics of War and Nuclear Deterrence* (Belmont, Cal.: Wadsworth, 1985), p. 10.

9 Actually, in Schelling's well-known terminology, the gunman's intention is *compellent* rather than deterrent, i.e., it tries to get you to do something rather than refrain from doing something. My response to Sterba does not depend upon this feature of his example, so I ignore it in the text.

10 Anthony Kenny, *The Logic of Deterrence* (Chicago: University of Chicago Press, 1985), p. 49. Kenny quotes the argument in question from Bishop B.C. Butler's letter to *The Times of London*, February 9, 1983.

11 Kenny, *Logic of Deterrence,* pp. 47–48.

12 Lackey, "Intentions of Deterrence," pp. 312–13.

13 Gerald Dworkin, "Nuclear Intentions," *Ethics* 95 (April 1985): 445–60. I treat his discussion as assuming that nuclear deterrence occurs in an SDS, so that his arguments are relevant to the first moral paradox of deterrence.

14 Dworkin, "Nuclear Intentions," p. 453.

15 It is not clear from Dworkin's description of bounce-back whether its point is partial defense or deterrence by threat of bounce-back damage.

16 Thus, as I interpret Dworkin, a defender who would retarget the bounce-back device (if he could) to achieve deterrence in the face of enemy missile sites isolated from cities would not be a genuine bounce-backer. The difference that matters is not between the mechanisms (autoretaliator or bounce-back), but between the action dispositions of those who build and use them.

17 Dworkin, "Nuclear Intentions," pp. 459–60.

18 This assumes that the practice in question is not part of a set of practices from which the same groups always benefit and suffer. If it were part of such a set, the practice in question would be wrong because of the part it played in the wider pattern of injustice.

19 Dworkin, "Nuclear Intentions," p. 460.

20 David Gauthier, "Deterrence, Maximization, and Rationality," and "Afterthoughts," both in MacLean, *The Security Gamble,* pp. 100–22, 159–61. For further discussion and criticism of Gauthier's position, see Daniel Farrell, "Intention, Reason, and Action."

21 I assume that the agent's substantive values remain the same. Obviously, if she came to be indifferent to the well-being of those who would be harmed by retaliation, she could have this intention while remaining fully rational in the instrumental sense.

22 Very roughly, a prisoner's dilemma is an interactive situation in which the actors all do worse if each performs the act that is best for him or her, given what the others do. See Chapters 8 and 10. For an explanation and full discussion, see, e.g., Brian Barry and Russell

Hardin (eds.), *Rational Man and Irrational Society?* (Beverly Hills, Cal.: Sage Publications, 1982).

23 I discuss this example more fully in "The Toxin Puzzle," *Analysis* 43 (January 1983): 33–36.

24 The term is due to McGeorge Bundy. See, for example, his "Existential Deterrence and Its Consequences," in MacLean, *The Security Gamble.*

25 See, e.g., Sterba's "How to Achieve Nuclear Deterrence Without Threatening Nuclear Destruction," in Sterba, *The Ethics of War and Nuclear Deterrence,* pp. 155–68.

26 See John Hare, "Credibility and Bluff," in Cohen and Lee, *Nuclear Weapons and the Future of Humanity,* pp. 191–99.

27 Something like the Scrupulous Retaliation policy seems to be advocated by David Lewis in his "Finite Counterforce," in Henry Shue (ed.), *The Shadow of the Bomb: Extended Deterrence and Moral Constraint* (forthcoming).

28 On the danger of such problems leading to nuclear war, see Paul Ehrlich and Anne Ehrlich, "Ecology of Nuclear War: Population, Resources, Environment," in Cohen and Lee, *Nuclear Weapons and the Future of Humanity,* pp. 85–101.

29 As suggested by David Lewis, letter to the author, April 1986. Lewis has emphasized in correspondence with the author (October 1986) that, in his view, retaliatory strikes must be directed at preventing further attacks rather than at achieving revenge or punishment.

30 If the second paradox of deterrence stands, fully rational agents cannot be influenced by considerations of deterrence in this way. But less than fully rational agents can be.

31 For further analysis of situations having this odd strucuture, see my "Rule by Fear," *Nous* 17 (November 1983): 601–20.

32 See, e.g., Paul Bracken, *Command and Control of Nuclear Forces* (New Haven, Conn.: Yale University Press, 1983).

33 Apparently common sense, in the form of the opinions of the American public, also supports propositions (1) and (2). For discussion of polling data which reveal that most Americans favor nuclear threats but oppose nuclear use, see Daniel Ellsberg, "Blind Men's Bluff," *Nuclear Times* (July/August 1985), pp. 20–22.

34 Since forming an intention – in the relevant "success verb" sense of "forming" – entails ending up having that intention, there is a price to be paid for accepting the Traditionalist intuitions while rejecting the unmodified WIP. We must allow that it can be permissible for an agent to perform an act that she knows entails the creation of a wrongful state in herself. This is a form of the third paradox of Chapter 1.

3. DETERRENCE, UTILITY, AND RATIONAL CHOICE

1   The utilitarian perspective is one, but by no means the only, useful perspective from which the morality of deterrence may be examined. See, for example, Chapter 4.

2   A similar conclusion is argued for in more detail in Douglas Lackey's utilitarian comparison between what he calls Victory and Détente strategies. See Lackey, *Moral Principles and Nuclear Weapons* (Totowa, N.J.: Rowman & Allanheld, 1984), 128–34. I agree with many, but not all, of the points Lackey makes in comparing these two strategies. Cf., however, Chapter 6.

3   That is, the nation is to choose on the assumption that the policy selected will be pursued until a significant change in circumstances occurs, or thirty years elapse, at which time a complete reassessment of the alternatives and a new choice are to be made.

4   I have further simplified the problem by presenting it as a choice between alternatives that have only two possible outcomes each: the status quo and either nuclear war or world domination by one's opponent. The effects of this assumption are discussed in section V.

   Our utilitarian dilemma may be compounded by uncertainty as to which is the best hope of achieving bilateral disarmament – providing an incentive to the other side by staying armed or providing an example by disarming oneself. For a discussion of bilateral disarmament following the incentive line, see Chapter 10.

5   I do not rule out identifying an individual's utility with the satisfaction of his subjective preferences. The idea is that the same concept of personal utility is applied to all people, and some objective scheme of aggregation is used to combine personal utilities into a measure of net human utility. Any conception of aggregate utility that identifies it with the subjective preferences of a single individual is not a possible interpretation of the concept of utility used by utilitarian moralists.

6   Other critiques of the application of EUP to nuclear weapons policy are: Robert Levine, *The Arms Debate* (Cambridge, Mass.: Harvard University Press, 1963), pp. 33–36; Anatol Rapoport, *Strategy and Conscience* (New York: Schocken, 1964), pp. 16–30, 84–104; Robert Paul Wolff, "Maximization of Expected Utility as a Criterion of Rationality in Military Strategy and Foreign Policy," *Social Theory and Practice* 1 (Spring 1970): 99–111.

7   One could deal with this problem by specifying the nature of the outcomes in more detail. (The limit of such a process would be to list all possible utility levels as the "ultimate outcomes," while realizing that various different paths might lead to the same ultimate outcome and that there might be no paths to some [potential] ultimate out-

comes.) This would simply transfer the difficulties inherent in determining the effects of war or domination onto the probability-estimating aspect of our problem.

8   If forced to make precise estimates of the relevant utilities and probabilities, I would probably come up with numbers that imply a higher expected utility for minimum deterrence than for unilateral disarmament. But these estimates would be controversial and largely impressionistic. In place of specific numerical estimates, one might use utility and probability intervals. However, the problem of fixing the end points of the intervals is similar to the problem of arriving at a single estimate. If the intervals are made wide enough to encompass all reasonable estimates, the application of EUP to different sets of values in the relevant intervals will yield different solutions to our choice problem.

9   This approach was originally outlined by Frank Ramsey in "Truth and Probability," in *The Foundations of Mathematics and Other Logical Essays* (London: Kegan Paul, 1931). It has been formally axiomatized by Jacob Marschak in "Rational Behavior, Uncertain Prospects, and Measurable Utility," *Econometrica* 18 (Arpil 1950): 111–41, and by Leonard Savage in *The Foundations of Statistics*, 2nd ed. (New York: Dover, 1972).

10 That the subjective utility theorist and the utilitarian moralist are not using the same concept of utility can be seen by noting that the latter's traditional foe – the rational egoist – would be viewed as a utility maximizer by the former (provided his preferences reflected the relevant sort of consistency).

11 See, e.g., Levine, *The Arms Debate*; Arthur Herzog, *The War-Peace Establishment* (New York: Harper & Row, 1965); William Van Cleave, "The Nuclear Weapons Debate," in Richard Head and Ervin Rokke (eds.), *American Defense Policy*, 3rd ed. (Baltimore: Johns Hopkins University Press, 1973). Note, however, that these experts are not usually making, or presupposing, judgments about the likelihood of *minimum* deterrence leading to war.

12 John Rawls, *A Theory of Justice* (Cambridge, Mass.: Harvard University Press, 1971).

13 Ibid., pp. 152–57.

14 For a description of a culture in which long-standing food shortages have eliminated nearly all of what makes human life worth living, see Colin Turnbull, *The Mountain People* (New York: Simon & Schuster, 1972).

15 See R. Duncan Luce and Howard Raiffa, *Games and Decisions* (New York: John Wiley & Sons, 1957), pp. 257–86.

16 At the suggestion of Jefferson McMahan, the example is constructed with these tiny chances included in order to preserve the exact

parallel to the deter-or-disarm choice. Since deterrence could result in enemy domination and unilateral disarmament could be followed by large-scale nuclear war (e.g., after a large nuclear buildup by a third nuclear power), the parallel would not be exact without the inclusion of these tiny chances.

17   Of course, the three principles will diverge in their recommendations only if, as in the deter-or-disarm situation, no single alternative minimizes both the probability and magnitude of potential disaster.

While I am here treating it as a normative principle of choice, DAP would also be worth investigating as a descriptive principle that may predict and explain how decision makers actually tend to choose when faced with choices between potential disasters. For example, what President Kennedy did in the Cuban Missile Crisis can perhaps best be understood as disaster avoidance behavior practiced under the wrong (from a normative perspective) conditions. See Chapter 9 for discussion. One might also expect organizations (or units thereof) to roughly conform their behavior to DAP if top decision makers know they are likely to lose their jobs should even a small disaster occur within the organization (or unit).

18   I do not claim that minimizing the probability of disaster occurrence is a generally acceptable strategy of choice under uncertainty. I should be content to establish, to the satisfaction of many, that under conditions that may well apply to the deter-or-disarm choice, DAP is superior to EUP and MMP as a principle of rational choice.

19   The first two conditions are, strictly speaking, redundant, as they are satisfied in any situation of two-dimensional uncertainty. Some of the conditions require some rough cardinal informatioin for application, but not the precise cardinal information needed to apply EUP.

20   See also the discussion of the thirty-year policy period in section V of this chapter.

21   Note, for example, that *all* of the reasons McMahan lists for why current deterrent policies have a significant probability of producing nuclear war either do not apply, or apply less strongly, to minimum deterrence. See Jefferson McMahan, "Nuclear Deterrence and Future Generations," in Avner Cohen and Steven Lee (eds.), *Nuclear Weapons and the Future of Humanity* (Totowa, N.J.: Rowman & Allanheld, 1986), pp. 325–26.

22   Recent studies of nuclear winter indicate that it is unlikely to produce extinction. See, e.g., S.L. Thompson and S.H. Schneider, "Nuclear Winter Reappraised," *Foreign Affairs* 64 (Summer 1986): 981–1005.

23   If this is so, then despite the problems inherent in applying EUP to

the deter-or-disarm situation, nuclear deterrence can serve to illustrate the paradoxes discussed in Chapter 1.

24 Transitivity would mean that if the principle of choice favors act A over act B and act B over act C, it must favor A over C.

25 Cf. Daniel Ellsberg, "Risk, Ambiguity, and the Savage Axioms," *Quarterly Journal of Economics* 75 (November 1961): 643–69, for Ellsberg's principle, which is a weighted average of EUP and MMP.

26 This regimentation is necessary because the other factors in the index are limited to a similar range of variation. The natural way to regiment is to assign a utility of one to the best outcome, and zero to the worst outcome. If one does not use the outcomes of all the alternatives in regimenting the utility scale, new transitivity problems may arise.

27 Consider the simplified case in which there are only two alternative acts, A_1 and A_2, and condition five is "maximally satisfied." A_1 and A_2 may lead to the status quo or to respective disasters D_1 and D_2 with probabilities P_1 and P_2. Given $P_1 > P_2$, and setting the utility of the status quo at one and the worse disaster (D_2) at zero, let x (between zero and one) be the utility estimate for D_1. The exact condition under which DAP and CP will agree is: $(P_2/P_1 + rx) < 1$. Now condition nine implies that P_2/P_1 is significantly less than one. If conditions one and four are satisfied, r is quite low and x is significantly less than one. Hence their product will be quite low, and the above inequality will likely be satisfied.

28 This objection was suggested to me by Thomas E. Hill, Jr.

29 McMahan, "Nuclear Deterrence and Future Generations," p. 330.

4. NUCLEAR DETERRENCE: SOME MORAL PERPLEXITIES

1 Adapted from James Mills's novel, *Report to the Commissioner* (New York: Pocket Books, 1973).

2 The question of whether the belief in question is reasonable might be regarded as normative, though not (directly) moral.

3 See Douglas Lackey, "Ethics and Nuclear Deterrence," in James Rachels (ed.), *Moral Problems,* 2nd ed. (New York: Harper & Row, 1975), pp. 343–44.

4 This point is also made in Micheal Walzer, *Just and Unjust Wars* (New York: Basic Books, 1977), p. 271.

5 Jefferson McMahan has pointed out that the elevator case differs from nuclear deterrence in precisely this respect, for if one keeps one's gun pointed at one's rival in the elevator, one only risks shooting the children *unintentionally.*

6 If in the Threat Principle we read "threaten" purely in the risk-

imposition sense (ignoring the declarative element), the principle is obviously inadequate. For in some situations, every alternative may involve a risk of death for large numbers of innocents.

7 When we combine elements like "deliberate killing" and "of the innocent," the two are related by the latter removing a plausible rationale for the former – in this case that the victim deserves to be killed. (Similarly, for "infliction of suffering" and "pointless," the latter removes the possibility that an act of the former kind is for the greater good.) In these cases, unlike the one in the text, there is perhaps some ground for contending that two nonabsolute prohibitions combine to form an absolute one.

8 This principle is nonabsolutist in that it fails to absolutely proscribe certain acts (i.e., risk-imposing threats) based on their intrinsic features. It may be absolutist in the sense of allowing no exceptions, once the notion of disproportion is built into the principle itself. Note, however, that even the supreme principle of a purely utilitarian system can be absolutist in this latter sense.

9 Richard Wasserstrom, "On the Morality of War: A Preliminary Inquiry," in Richard Wasserstrom (ed.), *War and Morality* (Belmont, Cal.: Wadsworth, 1970), p. 89.

10 See Locke's *Second Treatise of Government,* sec. 8.

11 Wasserstrom, "On the Morality of War," p. 90.

12 It might be suggested that protection from brainwashing (the closest personal analogue to a nation being conquered) supports a weaker right of self-defense than protection against the other harms mentioned. For liberty, sight, use of limbs, and higher faculties are necessary for living most lives in the normal human range, while possessing a particular set of values (that one might lose through brainwashing) is not. Still, if human life has value and meaning beyond mere survival and pleasure, involuntary loss of one's most basic values and commitments must be among the gravest injuries one can suffer. I am inclined then to ascribe equal strength to the right to defend fundamental values, provided that the values in question are not themselves evil ones.

13 See Judith Jarvis Thomson, "A Defense of Abortion," *Philosophy and Public Affairs* 1 (Fall 1971): 47–66.

14 For an explanation of how a nation's people might lack the capacity to replace unsatisfactory leaders, see my "Rule by Fear," *Nous* 17 (November 1983): 601–20.

15 See, e.g., the report on the *United States* v. *Holmes* lifeboat case, in Philip Davis (ed.), *Moral Duty and Legal Responsibility* (New York: Appleton-Century-Crofts, 1966), pp. 102–18.

16 The term "relevant" must be included because moral responsibility for one harm or danger does not render a person morally liable to just any harm or risk that might be imposed. There must be a rational

connection between the two, such as the imposed harm being the recognized penalty for creating the first harm, or a way of alleviating it. A more precise specification of the Immunity Thesis would spell this out in more detail and would introduce qualifications to take account of justified paternalism and consent of the victim.

17 We may define a "dangerous situation" as one in which not everyone's life can be protected, that is, one in which any action (including inaction) will place (or leave) some people at significant risk of losing their lives.

18 I say "apparently" here because one could interpret the causation view so that contributions to collective causation of harms would annul immunity.

19 These terms are taken from Robert Nozick, *Anarchy, State, and Utopia* (New York: Basic Books, 1974), pp. 34–35.

20 Here two wrongs may make a right. See my "When Two Wrongs Make a Right: An Essay on Business Ethics," *Journal of Business Ethics* 2 (1983): 61–66. Note, however, that this approach does not deal with the nuclear risks – from fallout or off – target missiles –imposed by the superpowers on citizens of other countries. Analysis of this problem would involve consideration of the moral significance of alliances, and of the distinctions between intended and unintended effects of actions, and direct and indirect imposition of risks. Also, if there are differing degrees of individual responsibility for nuclear threats, citizens of democratic nuclear powers typically bear a higher degree of such responsibility than citizens of other nuclear powers.

21 With the term "disproportionate" thus interpreted to take account of numbers, nature of the risks, alternatives, and degrees of innocence, we may reword and simplify the principle into the following: (1″) *Final Threat Principle*: It is wrong to disproportionately threaten and impose risks upon other people. The Necessity Claim must also be revised, so that superpower civilians are described as "partly innocent."

22 One crude way of doing it would be to choose broad categories (e.g., military-government, civilians, populations of uninvolved neighboring nations that would be harmed in the event of nuclear war) and to assign to each a weighting factor between zero (for the guilty or responsible) and one (for the purely innocent bystander), thought to represent the relative degree of immunity of members of the group. These weights would then be incorporated into one's utilitarian analysis.

23 Douglas Lackey, "Missiles and Morals: A Utilitarian Look at Nuclear Deterrence," *Philosophy and Public Affairs* 11 (Summer 1982): 189–231.

24 See "Current Policy No. 472," United States Department of State (Washington, D.C.: March 1983).

25   At current levels of offensive nuclear armaments, this may make little practical difference. For there are now enough weapons to cover all sensible targets. But the problems discussed below might become practical at some future time if defense systems are conjoined with substantial negotiated reductions in offensive systems, as proposed by the Reagan administration. (This administration proposal should not be confused with the suggestion of Chapters 8 and 10 that strategic defenses might be useful in the final stages of a complete bilateral nuclear disarmament process.)

The pros and cons of different targeting strategies are discussed briefly in the Introduction. The argument here is that strategic defense might encourage countervalue targeting without providing the stability advantages usually attributed to such targeting.

26   See, e.g., Robert Gessert and J. Bryan Hehir, *The New Nuclear Debate* (New York: Council on Religion and International Affairs, 1976); and Arthur Lee Burns, *Ethics and Deterrence;* Adelphi Paper 69 (London: Institute for Strategic Studies, 1969).

27   In addition to discussing this policy in my seminars some years ago, I have seen it discussed in an unpublished paper by James Sterba.

28   McGeorge Bundy, "Existential Deterrence and Its Consequences," in Douglas MacLean, (ed.), *The Security Gamble* (Totowa, N.J.: Roman & Allanheld, 1984).

29   That is, the probability of Soviet attack might increase more than the probability of U.S. retaliation to Soviet attack decreases. In that case, the probability of U.S. retaliation, which is the product of these two, would rise.

30   See, e.g., Walter Stein, "The Limits of Nuclear War: Is a Just Deterrence Strategy Possible?" in James Finn (ed.), *Peace, the Churches and the Bomb* (New York: Council on Religion and International Affairs, 1965), p. 83. Cf. Nozick, *Anarchy, State, and Utopia,* pp. 126–31.

31   Some of the intuitions underlying this judgment may coincide with those underlying the pure defense principle of Chapter 8. Note the limits on this principle discussed there.

32   As Jefferson McMahan points out, we cannot presume that your rival cares about the children as Soviet leaders care about their citizens and cities. For this reason, the missile-deflection device may be more easily justified than the shield – it is more likely to actually deter.

33   Being only 50 percent effective, it could not physically protect our cities from destruction in an all-out Soviet attack. Hence, warding off an actual attack would probably be only a secondary purpose: Note that because of its relative lack of defensive effectiveness and its capacity to punish an attacker with his own missiles, the deflector system would not provide its possessor with the retargeting incentives associated with the purely defensive system discussed earlier in this section.

Jefferson McMahan has raised the interesting question of how effective the deflection device would have to be before we were obligated to not target Soviet cities as deflection targets. There is no easy answer to this question. Obviously, if the device were 100 percent effective, we should target the oceans. But where exactly the effectiveness cutoff point is that would require not targeting Soviet cities as deflection targets depends on a complex balancing of risks to all concerned.

34 They also fire the missiles themselves. But, in a sense, they also fire our missiles if they attack our autoretaliator.

35 See, e.g., Jonathan Schell, *The Fate of the Earth* (New York: Avon Books, 1982), pt. II; and Jefferson McMahan, "Nuclear Deterrence and Future Generations," in Avner Cohen and Steven Lee (eds.), *Nuclear Weapons and the Future of Humanity* (Totowa, N.J.: Rowman & Allanheld, 1986).

36 National Conference of Catholic Bishops, *The Challenge of Peace: God's Promise and Our Response* (Washington, D.C.: Catholic Conference, 1983), secs. 186–88. It is unclear whether the bishops endorse the specific concept of conditional permissiblity discussed here. Note, however, that Rev. J. Brian Hehir, a key adviser to the bishops in drafting the document, writes (in "Moral Issues in Deterrence Policy," in MacLean, *The Security Gamble,* p. 62): "The American Bishops tie the justification for deterrence to an understanding that it be used as a framework for moving to a different basis of security among nations."

37 This problem was pointed out to me by Daniel Ellsberg.

5. DILEMMAS OF NUCLEAR PROTEST

1 On this last point see Richard Wasserstrom, "War, Nuclear War, and Nuclear Deterrence: Some Conceptual and Moral Issues," *Ethics* 95 (April 1985): 427–28; and Richard Ullman, "Denuclearizing International Politics," ibid., p. 587.

2 Using the bucket metaphor, we are concerned with the chance that one particular drop will be the one that causes the bucket to overflow (when it otherwise would not have).

3 Note that the drop-in-a-bucket problem is not an artifact of assuming that individual agents are motivated solely by self-interest. It can arise even when, as here, we assume the individual is concerned with promoting the well-being of all. On this point as it applies to the problem of revolution, see Alan Buchanan, "Revolutionary Motivation and Rationality," *Philosophy and Public Affairs* 9 (Fall 1979):65.

4 In the terms of economic theory, the objection to this solution is that it recommends acts leading to Pareto-inferior outcomes.

5 The most sophisticated defense of an approach like that embodied in the Collective Reasoning solution is Donald Regan, *Utilitarianism and Co-operation* (Oxford: Clarendon Press, 1980).

6 For similar solutions to other collective action problems see Regan, chap. 2, n. 6, p. 231; Brian Barry, *Sociologists, Economists, and Democracy* (London: University of Chicago Press, 1970), p. 32; and Derek Parfit, "Correspondence," *Philosophy and Public Affairs* 10 (Spring 1981): 180–81.

7 For further discussion of the rebellion case, see my "Two Solutions to the Paradox of Revolution," *Midwest Studies in Philosophy* 7 (1982).

8 Even supporters of symbolic protest may hesitate to endorse it when it threatens harm to others besides the protester, as counterproductive protest does. See, e.g., Thomas E. Hill, Jr., "Symbolic Protest and Calculated Silence," *Philosophy and Public Affairs* 9 (Fall 1979): 101–02.

9 George Will, "The Handicap of Intellect," *Newsweek*, October 14, 1985, p. 108.

It is worth noting that "honesty is the most effective policy" may well be true when applied to eductional, as opposed to political, means of moderating the nuclear arms race. Norms of truthfulness, rational argumentation, and objectivity are deeply enough entrenched – and rightly so – in educational institutions, that it would probably be dangerous and counterproductive to try to strengthen the nuclear peace movement by using propaganda in the schools. In any case, there is plenty of room for improving nuclear policy in the future by simply informing students and encouraging them to take a questioning attitude toward the status quo, without educators having to resort to antirational devices or the violation of existing norms of truthfulness, openness, or intellectual honesty.

10 See especially Bernard William's contribution to J.J.C. Smart and Bernard Williams, *Utilitarianism: For and Against* (Cambridge: Cambridge University Press, 1973).

11 This view is applied to the world hunger problem in Peter Singer, "Famine, Affluence, and Morality," *Philosophy and Public Affairs* 1 (Spring 1972).

12 I borrow this point from Virginia Warren, "Discussing World Hunger Over Dinner," typescript, Chapman College, 1984.

13 The nuclear arms race has substantial economic and psychological costs, but these are quite small compared to the costs of the actual use of the weapons.

14 For example, a 50 percent chance of 50 million more long-run starvation deaths worldwide (not an unrealistic estimate for the costs of present environmental and population policies compared to possible alternatives) produces as many "expected deaths" as does a 5 percent extra risk of a nuclear war entailing 500 million deaths.

15 The Marginal Utility view is an exception. It is equally implausible in either case.

16 Presumably one allocates one's protest resources on different issues so that the marginal benefit-to-cost ratios are the same for all issues. Otherwise a shift of resources could produce more benefits at equal cost or equal benefits at lesser cost.

17 This point is reinforced by noting that the efficiency and effectiveness of protests can usually be increased by forming coalitions of generally like-minded groups interested in somewhat different issues.

6. UNILATERAL NUCLEAR DISARMAMENT

1 Douglas Lackey, "Missiles and Morals: A Utilitarian Look at Nulcear Deterrence," *Philosophy and Public Affairs* 11 (Summer 1982): 189–231; Jefferson McMahan, "Nuclear Deterence and Future Generations," in Avner Cohen and Steven Lee (eds.), *Nuclear Weapons and the Future of Humanity* (Totowa, N.J.: Rowman & Allanheld, 1986), pp. 319–39.

2 See Lackey, "Missiles and Morals," pp. 203, 193; McMahan, "Nuclear Deterrence," pp. 320–23.

3 See Lackey, "Missiles and Morals," pp. 206, 208; McMahan, "Nuclear Deterrence," pp. 337, 324–25 (where he lists reasons current deterrent policies are risky, none of which would apply in the case of minimum deterrence). McMahan, in fact, does not deny my conclusion that minimum deterrence may be a lesser evil than unilateral nuclear disarmament.

4 Lackey, "Missiles and Morals," pp. 205, 212.

5 Ibid., p. 211.

6 H.R. Haldeman, *The Ends of Power* (New York: Times Books, 1978), pp. 88–94. See also Henry Kissinger, *White House Years* (Boston: Little, Brown, 1979), pp. 183–94, 764. McMahan (correspondence with the author, April 1986) expresses skepticism that the Soviets were deterred by a possible U.S. nuclear response. But they may have feared world opinion, because and only because they had to compete for influence with a roughly equally powerful United States. As noted at the end of this section, after U.S. unilateral nuclear disarmament they might well lose such fears.

7 Lackey, "Missiles and Morals," p. 222.

8 Not expecting the bank to be unlocked and unguarded, Lefty never even adopts the conditional goal of robbing it if it is. Like busy

Soviet leaders, she does not make contingency plans for fantastical contingencies.

9   McMahan, "Nuclear Deterrence," p. 327.

10 Lackey, "Missiles and Morals," p. 221.

11 Lackey, "Missiles and Morals," p. 221; McMahan, "Nuclear Deterrence," pp. 326–28.

12 If, improbably, unilateral nuclear disarmament were ever adopted by the United States, it would surely be over the opposition of powerful domestic forces that might later regain control of U.S. nuclear policy. On the dangers of nuclear attack to prevent rearmament, see Russell Hardin, "Risking Armageddon," in Cohen and Lee, *Nuclear Weapons,* pp. 205–07.

13 See Ronald Clark, *The Life of Bertrand Russell* (London: Jonathan Cape, 1975), chap. 19, which includes a number of relevant quotations from articles, speeches, and letters by Russell. See also Bertrand Russell, "The Future of Mankind," in his *Unpopular Essays* (New York: Simon & Schuster, 1950), pp. 34–44. McMahan (correspondence with the author, April 1986) notes this disanalogy between the situation Russell was considering and the hypothetical situation of U.S. unilateral nuclear disarmament: in the former situation, the main foe of the nuclear power was seeking to acquire nuclear weapons; in the latter case, the main foe would have given them up. The analogy is partly restored, however, by the real possibility of nuclear rearmament in the latter situation.

14 See Hardin, "Risking Armageddon," p. 206.

15 Lackey, "Missiles and Morals," pp. 196, 205, 214; McMahan, "Nuclear Deterrence," pp. 326–28.

16 Lackey, "Missiles and Morals," p. 212.

17 Some historians have suggested that the United States used the atomic bomb on Japan partly to frighten the Soviet Union.

18 Lackey, "Missiles and Morals," p. 230.

19 Lackey (in "Missiles and Morals," pp. 202–05) criticizes the original essay that Chapter 3 is based on, but his criticisms are largely off-target. He misrepresents the one condition in my analysis that he discusses, confusing two disasters being of "roughly the same *order* of magnitude," that is, the greater not being "a hundred or a thousand times as bad as the lesser" (my terms), with their being "roughly equal in magnitude" (his terms). Further, he contends that in comparing policies that risk unequal disasters, it is the *difference* rather than the *ratios* of the magnitudes of the disasters that matter in figuring utilitarian tradeoffs with increased chances of avoiding disaster. But this is just wrong.

Consider two choice situations, S1 and S2. In each situation, individual members of a base group of persons, numbering 1 in S1 and 99 in S2, will suffer equal-magnitude disasters if no action is taken. Action may save all from disaster, but if it fails, will cause the base group and an additional person to suffer the disaster. In both S1 and S2, the *difference* between the aggregate disasters that may follow from action and inaction is the same (that is, $2 - 1 = 100 - 99$). Yet the *ratios* are quite distinct: 2 in S1, and 100/99 in S2. So this can serve as a test of which matters. But it is obvious that, *ceteris paribus*, the action is more worth taking in S2 than in S1: we may save 99 at the hazard of harming 1 extra. Thus, contrary to what Lackey asserts, it is ratios rather than differences in magnitude than matter for trade offs with increased chances of disaster avoidance. As the interested reader may check, the way expected values are calculated confirms the point for all situations of this kind involving risk.

7. WORLD GOVERNMENT

1 As before, "minimum deterrence" is used as a shorthand for the sort of deterrent strategy advocated in the Introduction, combined with full-blown efforts toward multilateral nuclear disarmament as a long-range solution.

2 See Edward McClennan, "The Tragedy of National Sovereignty," in Avner Cohen and Steven Lee (eds.), *Nuclear Weapons and the Future of Humanity* (Totowa, N.J.: Rowman & Allanheld, 1986), pp. 391–405; David Gauthier, *The Logic of Leviathan* (Oxford: Clarendon Press, 1969), pp. 211–12; and Howard Warrender, *The Political Philosophy of Hobbes* (Oxford: Clarendon Press, 1957), p. 119. The argument in chap. 3 of Jonathan Schell's *The Fate of the Earth* (New York: Avon Books, 1982) may also be interpreted along these lines, though it does not mention Hobbes. Cf. my "Hobbes's War of All Against All," *Ethics* 93 (January 1983): 306–07; the present chapter may be viewed as an elaboration of my brief remarks there.

3 A similar task is undertaken in Mark Heller, "The Use & Abuse of Hobbes: The State of Nature in International Relations," *Polity* 13 (Fall 1980): 21–32. However, Heller discusses the use of Hobbes's state of nature as a general model of international relations. I focus on the nuclear-armed world and hence present a rather different line of argument. I am grateful to Sanford Lakoff for drawing my attention to Heller's useful article.

4 For more detailed elaboration of the argument, see my "Hobbes's War of All Against All" and *Hobbesian Moral and Political Theory* (Princeton, N.J.: Princeton University Press, 1986), chaps. 3–4. Hobbes's full argument against anarchy includes a third part designed to show that the problems of the state are not worse than those of the state of nature. See *Hobbesian Moral and Political Theory*, chaps. 5–6.

5 Thomas Hobbes, *Leviathan,* vol. 3 of William Molesworth (ed.), *The English Works of Thomas Hobbes* (London: John Bohn, 1839), chap. 13, p. 113 (Subsequent references to *Leviathan* will be to chapter and page number in this edition.)

6 *Leviathan,* chap. 13, pp. 112–13.

7 On the relationship, in Hobbes, between morality, prudence, and the laws of nature, see my "Right Reason and Natural Law in Hobbes's Ethics," *The Monist* 66 (January 1983): 120–33; and my *Hobbesian Moral and Political Theory,* chap. 9.

8 *Leviathan,* chap. 14, p. 117.

9 *Leviathan,* chap. 14. p. 118.

10 *Leviathan,* chap. 13. p. 115.

11 This last factor may, however, be outweighed by the greater costs and difficulties of punishing an aggressor nation (rather than individual) once identified.

12 There may be economic arguments for world government in the modern world, e.g., based on the need to divert resources from the rich to the poor, or from military programs to welfare programs. But these arguments are distinct from the Nuclear World Government Argument and will not be considered here.

13 Of course, leaders will generally take into account how the impact of their nation's acts on outsiders may lead to responsive acts that affect their nation, and sometimes they will act out of genuine concern for outsiders. The assumption, however, is that the motivational influence of the latter factor – international altruism – is small, except on rare occasions.

14 As is pointed out in Heller, "Use & Abuse of Hobbes." See also the first paragraph of section III of this chapter.

15 Gauthier and Warrender, for example, endorse only the proliferated-world version of the argument.

16 *Leviathan,* chap. 13, p. 110.

17 I argue in Chapter 8 that joint superpower development of systems to defend against third-party attacks is the only policy of strategic defense that makes moral or prudential sense in the foreseeable future.

18 *Leviathan,* chap. 10, p. 74. Note, however, the observation of our Introduction that in the current (largely bipolar) international situation, extended nuclear deterrence by the United States may be imprudent and immoral because it is probably unnecessary and excessively dangerous.

19 The so-called phony war between Great Britain and Nazi Germany immediately following the invasion of Poland in 1939 would constitute an example of a passive state of war. Obviously, the term "passivity" does not imply inactivity in the preparation for future fighting.

20 This argument may be what Schell has in mind when he writes *(Fate of the Earth,* pp. 183–84): "unless we rid ourselves of our nuclear arsenals a holocaust not only *might* occur but *will* occur – if not today, then tomorrow; if not this year, then the next."

21 Jefferson McMahan, correspondence with the author, June 1986. I present McMahan's argument, as I understand it, in my own terms.

22 The best-known use of a maximin rule of this type is in John Rawls, *A Theory of Justice* (Cambridge, Mass.: Harvard University Press, 1971), chap. 3.

23 An analogous argument can be used to argue the superiority of unilateral nuclear disarmament over continuing nuclear deterrence. (See, e.g., Douglas Lackey, "Missiles and Morals," *Philosophy and Public Affairs* 11 [Summer 1982]: 196–98.) This argument fails for the same reason as the argument in the text: the other alternative (here, unilateral nuclear disarmament) could lead to as bad a possible outcome – namely, extinction caused by environmental effects of a one-sided nuclear strike or a nuclear war between the remaining nuclear powers.

24 There is a growing literature on "nuclear winter" and other possible environmental effects of nuclear war. See, e.g., Anne Ehrlich, "Nuclear Winter," *Bulletin of the Atomic Scientists* 40 (special supplement, April 1984): 38–148. Note that the suggestion here that human extinction *could* result from a medium-sized nuclear war is consistent with the observation of Chapter 3 that even large-scale nuclear war is *not likely* to produce human extinction.

25 I especially have in mind the prediction by Grenville Clark in the introduction to Grenville Clark and Louis B. Sohn, *World Peace Through World Law*, 3rd ed. enlarged (Cambridge, Mass.: Harvard University Press, 1966).

26 See McClennan, "The Tragedy of National Sovereignty."

27 Clark and Sohn, *World Peace Through World Law.*

28 The use of strategic missile defense systems is suggested in Freeman Dyson, "Weapons and Hope (II)," *New Yorker,* February 13, 1984, pp. 98–99.

29 See Jonathan Schell, *The Abolition* (New York: Alfred Knopf, 1984).

8. STRATEGIC DEFENSE

1 On the likely effects of one thermonuclear bomb exploding over a major urban area, see Office of Technology Assessment, *The Effects of Nuclear War* (London: Croom Helm, 1980), chap. 2. The limited effectiveness of damage-limiting technologies is discussed below.

2   In principle, attaining goals 2 and 3 to a very high degree (i.e., assuring, by inexpensive means, that there would be little loss of life and property in a nuclear war) would vastly reduce the importance of goal 1. But since such attainment of goals 2 and 3 is not possible in practice, goal 1 should be given highest (though not absolute) priority.

3   See, e.g., Thomas Karas, *The New High Ground: Strategies and Weapons of Space-Age War* (New York: Simon & Schuster, 1983), chap. 8; and Kosta Tsipis, "Laser Weapons," *Scientific American* 245 (December 1981): 51–57. See also the following series of articles in *Aviation Week and Space Technology:* Clarence A. Robinson, Jr., "Panel Urges Defense Technology," October 17, 1983, pp. 16–18; Robinson, "Study Urges Exploiting of Technology," October 24, 1983, pp. 50–51, 55–57; Micheal Feazel, "Europeans Support U.S. Space-based Systems," October 24, 1983, p. 59; Robinson, "Panel Urges Boost-Phase Intercepts," December 5, 1983, pp. 50–61. These articles undertake to summarize the contents of the report of the Reagan administration's Defensive Technologies Study Team (Fletcher Committee), in which development of a multicomponent strategic missile defense system is recommended.

4   See Colin Gray, "Strategic Defense, Deterrence, and the Prospects for Peace," *Ethics* 95 (April 1985): 659–72.

5   For present purposes, I ignore the real possibility that deploying an SD system will influence the other side's targeting policy. For discussion, see Chapter 4.

6   I here ignore the possibility that mutual disarmament beyond a certain level may be dispreferred because it is less stable, since the same applies to mutual defense.

7   Even a superpower with purely defensive motives would prefer being the only side defended to having its opponents defended as well. For the absence of defense on the other side ensures the effectiveness of one's own deterrent and may also increase one's political bargaining power.

8   See Tsipis, "Laser Weapons"; and Richard L. Garwin, "Weapons in Space: Are We on the Verge of a New Arms Race?," *IBM Research Report,* February 25, 1981, pp. 9–12. The Fletcher Committee Report apparently acknowledges these difficulties but concludes that they are ultimately solvable. See, e.g., Robinson, "Study Urges Exploiting of Technology," pp. 51–52.

9   See Tsispis, "Laser Weapons," pp. 56–57. The Fletcher Committee Report deals with hardening (see Robinson, "Study Urges Exploiting of Technology," pp. 51, 56) but does not appear to have solved the problem of overloading, as its proposals are "predicated on providing the capability to defend the U.S. effectively against a near

simultaneous launch of 1000 ballistic missiles by the USSR" ibid., p. 56). The game-theoretic argument sketched below suggests that development of such a defensive capability would lead to the Soviets acquiring forces capable of making a larger strike.

10   For an argument along these general lines, see Herbert York, *Race to Oblivion* (New York: Simon & Schuster, 1970), pp. 190–91, 205–06. To achieve a high kill rate, the Fletcher Committee envisions a multilayered SD system that can attack ballistic missiles in their boost phase, post-boost phase, midcourse phase, and terminal (target-approaching) phase. Still, according to Robinson, "Study Urges Exploiting of Technology," its report acknowledges that "it is not technically credible to provide a ballistic missile defense that is 99.9% leak proof" (p. 51).

11   Robinson, "Study Urges Exploiting of Technology," p. 59; and Karas, *The New High Ground,* p. 186. After reading the description of the proposed multilayered system, it is easy to believe that the actual cost might reach (or exceed) the higher figure.

12   Concern about the dangers involved in a superpower race to complete an effective SD system has been expressed by such diverse sources as a former National Security Council staff member whom I heard speak and the coauthor of a booklet produced by an antinuclear protest group (see Jim Heaphy, "Militarization of Space," in *International Day of Nuclear Disarmament* [Berkeley: Livermore Action Group, 1983], p. 67).

13   This relative advantage might not be worth very much in war-fighting terms if both sides retain an overkill capacity. Nonetheless, both superpowers act as though strategic advantages are worth having, even when there is overkill on both sides, and such strategic advantages may in some cases yield political benefits.

14   Note that if we assume the opposite of the third assumption, that Arming yields a greater relative advantage in this case as well, Arming is then a dominant strategy. We would thereby reach more directly the conclusion offered below: that Arming is the rational strategy for each to follow.

15   Let '1' through '9' represent, for a given party, the outcome in Figure 3 that corresponds to that number (in preference order) for that party. (For example, for the United States, '7' stands for U.S.A. Defends and USSR Arms.) That the outcomes are preferred in the order indicated in Figure 3 can be seen as follows: T3 and M2 imply that 1 is preferred to 2 and 8 to 9; T4 and M2 imply that 2 is preferred to 3 and 7 to 8; T1, T2, and M1 imply that 3 is preferred to 4 and 6 to 7; and T1 and M3 imply that 4 is preferred to 5 and 5 to 6.

16   I am not claiming that the decision makers saw the alternatives in

precisely these same terms or that they explicitly reasoned in game-theoretic terms. My contention is that the underlying structure of that situation was like that of the present situation and can roughly be represented by Figure 3. The extent to which multiple-warhead missiles were designed as countermeasures to actual or possible SD systems is a matter of some controversy. See Graham Allison, "Questions About the Arms Race: Who's Racing Whom? A Bureaucratic Perspective," in Robert Pfatzgraff, Jr. (ed.), *Contrasting Approaches to Strategic Arms Control* (Lexington, Mass.: D.C. Heath & Co., 1974), pp. 31–72; Herbert York, "Multiple Warhead Missiles," *Scientific American* 229 (November 1973): 18–27; and Ted Greenwood, *Making the MIRV: A Study of Defense Decision Making* (Cambridge, Mass.: Ballinger, 1975).

17   Robert B. Cullen and John J. Lindsay, "A Shield or a Sieve?," *Newsweek,* June 25, 1984, p. 36.

18   Assuming a fixed percentage of effective missile "kills" by a first-striker, a second-striker's retaliatory capacity will be a fixed percentage of his original arsenal. But with small enough arsenals, this may not be enough to impose "unacceptable damage" on the first-striker. (See Thomas Schelling, *The Strategy of Conflict* [London: Oxford University Press, 1963], pp. 235–37.) A variant on the argument in the text is presented in Gray, "Strategic Defense, Deterrence, and the Prospects for Peace," where it is suggested that SD systems reduce the risks of bilateral disarmament by protecting each side against the negative effects of covert stockpiling of weapons by the other side. But at high levels of nuclear armament, such stockpiling represents little threat. At very low levels of nuclear weapons possession, the argument may make sense. But then the rational course of action is to reduce offensive arms to such levels and then co-operatively build (smaller and cheaper) SD systems.

19   Richard Sybert, special assistant to the secretary of defense, provides a typical example of such an appeal when he writes, "SDI [the strategic defense initiative] . . . is . . . ethical – defensive measures kill no one." (*Los Angeles Times,* January 27, 1986, pt. II, p. 9.) Even so vigorous a critic of SDI as Lord Zuckerman seems to endorse this argument when he describes as "fairly unassailable" the proposition that "defense . . . is always a good thing." ("The Wonders of Star Wars," *New York Review of Books,* January 30, 1986, p. 35.)

20   We could strengthen this criterion so that prevention of harm must be the *only* motive of the act, but then – given the complexity of human motives – very few acts would qualify as purely defensive, and strategic defense almost certainly would not. Also, pure defense of valuable objects other than persons (e.g., animals, artworks) is excluded to avoid unnecessary complications.

21 Aggression as a secondary motive is briefly explored by Jefferson McMahan ("A Note on Pure Defense," *Journal of Philosophy* 83 [November 1986]: 640–41), who points out that a secondary offensive motive for a purely defensive act may be reliably inferred from the larger pattern of activity in which that act is embedded. I de-emphasize this possibility here not because I disagree with Mc-Mahan, but because I want to analyze strategic defense without getting into the controversial substantive issue of what its proponents' motives are.

22 See Chapter 4.

23 See Bertrand Russell, "The Future of Mankind," in his *Unpopular Essays* (New York: Simon & Schuster, 1950), pp. 34–44; and Ronald Clark, *The Life of Bertrand Russell* (London: Jonathan Cape, 1975), chap. 19.

24 There is some evidence that the Soviets might have seriously contemplated such a strike in the late sixties. See H.R. Haldeman, *The Ends of Power* (New York: Times Books, 1978), pp. 88–94; and Marvin Kalb and Bernard Kalb, *Kissinger* (Boston: Little, Brown, 1974), pp. 226–28.

9. NUCLEAR COERCION

1 See Colin Gray and Keith Payne, "Victory is Possible," *Foreign Policy* 39 (Summer 1980): 14–27.

2 See Daniel Ellsberg, "Call to Mutiny," in E.P. Thompson and Dan Smith (eds.), *Protest and Survive* (Monthly Review Press, 1981).

3 See Daniel Kahnemann and Amos Tversky, "Prospect Theory," *Econometrica* 39 (March 1979): 263–92.

4 It hardly needs explaining why Soviet placement of the missiles was immoral – it was provocative, dangerous, unnecessary, and deceptive.

5 See Elie Abel, *The Missile Crisis* (New York: Bantam Books, 1966), pp. 36–39; and Robert F. Kennedy, *Thirteen Days* (New York: W. W. Norton, 1971), pp. 26, 97. On the theory of routine foreign-policy decision making with special application to the issue of antiballistic-missile deployment in the United States, see Morton Halperin, *Bureaucratic Politics and Foreign Policy* (Washington, D.C.: The Brookings Institution, 1974).

6 Abel, *Missile Crisis,* p. 25.

7 Texts of Kennedy's statements are in David Larson (ed.), *The "Cuban Crisis" of 1962: Selected Documents and Chronology* (Boston: Houghton Mifflin, 1963), pp. 3–4, 17–18.

8 Abel, *Missile Crisis,* pp. 48–50; Theodore Sorensen, *Kennedy* (New York: Harper and Row, 1965), p. 682.

9 This assessment by the military was based on faulty analysis and was later corrected. See Graham Allison, *Essence of Decision* (Boston: Little, Brown, 1971), p. 126. This book is a theoretical study of missile-crisis decision making.

10 Ibid., p. 60; Abel, *Missile Crisis,* pp. 78–79; Kennedy, *Thirteen Days,* pp. 26–27; Sorensen, *Kennedy,* pp. 684–85; Arthur Schlesinger, Jr., *A Thousand Days* (Greenwich, Conn.: Fawcett, 1965), pp. 738–39; and Richard Neustadt and Graham Allison, "Afterword" to *Thirteen Days,* pp. 128–29.

11 For texts of the U.S. Draft Resolution to the Security Council and Ambassador Stevenson's statement, see Larson *"Cuban Crisis,"* pp. 48, 66–81. The text of the O.A.S. resolution, adopted on October 23, is in ibid., pp. 64–66.

12 Text in ibid., pp. 41–46.

13 See, e.g., U.N. documents in ibid., pp. 49–54 and 90–102. See also Abel, *Missile Crisis,* pp. 116–17; and Kennedy, *Thirteen Days,* p. 44.

14 Bertrand Russell, *Unarmed Victory* (Baltimore: Penguin Books, 1963), pp. 31–32.

15 Text in ibid., pp. 36–38, and in Larson, *"Cuban Crisis,"* pp. 125–27.

16 Russell, *Unarmed Victory,* p. 45; Kennedy, *Thirteen Days,* p. 52.

17 For paraphrases of the letter, see Abel, *Missile Crisis,* pp. 158–62; Allison, *Essence of Decision,* pp. 221–23.

18 Text in Larson, *"Cuban Crisis,"* pp. 155–58.

19 Kennedy, *Thirteen Days,* pp. 86–87; Allison, *Essence of Decision,* pp. 65–66.

20 Text of Khrushchev's letter to Kennedy is in Larson *"Cuban Crisis,"* pp. 161–65.

21 On the Illyushin matter, see Abel, *Missile Crisis,* pp. 187–91; and Sorensen, *Kennedy,* pp. 719–21.

22 See Kennedy, *Thirteen Days,* p. 106 (Sorensen's note at the end of the text); Roger Hagan, "Righteous Realpolitik"; I.F. Stone, "What Price Prestige"; and Ronald Steel, "Lessons of the Missile Crisis," all in Robert Divine (ed.), *The Cuban Missile Crisis,* (Chicago: Triangle Books, 1971).

23 Thus, for present purposes, we need not determine whether, or to what extent, morality allows or requires national leaders to give priority in their deliberations to the welfare of their own people.

24 See, e.g., Kennedy, *Thirteen Days,* p. 84.

25 Abel, *Missile Crisis,* p. 128.

26 Russell, *Unarmed Victory,* p. 28. Ordinary people's reactions were similar. Abel reports (p. 146) that Prague housewives were panic-buying. I myself remember this as the one time in my growing-up years when adults around me were genuinely worried about events in the political world.

27 Nikita Khrushchev, *Khrushchev Remembers,* trans. and ed. Strobe Talbott (New York: Bantam Books, 1970), p. 550.
28 Kennedy, *Thirteen Days,* p. 71.
29 Abel, *Missile Crisis,* p. 110.
30 Kennedy, *Thirteen Days,* p. 61.
31 Ibid., p. 105.
32 Sorensen, *Kennedy,* p. 693.
33 Ibid., p. 705. See also Schlesinger, *A Thousand Days,* p. 734.
34 Kennedy, *Thirteen Days,* p. 40.
35 Ibid., p. 76.
36 On the submarine incidents, see Allison, *Essence of Decision,* p. 138.
37 Kennedy, *Thirteen Days,* p. 26.
38 See, e.g., Dean Rusk, "Co-existence without Sanctimony," in A.R. Urban (ed.), *Detente* (New York: Universe Books, 1976), pp. 245–46; and Bernard Brodie, *War and Politics* (New York: Macmillan, 1973), p. 430–32.
39 Kennedy, *Thirteen Days,* pp. 9–11. Emphasis added.
40 Sorensen, *Kennedy,* pp. 674–75. Emphasis added.
41 Abel, *Missile Crisis,* p. 38; Allison, *Essence of Decision,* pp. 195–96.
42 Kennedy, *Thirteen Days,* p. 45. Compare Neustadt and Allison, "Afterword," pp. 115–16.
43 See, e.g., Abel, *Missile Crisis,* p. 35; and Neustadt and Allison "Afterword," pp. 115–16.
44 In his televised speech of October 22, Kennedy said the missiles in Cuba "cannot be accepted by this country if our courage and our commitments are ever to be trusted again by either friend or foe." See Larson, *"Cuban Crisis,"* p. 43.
45 Sorensen, *Kennedy,* pp. 676–78.
46 See, e.g., Allison, *Essence of Decision,* pp. 47–55. Compare Khrushchev's own suggestion that these were his two motives, in Khrushchev, *Khrushchev Remembers,* p. 547.
47 See Sorensen, *Kennedy,* p. 688.
48 See, e.g., Divine, *Cuban Missile Crisis,* p. 155.
49 See Chapter 3.
50 Ibid.
51 Kennedy, *Thirteen Days,* p. 45.
52 On previous acceptance of the bombers, see Allison, *Essence of Decision,* pp. 236–37.
53 Abel, *Missile Crisis,* p. 187.
54 Kennedy, *Thirteen Days,* pp. 44–48, 72–75.

55 As the president had the final decision making authority, I shall focus in this section on the factors influencing him. It is clear, however, that many of his top advisers shared his views.

56 Robert Kennedy once said of the members of the fourteen-man Executive Committee, "If six of them had been President of the U.S., I think that the world might have been blown up." Quoted in Steel, "Lessons of the Missile Crisis," p. 233.

57 See, e.g., ibid., pp. 217–20; Hagan, "Righteous Realpolitik," in Divine, *Cuban Missile Crisis,* p. 74; Stone, "What Price Prestige," in ibid., pp. 158–59; and Leslie Dewart, "The Kennedy Trap," in ibid., p. 169.

58 Sidney Hook, (ed.), *Psychoanalysis, Scientific Method, and Philosophy* (New York: New York University Press, 1959).

59 Morris Lazerowitz, "The Relevance of Psychoanalysis to Philosophy," in ibid., pp. 133–54.

60 See, e.g., "Philosophy and Psychoanalysis," Donald William's vigorous reply to Lazerowitz, in Hook, *Psychoanalysis,* pp. 157–79.

61 See, e.g., Sorensen, *Kennedy,* p. 683; and Abel, *Missile Crisis,* pp. 35–36, 47–48.

62 Larson, "*Cuban Crisis,*" p. 43.

63 Sorensen, *Kennedy,* p. 683; and Abel, *Missile Crisis,* p. 171.

64 Kennedy, *Thirteen Days,* pp. 17, 27; Abel, *Missile Crisis,* pp. 66–67, 74; Allison, *Essence of Decision,* p. 203; and Neustadt and Allison, "Afterword," p. 128.

65 See references in notes 62 and 63. Also see Kennedy, *Thirteen Days,* p. 11; and Schlesinger, *Thousand Days,* p. 729.

66 Schlesinger, *Thousand Days,* p. 759; Kennedy, *Thirteen Days,* pp. 14, 102.

67 Schlesinger, *Thousand Days,* pp. 728–29; Sorensen, *Kennedy,* pp. 676–78.

68 See references in note 46.

69 See Dewart, "The Kennedy Trap," for the suggestion that the administration deliberately created the crisis.

70 Sorensen, *Kennedy,* p. 674.

71 Allison, *Essence of Decision,* 189–90. Emphasis added.

72 Sorensen, *Kennedy,* p. 688.

73 Kennedy, *Thirteen Days,* p. 45.

74 Allison, *Essence of Decision* pp. 193–94; Neustadt and Allison, "Afterword," pp. 122–23.

75 Allison, *Essence of Decision,* p. 193. (From Richard Neustadt, "Afterword: 1964," *Presidential Power* [New York, 1964], p. 187).

76 Allison, *Essence of Decision,* pp. 194–95.

77 Ibid., p. 203.

78 See Irving Janis, *Victims of Groupthink* (Boston: Houghton Mifflin,

1972), chap. 6; and Allison, *Essence of Decision,* pp. 127–32. The Janis chapter is a theoretical study of missile-crisis decision making.

79　By contrast, an important false *factual* assumption about the likelihod of success of a surgical air strike was reexamined and corrected during the crisis. See Allison, *Essence of Decision,* pp. 124–26.

80　Kennedy, *Thirteen Days,* pp. 45–46.

81　McGeorge Bundy, "The Missed Chance to Stop the H-Bomb,"*New York Review of Books,* May 13, 1982, p. 16.

82　On rule worship, see J.J.C. Smart, "An Outline of a System of Utilitarian Ethics," in Smart and B. Williams, *Utilitarianism: For and Against* (Cambridge: Cambridge University Press, 1973), p. 10.

83　Kennedy, *Thirteen Days,* p. 97.

84　Ibid., p. 26.

85　See Russell, *Unarmed Victory,* p. 31, for the text of the telegram.

86　For the text, see Larson, *"Cuban Crisis,"* p. 142.

87　Russell said, "I don't suppose I have altered the course of events by a fraction of an inch," and wrote, "Probably Khrushchev only does what I ask if he had decided to do it anyhow." See Ronald Clark, *The Life of Bertrand Russell* (London: Jonathan Cape, 1975), p. 600.

88　At the time this argument was made and had its effect, the participants believed that an air strike against only the missiles themselves was not feasible, and that any attack sufficient to wipe out the missiles would entail large numbers of civilian casualties. See Kennedy, *Thirteen Days,* pp. 15–17; and Allison, *Essence of Decision,* pp. 123–26.

89　Dean Acheson, "Homage to Plain Dumb Luck," in Divine, *Cuban Missile Crisis,* p. 197.

90　Ibid., p. 199.

91　See, e.g., Richard Brandt, *A Theory of the Good and the Right* (Oxford: Clarendon Press, 1970), pp. 273–77.

10.　MUTUAL NUCLEAR DISARMAMENT

1　According to some accounts, complete nuclear disarmament was seriously discussed by top U.S. and Soviet leaders at the October 1986 Iceland summit. (See "Elimination of Nukes Discussed, Officials Say," *Houston Chronicle,* October 26, 1986; sec. 1. p. 20.) Although these talks did not result in agreement, this lends plausibility to the claim that bilateral nuclear disarmament may well be possible at some time in the future.

2　Robert Axelrod, *The Evolution of Cooperation* (New York: Basic Books, 1984). On iterated prisoner's dilemma, see also Michael Taylor, *Anarchy and Cooperation* (London: John Wiley & Sons, 1976);

and Anatol Rapoport and Albert Chammah, *Prisoner's Dilemma* (Ann Arbor: University of Michigan Press, 1965).

3   There are two complications. First, tit-for-tat perpetuates past non-cooperation as well as past cooperation. So (given the rather dismal record of the past) the superpowers would have to begin anew: a treaty or a farsighted unilateral move could effectively signal and constitute such a new beginning. Second, the payoff structure may change in late plays of the bilateral disarmament game. See the discussion of the Dangers of Transition Argument in section II below.

4   A lexical ordering of goals means that alternatives are ranked by how they fare on the first goal, the second goal mattering only if alternatives equally satisfy the first, and so on. Alphabetical ordering of entries in a dictionary is the paradigm of lexical ordering.

5   The same conclusion follows even if we weaken the assumptions by making them disjunctive. It does not matter, for example, if we switch Opposition's second and third priorities, or switch which odd man-out disadvantage is larger. The key assumptions are that the odd-man out loses in domestic politics and that domestic politics is Opposition's dominant interest. I might add that I was initially surprised by the conclusion – I began the present analysis in an attempt to represent, rather than refute, the Domestic Politics Argument!

6   Leaders may rationally avoid marginal military disadvantages for fear of what the other side might try to do with its advantage, while not valuing gaining such an advantage because it is likely to be short-lived and unexploitable.

7   The lack of political democracy in the Soviet Union greatly limits the significance of possible bottom-up pressures there. This means that more of the burden of applying bottom-up pressures for a rational solution to the arms race falls upon citizens of the West.

8   See Russell Hardin and John Mearsheimer, introduction to Russell Hardin et al. (eds.), *Nuclear Deterrence: Ethics and Strategy* (Chicago: University of Chicago Press, 1985), pp. 10–12.

9   Actually, the relevant risk of nuclear war is the *net* risk under armament, i.e., the risk of nuclear war under armament minus the risk of nuclear war after nuclear disarmament (as a result of rearmament). On the latter risk, see note 12 of this chapter and the accompanying text.

10 There is no inconsistency here with the disaster avoidance analysis of Chapter 3 for two reasons. First, a conventional war may be a significantly lesser disaster than world domination by one's opponent. Second, and more important, Chapter 3 compared the *short-run* (e.g., thirty-year) risks of nuclear deterrence to the risks of unilateral

nuclear disarmament and found preference for the former risks potentially rational and moral. But the present comparison is between the *long-run* risks of continued nuclear deterrence and an increased risk of conventional war.

11   This is not to say that the current (February 1987) U.S. government policy of pursuing strategic defense rather than mutual reductions makes sense. Strategic defenses would be needed only *after* nuclear arsenals were reduced to a small fraction of current levels. Transition-to-zero problems need not be solved in the first stage of bilateral nuclear disarmament.

12   Similar considerations indicate why nations would be disinclined to rearm themselves with nuclear weapons once the zero level had been reached.

13   A margin of error might be prudently allowed for here. But no reasonable margin would be large enough to permit anything approaching present levels of overkill and present numbers of weapons with first-strike characteristics.

14   Safe implementation of a no-first-use policy by the West might require lengthy negotiations among the Western allies and either a conventional arms buildup by NATO or negotiated mutual force reductions with the Warsaw Pact.

Index